MW01182198

To Nina
from Herb

C. Herbert Duncan

2013

HISTORY OF MISSOURI BANDS

1800 - 2000

HISTORY OF
MISSOURI BANDS
1800 - 2000

BY
C. HERBERT DUNCAN

Published by:
Missouri Bandmasters Association

And

Lambda Foundation–Phi Beta Mu
International Bandmasters Fraternity

Two Harbors Press
Minneapolis, MN

Copyright © 2012 by C. Herbert Duncan.

Two Harbors Press
212 3ʳᵈ Avenue North, Suite 290
Minneapolis, MN 55401
612.455.2293
www.TwoHarborsPress.com

All rights reserved. No part of this publication may be reproduced, stored in a retrieval system, or transmitted, in any form or by any means, electronic, mechanical, photocopying, recording, or otherwise, without the prior written permission of the author.

ISBN-13: 978-1-937928-14-8
LCCN: 2011944539

Distributed by Itasca Books

Cover and graphic design: Wade Howell Design, St. Louis
Cover photo: Triplett Concert Band, Chariton County–1913
Back cover photo: Nathan Frank Bandstand, St. Louis Forest Park–1925

Printed in the United States of America

TABLE OF CONTENTS

HISTORY OF
MISSOURI BANDS
1800 - 2000

TABLE OF CONTENTS

DEDICATION

DEDICATION

To my wife, Sally
For her love and support…always.

A TRIBUTE

———⊶⟨⟩⊷———

To Wilford B. Crawford, director of band, orchestra, chorus,
Ferguson High School (1939-1947),
the person who terrified and inspired me at the same time.

To Robert "Doc" Watson, teacher of biology,
Ferguson High School (1944-1948)
who taught that nothing can be accomplished until it is organized.

To Keith K. Anderson, Director of Bands,
Central College, Fayette (1925–1952),
who set a standard of excellence that I had never known.

To Dr. E. Thayer Gaston– Chair, Department of Music Education,
University of Kansas, Lawrence,
who saw something in me that I did not.

———⊶⟨⟩⊷———

Great people change lives. These people changed mine.
CHD

The greatest good you can do for another is not to share your riches but to revel to him his own.

DISRAELI

PRELUDE

PRELUDE

Three thousand came to listen.

There is no one thing that goes so far toward making any affair a success as a band. Many people in town were not going to this year's county fair owing to the bad weather. But when they heard that the best band in the state was going to play they paid twenty-five cents to hear the music by the Novinger Cornet Band. Three thousand came to listen.

"County Fair Draws Crowd," *Shelby County Torchlight,* Shelbina, Missouri, 1907.

Novinger Cornet Band – 1893
All members were farmers in Adair County
Adair County Historical Society Museum photo

INTRODUCTION

Chapter 1

INTRODUCTION

————◆—————

Bands in Colonial America

There are many references to wind music in the early American colonies, mostly related to militia activity. In 1635 the New Hampshire colony had at least two drums for training the militia and fifteen hautboys and soft recorders to cheer the colonists' spirits. Hautboys were oboe -type instruments popular during the Renaissance for outdoor use. In 1660 drums and trumpets were used for military and civic purposes throughout New England, and in 1687 Virginia counties voted to use tax money to purchase drums, trumpets, and flags for the local militia. According to M. L. Mark and C. G. Gary in *A History of American Music Education*, a 1999 MENC publication, "Drums and trumpets substituted for bells in calling people to church and warning them of Indians" (1).

Paired woodwinds were originally known as *harmoniemusik* (2). In early America these ensembles were primarily associated with military functions and consisted of pairs of oboes, clarinets, bassoons, and horns similar to the classic Mozart orchestra wind section. Music written for harmoniemusik ensembles included compositions by J. C. Bach, Haydn, and Mozart, and later Beethoven and Schubert. These works and ensembles are the foundations of the wind band and the wind band literature heard on concert stages and performed by schools and universities across North America today.

"Bands of Musik" were apparent in the society of the colonies. The year 1756 marked the first recorded mention of an American military band. It was modeled on the British style of bands. Benjamin Franklin, as commander of a militia regiment, is reported to have marched in a Philadelphia parade led by a group of "hautboys and fifes in rank." The term "hautboy" had become used as a generic term for bandsmen in general (3).

The growth of bands leading up to the Revolutionary War, as well as in the aftermath, is documented in letters from notable figures of the period. These letters sometimes reveal instrumentation, however early historians saw the term "band" as referring to fife and drums, with no distinction between the terms "band" and "Band of Musik." Letters from the period indicate that wind music was vibrant in the early days of America.

Band Development: 1800–1920

In 1832, Indiana University became the first educational institution in the United States to form a brass band (4). In 1842, Notre Dame University was founded and immediately established what is considered to be the first university band comprising both woodwinds and brass (5). Shortly after, in 1847, the University of Michigan established a band. In 1848, the Boston Farms and Trade School, a boarding school for boys, formed the first [high] school band in the United States (6).

By 1850 there were an estimated 3,000 brass bands in the United States. In 1861 the Union Army had 500 bands with more than 9,000 musicians. The popularity of bands caused such an explosion within the military ranks that Congress, threatened by a string of defeats in the Civil War and facing the potentiality of defeat by General Robert E. Lee, eventually was required to limit the number of bands in the army to make more men available for combat service.

Following the Civil War, bands continued to flourish in America. Concerts in parks and town squares became an American tradition. Bands grew with the increasing numbers of soldiers returning from the war, and communities throughout the country were embracing town bands. The town band had become a mark of a town's social status. W. H. Dana wrote that "a town without a brass band is as much in need of sympathy as a church without a choir. The spirit of a place is recognized in its band" (7).

This community spirit began to infuse the educational systems of towns as more school bands began to appear. By 1889 Harper's Weekly estimated there were over 10,000 "military" bands in the United States (8).

Pre-World War I

Bands and band music steadily developed through the late nineteenth and early twentieth centuries as cornerstones of town culture, education, and even higher learning. New concepts of teaching instrumental music on a classroom basis were explored by Albert G. Mitchell. As a result, bands became a more visible part of society.

World War I

The development of instrumental music in America had another period of growth created by the war in Europe. With the onset of World War I, American military leaders encountered for the first time the substantially well-trained European military bands. They found that American bands were lacking in comparison. In 1918 General John J. "Blackjack" Pershing was appointed as Commander of the Allied Expeditionary Forces in Europe. Pershing was born on a farm near Laclede, Missouri, in Linn County. In 1880 he enrolled in the Missouri State Normal School # 1

(Truman State University) before being accepted as a cadet at the United States Military Academy at West Point. Upon his arrival in Europe, he and his staff found the band performance level of military ensembles from France and Great Britain much higher than the bands in the United States. Pershing believed bands were indispensable to troop morale, and he was a great supporter of them (10).

General Pershing created a band school at Chaumont, France, in 1918. Walter Damrosch, conductor of the New York Symphony, designed the course of study. The eight-week course covered harmony, instrumentation, and conducting. In addition, bandsmen learned to play the oboe, bassoon, and French horn—instruments that were not included in many bands of the Army Expeditionary Forces. Teachers for the army music school were selected from the Paris Conservatory, and each was selected for his or her expertise and musicianship (11).

Pershing and Damrosch helped raise the level of musicianship in the bands of the United States Army. Their endeavors were undertaken to address the immediate problem regarding musicianship in army bands. The unforeseen consequence proved to be the seminal moment for bands in music education in America.

The bandsmen and band leaders returning from Europe after World War I brought their experiences and music training while applying for jobs as teachers in public schools. Many of them became directors, putting to use their skills and contributing to the growth of school bands (12).

The importance General Pershing placed on training American bands also created a need for quality instruments. Instrument manufacturers rose to the occasion and turned to the new growth area, school bands, to create the sustainable market they experienced during the conflict. These two events, more teachers, and better instruments laid the groundwork for the future of bands in America. They not only provided trained educators to teach the bands, but also used the advertising strength of the music manufacturing industry to market and promote the importance of bands in schools.

In 1922 there were 200 school bands in the United States. By 1929, the number had grown to 20,000. In 1923 the first National Band Contest was held in Chicago, sponsored by the music industry. This single event brought national attention to the school band program. The last national contest was in 1938.

The existence of bands from American colonial times through the present helps us anchor and acknowledge the lineage of the American school band in the United States and the importance that bands had in everyday life of the community, the military, and in schools. The incredible growth of bands in the years following times of war explains the influence of military tradition on bands today and portrays a country enthralled with the band, its music, and its celebrities.

Used by permission:
Alexander R. Treveno, "A Revisionist View of Band Development in American Music Education," *NBA Journal*, Baton Rouge, National Band Association, 2007, Vol. 47, No. 3, 40–43. Dr. Trevino is Associate Director of Bands at Old Dominion University, Norfolk, Virginia.

Early Education in Missouri

"As early as 1774 there was a school in the City of St. Louis taught by one J. B. Tribeau. This was the first school established within the territory which is now Missouri. It is generally conceded that this man remained in the same place and conducted school for about forty years; in fact, this seems to have been the only school in St. Louis, and he the only teacher during most of that long period" (13).

The first legislation concerning schools was enacted by the Territorial Legislature of Louisiana on June 21, 1808, when Thomas Jefferson was President. The Legislature, sitting in session in New Orleans, passed an act incorporating St. Genevieve Academy. This institution was the first legally organized school in the Territory of Missouri (14).

Education in the Missouri Territory fell into one of several categories (15):

Home	Provided by parents to teach skills of a craft or homemaking
Academy	Rooted in the New England educational tradition
Subscription	Formed by small groups of families paying a fee
Governess	Conducted in the household by a cultured person
Parochial	Organized by churches and taught by ministers
Seminaries	Established as boarding school for girls
Mission Schools	Established for poor students (16)

Among the most popular sources of early instruction were the parochial schools, opened by various orders of Catholic nuns and priests and Lutheran ministers. Instruction included the classics: Latin, Greek, French, German, grammar, writing, and mathematics. Many schools formed clubs that included music, crafts, and physical activities (17).

Normal Schools

The term "normal school" originated in the early 19th century from the French *ecole normale*, meaning "model school." The French concept of the *ecole normale* was to provide a model classroom for future teachers. The purpose of the normal school was to establish teaching standards or norms; hence its name. In 1685, Saint John Baptist de La Salle, founder of the Institute of the Brothers of the Christian Schools, founded what is generally considered the first normal school in France.

The first normal school in the United States was formed in Concord, Vermont, by the Reverend Samuel Hall in 1823. The earliest normal school in Missouri was Harris Teachers College, founded by the St. Louis Public Schools in 1857. It was the first public teacher education institution west of the Mississippi River and the 12th such school in the United States.

Harris Teachers College was named in honor of William Torrey Harris, who was the Superintendent of Instruction in the St. Louis Public Schools and later became the United States Commissioner of Education. Harris Teachers College was for the training of white teachers while Stowe Teachers College, established in 1890, was for future black teachers of elementary schools in St. Louis. These two teaching institutions were merged in 1954 as the first of several steps to integrate the public schools of St. Louis. In response to the many requests from alumni of Stowe Teachers College, the Board of Education changed the name to Harris-Stowe Teachers College in 1979 and Harris-Stowe State University on August 25, 2005 (18).

Missouri Normal Schools

Harris Teachers College	St. Louis	1857
Missouri State Normal School # 1	Kirksville	1867
Missouri State Normal School # 2	Warrensburg	1871
Missouri State Normal School # 3	Cape Girardeau	1873
Northwestern Normal School	Stanberry	1881
Stowe Teachers College	St. Louis	1890
Springfield Normal School	Springfield	1894
Missouri State Normal School # 4	Springfield	1905
Missouri State Normal School # 5	Maryville	1906

Kirksville Boys Band – 1905
Kirksville Daily Express photo

TIME LINE
1800 TO 2000

Chapter 2

TIME LINE: 1800–2000

Year	President	Historic Musical Event
1819	James Monroe	*Trout Quintet*—F. Schubert

FIRST MISSOURI TOWN BAND

First Missouri "Town Band" organized by the LaFrenier Chauvin family in St. Charles. The band played free concerts in a small park at 624 South Main.

1821	James Monroe	*Der Freischutz*—Carl Marie von Weber

August 10, 1821, Missouri admitted into the Union. The first Missouri capital was established in St. Charles, winning over eight other cities for the title.

1827	John Quincy Adams	Beethoven dies on March 26th

Missouri state capital moved from St. Charles to Jefferson City.

1832	Andrew Jackson	US requires bandsmen to serve as regular soldiers.

Indiana University becomes the first educational institution in the United States to form a brass band.

1842	John Tyler	*Rienzi*—Richard Wagner

Notre Dame University founded; immediately established what is considered to be the first university band comprising both woodwinds and brass.

1848   James Polk   *Oh, Susana*—Stephen Foster

The Boston Farm and Trade School, a boarding school for boys, formed the first high school band in the United States.

1853   Millard Fillmore   *Il Trovatore*—Giuseppe Verdi

FIRST HIGH SCHOOL IN MISSOURI

Central High School, the first high school in Missouri, was organized in St. Louis. The school opened with 70 students.

1855   Franklin Pierce   *Mikado*—Gilbert & Sullivan

MUSIC IN MISSOURI SCHOOLS

The State Superintendent of Schools advocates a uniform course of study, which should include music to be taught by a lady.

1866   Andrew Johnson   *Light Calvary*—Franz von Suppe

First high school in St. Joseph opens. The courses of study included: Natural Philosophy, Astronomy, Physiology, Rhetoric, Political Economy, Latin, and Greek.

1867   Andrew Johnson   *Blue Danube,* Waltz—Johann Strauss

Public education introduced in Cape Girardeau.

Central High School opens in Kansas City.

Joseph Baldwin opens the North Missouri Normal School and Commercial College in Kirksville.

1870   Ulysses S. Grant   *Romeo and Juliet*—Peter I. Tchaikovsky

Union Volunteer Fire Company Band was formed for a July 4th celebration parade in St. Charles. Joseph Decker was the leader.

Missouri General Assembly makes Joseph Baldwin's North Missouri Normal School the Missouri First District Normal School.

Arthur Willard Pryor born on September 22nd in St. Joseph. He became known as the "World's Greatest Trombone Player." Pryor was a member of Sousa's band for 12 years.

1871   Ulysses S. Grant   *Aida*—Giuseppe Verdi

Central High School opens in Springfield.

Missouri Second District Normal School established in Warrensburg.

1873   Ulysses S. Grant   Birth of Caruso, W. C. Handy, and Rachmaninoff
Missouri Third District Normal School established in Cape Girardeau.

1880   Rutherford B. Hayes   *Overture 1812*—Peter I. Tchaikovsky
Eustonia Silver Cornet Band, directed by William G. Bock, organized in Cape Girardeau.

1882   Chester Arthur   *Parsifal*—Richard Wagner
Concordia Cornet Band organized by the conductor, Wihelm Wilk.

1883   Chester Arthur   Richard Wagner dies on February 13th.
Central High School in Kansas City opened.

1884   Chester Arthur   *Symphony # 7*—Anton Bruckner
FIRST UNIVERSITY BAND
The State University of Missouri Agriculture College and University in Columbia organized a
Cadet Corps Military Band. It was the first college or university band formed in Missouri.

1885   Chester Arthur   *Symphony # 5*—Johannes Brahms
Board of Curators at the State University of Missouri Agriculture College and
University in Columbia issued a warrant for $125 for the new Cadet
Corps Military Band to purchase music, uniforms, and payment for a director.

1886   Grover Cleveland   *Carnival of the Animals*—Camille Saint-Saens
First concert given by the new State University of Missouri Cadet Band.

1887   Grover Cleveland   *Otello*—Giuseppe Verdi
FIRST BAND ASSOCIATION FORMED
Southwestern Band Association formed; first of its kind in Missouri.
Lincoln High School opens in Kansas City for African-American students.

1889   Andrew Johnson   *The Gondoliers*—Gilbert & Sullivan
The Southwestern Band Association sponsors a band concert on May 21st in
Sicher's Park in Rolla. Town bands came from California (Mo.), Warrensburg, Carthage,
Concordia, Hermann, Clinton, and Springfield.

1891   Benjamin Harrison   Cole Porter born on June 9th
The St. Charles County Fair holds a band contest with five bands participating:
The St. Charles Cornet Band, Clay Street Band, New Melle Band, Augusta Band, and the
O'Fallon Band. First prize of sixty-five dollars went to the St. Charles Cornet Band.

1893   Grover Cleveland   *Symphony # 9*—A. Dvorak
Central High School in Springfield moves into newly constructed building. At the time of its
construction it was the largest high school west of the Mississippi River and graduated its first
class of 41 students in 1894.
Central high School in St. Louis moved to a new building at 15th and Olive. It was the first
coeducational high school in the United States.

1897   William McKinley   *Sorcerer's Apprentice*—Paul Dukas
Manual Training high School in Kansas City opened.
On June 15th, the St. Charles Cornet Band started a tradition that survived for
more than 100 years. The first open-air concerts were inaugurated at Clerk's Office Hill, where
a new bandstand had been erected for the weekly concerts.

1903   Theodore Roosevelt   *Babes in Toyland*—Victor Herbert
Burr H. Ozment becomes Director of the Cadet Band at the State University of Missouri.
He continued in that position until 1909.

1904   Theodore Roosevelt   *Meet Me in St. Louis*—Sterling & Mills
April 30—Opening of the "Louisiana Exposition"—The St. Louis World's Fair.
Three bands performed on opening day—The Sousa Band, The Innes Band, and The Philippine
Scout Band.

1905   Theodore Roosevelt   *La Mer* and *Clair de Lune*—Claude Debussy
FIRST INSTRUMENTAL MUSIC CLUB IN MISSOURI SCHOOLS
First instrumental music club organized at Central High School in St. Louis,
consisting of 4 violins, 1 cornet, 1 flute, 1 drum, and a piano.
Fourth District Normal School founded in Springfield.
Fifth District Normal School founded in Maryville.

1907   Theodore Roosevelt   *La Coq d'Or*—Nikolai Rimsky—Korsakov
Missouri State Legislature sends the University of Missouri Cadet Corp Band to Jamestown
Exposition, commemorating the founding of the first settlement in America.
Music Supervisors National Conference is organized, later to become MENC.
Westport High School in Kansas City opened.

1908   Theodore Roosevelt   *Rapsodie Espagnole*—Maurice Ravel
The Missouri State Normal School Number Three Band was organized in Cape
Girardeau by Earl G. Beck.

1910   William H. Taft   *Symphony # 9*—Gustav Mahler
George Venable hired as Director of the Cadet Band at the University of Missouri. He stayed
as director for 36 years until 1946.

1915   Woodrow Wilson   Frank Sinatra born in Hoboken, New Jersey
Marie Turner Harvey forms the Porter Community Band for boys as part of their education in a
"progressive" school system. In 1917 girls were included in the band, which was a one-room rural
school building nine miles northwest of Kirksville.

1916   Woodrow Wilson   Start of World War I in Europe
R. Richie Robertson becomes head of Springfield's Central High School music department.
He previously taught in the schools of Paola, Kansas.

1919   Woodrow Wilson   World War I ends, Prohibition goes into effect
The names of the five area normal schools were changed:
Normal School # 1 became Northeast Missouri State Teachers College.
Normal School # 2 became Central Missouri State Teachers College.
Normal School # 3 became Southeast Missouri State Teachers College.
Normal School # 4 became Southwest Missouri State Teachers College.
Normal School # 5 became Northwest Missouri State Teachers College.

1920 Woodrow Wilson *The Planets*—Gustav Holst
LARGEST BOY SCOUT BAND IN THE WORLD
R. Richie Robertson organizes a Boy Scout Band in Springfield with 50 boys.
Under his direction the band grew to over 400 Scouts in the next ten years—the largest Boy Scout
Band in the world.

1921 Woodrow Wilson Paul Whiteman's Orchestra most popular in US
J. R. Huckstep organized the first band at Bowling Green High School. He later taught at
Brunswick, Chillicothe, and Raytown. He was the first bandmaster to be inducted into the Missouri
Bandmasters Association Hall of Fame (1970).

1922 Warren Harding Louis Armstrong joins King Oliver's Jazz Band
STATE BAND LAW OF 1922
Arthur Harrison and Clarence Schuchert, from Cape Girardeau, along with State Senator
Snodgrass from El Dorado Springs, helped pass the State Band Law. The legislation allowed cities
in Missouri to levy a tax to support town bands.

1923 Calvin Coolidge Composer Clifton Williams born on March 26
NATIONAL BAND CONTEST
The first National Band Contest was held in Chicago. It continued until 1937.
Douglass High School from Hannibal was the only Missouri participant.

1924 Calvin Coolidge *Rhapsody in Blue*—George Gershwin
First band at Jackson High School organized by A. W. Roloff. There were 11 members.
Cape Girardeau Central High School yearbook of 1924 shows a "Tiger Tooter" Band under
the direction of Miss Frieda Riech.
Winston Lynes, at the age of 18, named band director at Southwest Missouri State College in
Springfield.

1925 Calvin Coolidge *Piano Concerto in F*—George Gershwin
Hans Lemcke, former cornet player in the Sousa Band, named band director at Webster Groves
High School in St. Louis County. He also taught German.
Keith K. Anderson joins faculty at Central College, Fayette. He continued as Director of Bands
for 27 years until his retirement in 1972.

1926   Calvin Coolidge   *Desert Song*—Sigmund Romberg

MENC (Music Educators National Conference) takes over sponsorship of the National Band Contest. Thirteen bands from 10 states took part in the Contest held in Fostoria, Ohio. The National School Band Association was formed during this time.

1927   Calvin Coolidge   *Jazz Singer*, with Al Jolson, was first talking movie

John Philip Sousa conducts concert with the Webster Groves High School band.
First band in University City High School organized by George Mechalson.

1928   Calvin Coolidge   *Bolero*—Maurice Ravel

Maplewood High School organizes an after-school band with 22 students,
directed by Mr. Van Meter.
Northeast Missouri State Teachers College Band started by Professors R. E.
Valentine and Biggerstaff. The band replaced a "noise-maker" group at ball games that
had been organized by students in 1923.

1929   Herbert Hoover   *Stardust*—Hogie Carmichael

State Band Contest moved to three district contest in Kirksville, Springfield, and Warrensburg.
First school band organized at St. Charles High School. Mr. Snyder, a graduate of Otterbein
College in Ohio, was founder and director.

1930   Herbert Hoover   *Embraceable You*—George Gershwin

Hans Lemcke, Webster Groves, organizes the St. Louis All-County Band,
sponsored by the St. Louis County Band Directors Association. It later merged into the St. Louis
Suburban Music Educators Association.

1931   Herbert Hoover   *Star Spangled Banner* adopted as National Anthem

Norman Falkenhainer takes position as band director at University City High School. He was a
graduate of Missouri University and Assistant Band Director at the university.
William Shivelbine becomes band director at Central High School in Cape Girardeau. He retired
in 1940 to devote full-time to Shivelbine Music Company.

1933   Franklin D. Roosevelt   *Peter and the Wolf*—Sergi Prokofiev
National Band Contest canceled because of economic conditions.

1935   Franklin D. Roosevelt   *Porgy and Bess*—George Gershwin
FIRST PRESIDENT OF THE MISSOURI MUSIC EDUCATORS ASSOCIATION
Clarence Best, orchestra director at Webster Groves High School, elected as the first president of
the Missouri Music Educators Association. Best served as the instrumental president, and T. Frank
Coulter, from Joplin, as choral president.

1936   Franklin D. Roosevelt   Count Basie's Orchestra makes first recording
J. R. Huckstep accepts position of instrumental and vocal music at Chillicothe.
He continued until 1945.

1937   Franklin D. Roosevelt   *One O'clock Jump*—Count Basie
Last National Band Contest held with over 400 bands participating. Contest was later reorganized
with regional contests to accommodate the large number of entries. Kansas City's Muhlbach Hotel
became a regional contest center.

1938   Franklin D. Roosevelt   Benny Goodman plays Carnegie Hall in New York
LeRoy Mason named Director of Bands at Jackson High School. He remained for 19 years until
1957.

1939   Franklin D. Roosevelt   Marian Anderson sings at Lincoln Memorial
FIRST MISSOURI BAND CAMP
First Missouri band camp held in Fayette City Park organized by K. K. Anderson,
Director of Bands at Central College. Camp lasted three years until the beginning of World War II.
The band members—all boys—slept in tents provided by the local Boy Scouts.

1941   Franklin D. Roosevelt   Glenn Miller's *String of Pearls* tops music charts
US enters World War II.

1942   Franklin D. Roosevelt   *Fanfare for the Common Man*—Aaron Copland

Arthur Pryor, "World's Greatest Trombone Player," dies on June 18. He played in the Sousa band for 12 years. Pryor was born in St. Joseph and considered it his family home throughout his professional career.

1944   Franklin D. Roosevelt   D-Day in Europe, Glenn Miller missing in action

FIRST HIGH SCHOOL MARCHING BAND FESTIVAL IN MISSOURI

LeRoy Mason organizes the Jackson Marching Band Festival—first in the state.

1945   Harry S. Truman   *Carousel*—Rogers & Hammerstein, WWII ends

SOUTHEAST MISSOURI BAND DIRECTORS ASSOCIATION FORMED

LeRoy Mason (Jackson), Keith Collins (Sikeston), and other directors form the Southeast Missouri Band Association.

J. R. Huckstep employed as band director at Raytown High School. He retired in 1959 at the age of 69. He died in 1989 at age 89.

Southwest Missouri State Teachers College, Springfield, changes name to Southwest Missouri State College.

1946   Harry S. Truman   *Annie Get Your Gun*—Irving Berlin

George Wilson appointed Director of Bands—University of Missouri, Columbia.

He stayed 11 years until 1957 then resigned to accept the position as Vice President of the National Music Camp at Interlochen, Michigan.

Southeast Missouri State Teachers College, Cape Girardeau, changes name to Southeast Missouri State College.

Northwest Missouri State Teachers College, Maryville, changes name to Northwest Missouri State College.

1950   Harry S. Truman   *Guys and Dolls*—Frank Loesser

Raytown High School Band, directed by J. R. Huckstep, achieves a "1" rating at the Tri-State Music Festival in Enid, Oklahoma. He achieved equal success with the Raytown Chorus, Glee Club, and Orchestra. All performing groups under his direction received the highest award in the same year.

1951   Harry S. Truman   *King and I*—Rogers and Hammerstein

NORTH CENTRAL MISSOURI BANDMASTERS ASSOCIATION FORMED

North Central Bandmasters organized in the fall of 1951. Frank W. Fendorf,
Chillicothe High School, and businessman Harold Linton were leaders in the formation
of the new organization.

1956   Dwight D. Eisenhower *My Fair Lady*—Learner and Lowe

FIRST HIGH SCHOOL JAZZ BAND CONTEST IN MISSOURI

First Jazz Band Contest for high schools held at Boonville High School. Gerald McCollum,
band director, organized the contest until 1969. Jefferson City High School, directed by Don Verne
Joseph, won first place.

1957   Dwight D. Eisenhower *The Music Man*—Meredith Willson

LeRoy Mason named Director of Bands at Southeast Missouri State College in Cape Girardeau.
He remained for 19 years until his retirement in 1976.
Ed Carson replaces Mason at Jackson as Director of Bands.
Charles Emmons named Director of Band, University of Missouri – Columbia.

1959   Dwight D. Eisenhower *Gypsy*—Styne and Sondheim

LAMBDA CHAPTER OF PHI BETA MU FORMED

January 8, 1959—Lambda Chapter (Missouri) of Phi Beta Mu, National
Bandmasters Fraternity organized with 26 charter members. Charles Emmons, University of
Missouri – Columbia, elected president.
Girls admitted to University of Missouri Marching Band for the first time.

1960   Dwight D. Eisenhower *Camelot*—Lerner and Lowe

FIRST MISSOURI BAND IN ROSE BOWL PARADE

Ruskin High School first Missouri band to march in the Rose Bowl Parade in Pasadena, California.
Directors were Kenneth and Nancy Seward.

1964   Lyndon Johnson   *Hello, Dolly*—Jerry Herman

FIRST MISSOURI BAND INVITED TO MIDWEST BAND CLINIC

University City High School Band directed by Roger Warner, invited to the Midwest Band Clinic
along with four other US bands. It was the first band from Missouri to play at Midwest. Guest

conductors were Charles Emmons, University of Missouri – Columbia, Commander Charles Brendler, US Navy Band, retired. Trumpet soloists were Alexander Pickard, University of Missouri – Columbia and Haskell Sexton, Professor of Trumpet, University of Illinois.

Dr. Thomas E. Birch, Director of Bands at Central Methodist College, collapses and dies while conducting the first selection at a concert in Fayette before the start of a six-day band tour.

1966   Lyndon Johnson   *Sweet Charity*—Coleman and Fields

Charles Emmons retires as Director of Bands, University of Missouri – Columbia.

Alexander Pickard appointed to direct Missouri University band program.

1967   Lyndon Johnson   Chicago (group) and REO Speedwagon formed

Northeast Missouri State Teachers College, Kirksville, changes name to Northeast Missouri State College.

1968   Lyndon Johnson   *Hair*, rock musical opens

MISSOURI BANDMASTERS ASSOCIATION FORMED

Missouri Bandmasters Association organized with Bob Scott, Ruskin High School, as first president.

First University of Missouri – Columbia Jazz Festival.

Northeast Missouri State Teacher College, Kirksville, officially changes name to Northeast Missouri State College.

1969   Richard Nixon   Woodstock rock concert

First Missouri Bandmasters Association Convention held at Millstone Lodge, Gravois Mills, Missouri, July 13–15, 1969.

1970   Richard Nixon   Beatles break up—go solo

Richmond High School Band plays at Midwest Band Clinic in Chicago under the direction of Kenneth and Nancy Seward.

Carrollton Band Day organized by director Robert Ward.

J. Roy Huckstep, Raytown High School, receives first Missouri Bandmasters Association Hall of Fame award.

1971   Richard Nixon   *Jesus Christ Superstar*—Andrew Lloyd Weber
FIRST MISSOURI BAND TO PERFORM AT NFL SUPERBOWL
Southeast Missouri State University "Golden Eagle" Marching Band is first
Missouri band to perform at Super Bowl in Miami, Florida.
Central Missouri State Teachers College, Warrensburg, officially changes name to Central
Missouri State University.
First Greater St. Louis Marching Band Festival organized by Dr. Warren Bellis,
University of Missouri – St. Louis and C. Herbert Duncan, Normandy High School. Eight bands
participated at Francis Field, Washington University. Paris, Illinois, was the first place winner.

1972   Richard Nixon   Elvis Presley sells out Madison Square Garden
Ozarko Marching Band Festival organized at Southwest Missouri State College by newly
appointed Director of Bands, Robert Scott.
Northeast Missouri State College, Kirksville, changes name to Northeast Missouri
State University.
Southeast Missouri State College, Cape Girardeau, changes name to Southeast Missouri
State University.
Southwest Missouri State University, Springfield, changes name to Southwest Missouri
State University.
Northwest Missouri State University, Maryville, changes name to Northwest Missouri
State University.

1973   Richard Nixon   *A Little Night Music*—Stephen Sondheim
Southwest Missouri State University Jazz Festival held in Springfield under the direction of
founder Robert Scott, Director of Bands.

1976   Gerald Ford   *A Little Night Music*—Stephen Sondheim
LeRoy F. Mason, Director of Bands emeritus, Southeast Missouri State University, Cape
Girardeau, dies on July 14 at age 64 in St. Louis.

1977   Jimmy Carter   *Annie, the Musical*—Strouse & Charnin
FIRST MISSOURI ALL—STATE BAND ORGANIZED
The first Missouri All-State Band, sponsored by the Missouri Bandmasters Association, performs
for the Missouri Music Educators Association conference at Ramada Inn in Jefferson City.

1980   Jimmy Carter   *Barnum* and *42nd Street* opens on Broadway

J. Roy Huckstep, long-time Director of Bands at Raytown High School from 1945–1959, dies at age 89. He was the first recipient of the Missouri Bandmasters Association Hall of Fame Award.

1982   Ronald Reagan   *Joseph and the Amazing Technicolor Dreamcoat*

Alexander Pickard appointed Assistant Chairman of the University of Missouri–Columbia Music Department. He retires as Director of Bands. Dale Kennedy from Wichita State University appointed to replace Pickard.

1996   William Clinton

Northeast Missouri State University, Kirksville, officially changes name to Truman State University.

Firsts

First   SCHOOL in Missouri

1774 – Established in St. Louis, Territory of Missouri, and taught by J. B. Tribeau for 40 years

First   MUNICIPAL BAND in Missouri

1819 – St. Charles – The La Frenier Chauvin family gave free concerts at a small park at 624 South Main Street

First   HIGH SCHOOL in Missouri

1853 – Central High School, St. Louis – 70 pupils

First   SCHOOL BAND in Missouri

1884 – Cadet Corps Military Band, State University of Missouri, Frederick Pannell, Director

First   HIGH SCHOOL BAND in Missouri

1908 – McKinley High School, St. Louis, Mr. Burr, Director

First   MISSOURI BAND AT THE NATIONAL BAND CONTEST

1923 – Douglass High School, Hannibal, Martin A. Lewis, principal and band director

First   PRESIDENT OF MISSOURI STATE BAND & ORCHESTRA DIRECTOR'S ASS'N.

1935 – Clarence Best, Director of Orchestra, Webster Groves High School

First   BAND CAMP

1939 – Central College, Fayette, organized by Keith K. Anderson, held in city park

First   MARCHING BAND FESTIVAL

1944 – Jackson High School, LeRoy Mason, Director

First   HIGH SCHOOL JAZZ FESTIVAL

1956 – Boonville High School, Gerald McCollum, Director

First   LAMBDA CHAPTER / PHI BETA MU PRESIDENT
1959 –Charles Emmons, University of Missouri – Columbia

First   MISSOURI BAND TO MARCH IN ROSE BOWL PARADE
1960 – Ruskin High School, Kenneth and Nancy Seward, Directors

First   MISSOURI BAND TO PLAY AT MIDWEST BAND CLINIC
1964 – University City High School, Roger Warner, Director

First   MISSOURI BANDMASTERS ASSOCIATION PRESIDENT
1969 – Robert Scott, Ruskin High School

TOWN BANDS

Chapter 3

Town Bands

1900 America

As the United States entered the twentieth century, Missouri, along with all of the Midwest, was an agricultural state with many small towns. Towns along the two major rivers and the several railroads that supplied goods and transportation had their own churches, fire house, courthouse, and schools. There were no department stores or retail chains. Small independent businesses were the staple of every community. In 1912, F. W. Woolworth was incorporated and would become the biggest retail chain in America. The A&P (Atlantic and Pacific) grocery store chain had 500 stores by 1915 and boasted of opening a new store every three days. Fifty percent of all cars were manufactured by Henry Ford.

Anne Marvin, writing for the Kansas Historical Society, states in *The Turn-of-the-Century Hometown Band:*

> It is difficult to comprehend the tremendous popularity of town bands during the late nineteenth and early twentieth centuries. In those days before the phonograph, radio, movies, and television, bands had a monopoly on popular, light entertainment, and band music was considered appropriate to almost any setting. Until the mid-nineteenth century, most bands were affiliated with the military, but as the popularity of band music grew, more and more civilian ensembles were organized. Most of these organizations retained military-style uniforms that, along with their dynamic music, appealed to the American fascination with energy, progress, and patriotism. A brass band came to be considered essential to the life of a community, and by the turn of the century almost every town of any size had a band. It is estimated that by 1908, the United States was home to some eighteen thousand bands, many of them amateur civic organizations (19).

The social fabric of America was the church followed by fraternal organizations and societies. The pride of any community was the town band. Bands followed the European music tradition and were military in nature; that is, men only, military-type uniforms, and marches as the music of choice. Bands were needed for celebrations, holidays, and community events. Many took the name of the leader or the name of the town and were often called "Military Band" or "Cornet Band."

What caused the wide-spread popularity of this form of indigenous cultural entertainment in the era between the industrial revolution and World War I?

David E. Fulmer, a music and history researcher at the University of California, Berkeley, writes:

> On the one hand we generated a small amount of spare time for our hard-working pioneering forefathers; on the other, they did not have the means to get out of their immediate environment to enjoy it. Horse-drawn buggies were slow; automobiles were yet to come in profusion. Telephones were scarce and expensive; and, of course, radios and other forms of communication were non-existent. So, we turned inward and became our own entertainment. The sale of parlor pianos skyrocketed. Band instruments were available through mail-order houses, along with the music, music stands, and even instruction books needed to form a town band. A town that could pay $300 cash could get delivery of all the accouterments for a band in about three weeks. Then all remained was to come up with the musicians to play them. The results were, to say the least, uneven. But the enjoyment and home-grown sense of achievement must have far overshadowed any lapses in musicianship. It must have been a colorful, though cacophonous time (20).

Bands were often formed around the town's volunteer fire department. The origin of this is not clear. However it is speculated that the fire house provided a convenient meeting space for such activities. Community centers had yet to be discovered, and using a church facility would be unpopular for a segment of the town's population. Band practice in a church, no matter the denomination, would find little support with many community members. The fire house was a center for town gatherings, picnics, ice cream socials, and political debates before the introduction of radio, television, telephones, and automobiles.

Today, town bands continue to provide musical opportunities in many communities, primarily performed by non-professional musicians. Summer band concerts in the city park are strong reminders of the heritage enjoyed by family and friends. The town band became the foundation on which bands were then to find their way into the school first as a club activity, and then as part of the curriculum.

O'Fallon Cornet Band – 1900
St. Charles Historical Society photo

Town Bands

County		County Seat
Adair	Brasher Concert Band – 1915	Kirksville
	Novinger Cornet Band – 1893	
	Novinger Chautauqua Band –1890	
	Kirksville Boys Band – 1905	
	Kirksville Military Band	
	Knights of Pythias Band –1904	
	Porter Community Band –1915	
Audrain	Vandalia Band – 1910	Mexico
Bollinger	Quartette String Band – 1875	Marble Hill
	Marble Hill Cornet Band – 1876–1878	
	Marble Hill Silver Cornet Band – 1876–1920	
Boone	Columbia Community Band – 1981	Columbia
Buchanan	Rosenblatt's Band – 1868	St. Joseph
	Samuel Pryor's Military Band – ca 1871	
	Parland-Hamm All American Band – ca 1918	
	Willis C. Maupin's Band – ca 1920	
Callaway	New Bloomfield Town Band 1894	Fulton
Cape Girardeau	Cape City Band –1893	Jackson
	Cape Eureka Band – 1892	
	Cape Municipal Band (reorganized) – 1927	
	Commerce Band – 1892	
	Estonia Silver Cornet Band – 1880	
	Jackson Municipal Band – 1920	
	Schuchert Concert Band – 1910	
Cass	Harrisonville Town Band – 1885	Harrisonville

Harrisonville Citizens Cornet Band – 1887
Harrisonville Cornet Band – 1898
John N. White's Cornet Band

Cedar   Wonder City Rube Band – 1885   Stockton
Henry's Park Band –1897
El Dorado Springs Municipal Band – ca 1903
American Maiden's Band – 1925

Chariton   Forest Green Band – 1886   Keytesville
Brunswick Silver Cornet Band – 1908
Keytesville Band
Triplett Cornet Band – 1913

Christian   Billings Citizens Band – 1910   Ozark
Nixa Band – 1905

Clay   Liberty Band – 1900   Liberty

Clinton   Cameron Military Band – 1867   Plattsburg
Plattsburg Chautauqua Band – 1906
Cameron Community Concert Band – 1922
Rotary Boys Band – 1927
Cameron Municipal Band – 1929

Cooper   Picture only of band playing – 1870   Boonville
Otterville Silver Cornet Band – 1910

Dade   Dadeville Concert Band – undated   Greenfield
Greenfield Silver Band –1901

Dallas   Buffalo Concert Band – ca 1900   Buffalo

DeKalb   Fairport Cornet Band – 1896   Maysville

Dent   Stonehill Band – 1893   Salem

Franklin	Washington Town Band – ca 1874	Union
	later to be known as the:	
	William Lang Silver Cornet Band – 1874	
	Washington Philharmonic Reed Band – 1881	
	Washington Cornet Band – 1894	
	Washington Concert Band – 1918	
	International Shoe Company Band – 1907	
	Washington Golden Rod Concert Band – ca 1920	
	Washington Boys Band – 1930	
	Washington Elks Band – 1930	
	Washington VFW Band – 1950	
	Washington Brass Band – 1960	
Gasconade	Bray Brass Band – 1890	Hermann
	Stonehill Band – 1893	
	Hermann Apostle Band – 1890	
	Enterprise Military Band – 1919	
	Hermann Municipal Band – 1946	
Gentry	Albany Municipal Band – 1927	Albany
Greene	Dumar's Springfield Band – 1877	Springfield
	Hobart Band – 1884	
	Springfield Military Band – 1887	
	Marine Band – ca 1898	
	Hoover's Band – 1907	
Howard	Fayette Town Band – 1910	Fayette
	Roanoke Military Band – 1915	
Jasper	Carthage Light Guard Band – 1878	Carthage
	Carthage Silver Cornet Band	
	Queen City Band	
Jefferson	DeSoto Concert Band – 1903	Hillsboro
	DeSoto Veterans Drum and Bugle Corps	

Laclede	Lebanon Concert Band – 1912	Lebanon
Lafayette	Mount Hope Band – 1874	Lexington
	Wilks Band of Concordia – 1882	
	Concordia Cornet Band – 1882	
	Emma Cornet Band	
	Ernestville Band	
	Lexington Town Band – 1889	
	Mayview Cornet Band – 1890	
	Odessa Band – ca 1900	
	Lafayette Military Band of Higginsville – ca 1915	
	Lexington Boys Band –1922	
Lawrence	Lawrenceburg Village Band – 1892	Mount Vernon
	Mount Vernon Fireman's Band – 1903	
	Aurora Rotary Boys Band – 1929	
Linn	Bucklin Concert Band – 1898	Linneus
	Marceline Band –1902	
Macon	New Cambria Cornet Band	Macon
	Conter's Cornet Band – 1894	
	Callao Cornet Band – 1894	
	Blee's Military Academy Band – 1900	
Moniteau	California Brass Band – 1867	California
	California Silver Cornet Band – 1870	
	McGirk's Band – 1921	
Morgan	Florence Cornet Band – 1908	Versailles
Newton	Granby Silver Cornet Band –1880	Neosho
	Newtonia Band – ca 1880	
	Neosho Hayseed Band – 1892	

Diamond Cornet Band – 1894
Seneca Town Band
Stella Clown Band

Oregon	Alton Brass Band – 1910	Alton
Ozark	Gainesville Brass Band	Gainesville
Perry	Altenburg Band – ca 1880 Frohna Town Band East Perry County Band – 1945 Neislein's Band Uniontown Band Whittenberg Town Band	Perryville
Pettis	MKT Railroad Coach Shop Band – 1930	Sedalia
Phelps	Rolla Town Band – ca 1900 Russell Brothers Circus – 1930	Rolla
Polk	Bolivar Band – 1905 Humansville Concert Band – 1915	Bolivar
Randolph	Huntsville Knights of Honor Band – 1874 Higbee Silver Cornet Band – 1891	Huntsville
Saline	Miami Community Band – 1930	Marshall
Shannon	Ozark Land and Lumber Company Band – 1900	Eminence
Ste. Genevieve	Knights of Columbus Band Lions Band (prior to WW II) Ste. Genevieve Municipal Band – 1946	Ste Genevieve

St. Charles	LaFrenier Chauvin family band – 1819	St. Charles
	St. Charles Municipal Band – 1870	
	St. Charles Cornet Band – 1880	
	Rummel's Military Band – 1890	
	O'Fallon Cornet Band – 1900	
	St. Charles Military Band – 1913	
	St. Charles Municipal Band – 1929	
St. Clair	Osceola Town Band – 1891	Osceola
St. Louis County	Webster Groves Municipal Band – 1930	Clayton
Warren	Dutzow Cornet Band	Warrenton
Washington	Caledonia Band –1908	Potosi
Webster	Grand Army of the Republic Band	Marshfield
	Marshfield Cornet Band – 1878	
	Marshfield Cyclone City Band – ca 1888	
	Marshfield Concert Band – 1930	
Wright	Hartville Community Band – 1925	Hartville

Adair County

County Seat: Kirksville

The Novinger Cornet Band

"The Shelbina fair this year has made a feature of the band. There is no one thing that goes so far toward making any affair a success as a band. Without any band at all, any event is a dismal failure. With an ordinary band it's perhaps a little better, but with a band such as few people ever heard it is an assured success. Many people that otherwise were not going to see the fair owing to bad weather, are going to hear the famous Novinger Cornet Band. It is without doubt the best twenty–piece band in the state. This band gave a concert Friday afternoon, August 2, at Kirksville, and three thousand people came. They paid 25 cents each admission" (21).

"All who were so fortunate as to hear the Novinger Cornet Band at Crystal Lake Park last Saturday evening unite in praise of the splendid music made by this well-drilled organization. The band gave a most pleasing entertainment. The program included a number of high-class selections rendered in a most admirable manner, and that the audience was pleased was manifested by the hearty applause" (22).

For more than twenty-five years Novinger was noted for the fine quality of its concert band. Originally this band was organized in the early 1890's, and it continued to be a rather widely applauded organization. The members at first were a few farm boys who got together and were taught themselves to play the various instruments. In about 1903 they hired a director and instructor and began recruiting new members among the young people of the town and the area. Regular practice meetings were held several times each week until the band became very well rehearsed and proficient in the playing of many types of music; therefore, they had a wide popular appeal. They played for nearly all of the political rallies, school activities, and furnished music for any type of celebration throughout the area.

From the official Clinton County Chautauqua program of 1906: "Music lovers at this years [*sic*] Chautauqua will be more than pleased by the Novinger Band, which will furnish music every day. Its twenty members are nearly all Germans and they have worked together many years. Their band is their pride. They have arrived at high standards in music and are consequently able to present a record of successes" (23).

Lee Hoy was the director in 1906 and was photographed with the members of the band in their white uniforms. Professor W. A. Howland then took over the direction of the band in the summer of 1907 and was photographed with the band in the darker uniforms. Many of the members became professional musicians who traveled with circus or carnival bands in later years.

The Porter Community Band

The Adair County Porter School was built in 1892, three miles north and west of Kirksville via Industrial Road and Route B. Before 1912, Porter was just one of the hundreds of one-room schools found everywhere in rural America. It suffered from the same problems all rural districts faced: lack of funding, low attendance, and apathy by the community. Few of the students made it to high school, and many left for the cities as soon as they were of age.

One of the new "progressive educators" was Marie Turner, who taught elementary school in St. Louis County before coming to Kirksville and marrying State Normal School professor H. Clay Harvey. Her innovations in education brought attention to the Porter community where she taught. Articles in national and international newspapers and magazines attracted visitors interested in progressive education.

Marie Turner Harvey advocated music "as the one thing that would organize, harmonize, and stabilize a community" (24), and in 1915 put this theory into practice at Porter with the creation of the Porter Community Band, originally made up of the senior boys in the school. By 1917, women were included, a professional musician was engaged as director, and a Junior Band was established. Through the years the Porter Community Band became one of the best known ambassadors for the Porter School. Included among its accomplishments was an appearance at the State Fair in Sedalia in 1920, and a contract with the City of Kirksville for regular Saturday night concerts during the summer.

Many activities at Porter School emphasized patriotism and the responsibilities of citizenship. The Fourth of July provided an excellent opportunity for Mrs. Harvey to promote patriotism. Elaborate programs included performances by the band, community singing, recitations, and "living pictures." The latter was a popular turn-of-the-century entertainment in which costumed figures, frozen in place, imitated famous political cartoons.

Novinger Concert Band – 1909
Adair County Historical Society photo

Audrain County

County Seat: Mexico

Vandalia Town Band – ca 1910
Outside the Vandalia Grain Palace
The State Historical Society
of Missouri photo

Bollinger County

County Seat: Marble Hill

The Western Historical Manuscript Collection in Rolla at Missouri University of Science and Technology indicates there are two record books of the community bands at Marble Hill in Bollinger County. The records include constitutions, membership lists, minutes of meetings, and financial accounts of the Quartette String Band (1875), the Marble Hill Cornet Band (1876–1878), and the Marble Hill Silver Cornet Band (1876–1902). Although this collection was acquired from two separate donors, the combined material forms a unified history of the Marble Hill bands. The long association of Dr. August Sander with the bands explains the continuity of the records.

On June 22, 1875, the Lutesville and Marble Hill String Bands combined to form the Quartette String Band. Dr. August Sander was elected president. The band's rules established a minimum fee of fourteen dollars for an engagement, and prohibited "freelance" engagements by the individual musicians. The band performed at a ball on July 5, 1875, but further bookings were not forthcoming and the last entry by the treasurer was dated September, 1875.

On May 15, 1876, many of the same individuals organized the Marble Hill Cornet Band. Again, August Sander was elected president and J. M. Welch was named leader. There are detailed financial accounts for this organization extending into 1878.

There is a gap in the records from 1878 until May 15, 1887, when August Sander, now the secretary of the "Marble Hill Silver Cornet Band," essayed a brief account of the eleven-year history of the organization. This memoir includes a list of all members during the period, and noted that in late 1886 the band had been reorganized, with Robert W. Fisher as leader and Charles A. Sander as president.

There were subsequent reorganizations in 1891, 1897 (after the resignation of R. W. Fisher), 1899, and 1902 (when Fisher returned as leader). These reorganizations were reflected in new constitutions and bylaws. Financial accounts are most complete for the years 1895 through 1898 (25).

Boone County

County Seat: Columbia

The Columbia Community Band

The Columbia Community Band was founded in 1981 as part of the Columbia Public Schools Adult Education Program. It is comprised of a group of dedicated volunteer musicians. Since its inception, the Columbia Community Band has become one of the Midwest's premier symphonic concert bands, and has grown from an initial membership of twenty, to seventy musicians.

The Columbia Community band's first conductor, Butch Antal, played trumpet with the Henry Mancini Orchestra and other professional bands. Antal established and guided the Columbia Community Band through its first six years.

Alan Nellis led the band from 1986–1988, followed by Professor Keith House, Director of Bands at nearby Central Methodist College in Fayette. House led the band from 1989–2005. John Patterson became assistant director in 1999 and assumed the duties of director in 2005. He was the Director of Bands at Hickman High School in Columbia and continued as director of the community band after his retirement at Hickman. Paul Copenhaver joined the Columbia Community Band in 2008 as assistant director.

The band was the first concert band to perform in the historic Missouri Theatre in Columbia, and the first community band to perform at the International Scott Joplin Festival in Sedalia. By invitation, the Columbia Community Band has performed at the Missouri Bandmasters Association annual convention in 1991 and 2007, as well as the Missouri Music Educators Association Conference and the Association of Concert Bands.

In 1999, the Columbia Community Band expanded its performance venues when it traveled to England and Scotland to perform a ten-day concert tour. In 2006, the band celebrated its 25th anniversary with a concert at the Missouri Theatre in Columbia.

Area town band at
Columbia Fair, ca 1905
Boone County Historical Society
Westhoff collection photo

Buchanan County

County Seat: St. Joseph

The program reprinted by the Clinton County Historical Society in 1926 gave a history of the Plattsburg Chautauqua of 1918:

> The 1918 Chautauqua will open with a concert on Saturday evening, August 17th with the Parland-Hamm All American Band from St. Joseph. This is a new organization formed this season to furnish music in the city parks of St. Joseph. The band will be in performance throughout the Chautauqua Assembly. Mr. Fred Hamm, the director, is a cornetist of exceptional ability and brings the best out of a band (26).

Pryor's Military Band – ca 1871

Samuel Pryor was the town bandmaster in St. Joseph, Missouri. His wife was a pianist. The Pryors had two sons, one of whom was Arthur (see Pioneers), later to become known as the "world's greatest trombone soloist." The St. Joseph City Directory of 1871 had the following listing: Pryor, S.D., musician, residence, corner of 6th and Francis.

Wills C. Maupin's Band – ca 1920

Although not mentioned in the records of the Buchanan County Historical Society, the Maupin Band from St. Joseph, Missouri, is listed as one of the performing groups at the Plattsburg (Clinton County) Chautauqua in 1926. Program notes from that event indicate: "Willis C. Maupin's Band of St. Joseph, Missouri, will furnish the music for the entire session of the Plattsburg Chautauqua. They were here several years ago and so delighted that the crowd management was requested to return them again this year. They will give three programs daily and also will furnish a five-piece orchestra for the motion pictures" (27).

Fourth Infantry Band – Buchanan County – 1897
Missouri State Historical Society photo

Rosenblatt's Band, St. Joseph – 1868
Missouri State Historical Society photo

Callaway County

County Seat: Fulton

New Bloomfield Town Band –1894
Missouri State Archives photo

Cape Girardeau County

County Seat: Jackson

Jackson Municipal Band

Albert William Roloff (1880–1972) was the first director of the Jackson Municipal Band. Roloff graduated from the Jackson Military Academy in 1902. At the academy he received "thorough and modern instruction in music, art, and education," which indicates that the community perceived music as a valuable part of a student's education. It was at the academy that Roloff took lessons and learned to play most of the instruments.

The Chamber of Commerce wanted a musical organization to represent the city at patriotic events and other activities in the area, and asked Mr. Roloff to form a community band. One charter member, Paul Bruening, remembers that in September, 1920 Roloff recruited 29 boys to become band members. The boys rented or borrowed instruments and met every week in the Roloff wood shop, a free-of-charge rehearsal hall where they sat on wooden horses, coped with the sawdust, and practiced. Herr Roloff, their only teacher, gave individual and group lessons, and on November 11, 1921, the Jackson Junior Band (as it was known then) gave its first performance. Bruening remembers performing two selections: a march entitled *The Captain* (possibly Sousa's *El Capitan*) and a waltz called *Rustling Leaves*.

Although the band earned money (ten dollars for local events and fifty dollars for out-of-town concerts), band members still paid twenty-five cents in monthly dues to provide for music and other expenses. Roloff often gave money out of his own pocket when there was not enough money for necessary purchases, even though he received no salary for years. The group could not afford uniforms and they wore white shirts, white trousers, and black ties until 1938, when they purchased black pants, red coats, black caps, and Sam Browne belts.

Jackson residents had become proud of their community band and in 1930 voted for a special tax levy to provide funds for building a bandstand on the courthouse lawn. The bandstand was completed in 1932, and Jackson still maintains a tax to support the community band. Jackson is one of the few towns in Missouri that maintains such a tax. The name of the band changed to Jackson Municipal Band in 1935, and it now performs in a band shell that was built for them in the city park in 1976 and dedicated to A. W. Roloff (28).

Jackson Municipal Band directors have included Albert W. Roloff, LeRoy Mason, Ed Carson, Richard Partridge, Linton Luetje, Allen Rowland, James Rhodes, and Nick Leist.

Cape Girardeau Municipal Band

The Eutonia Silver Cornet Band, directed by William G. Bock, was organized in 1880 in Cape Girardeau. This was followed in 1892 by the Cape Eureka Band. In that same year, John F.

Schuchert organized the Silver Cornet Band. In 1893 the original Eutonia Silver Cornet Band became the Cape City Band under Willam G. Bock's direction. Records also list a Commerce Band in 1892, which was directed by John F. Schuchert as well.

John F. Schuchert started the band so men of the community could play an instrument, as a hobby, for picnics and public gatherings within a 50-mile radius of Cape Girardeau. The original band had 12 members and was called "Schuchert's Cornet Band."

In 1910, Dr. Clarence Schuchert, a dentist, followed his father as director, changing the name to "Schuchert's Concert Band." Soon several of the younger men were being mustered into military service, so the band enlisted as a unit and became the 140th National Guard Band. In 1917 the entire band was mustered into the regular army, and all 40 members left for camp. After three months, the band was broken up and the older men were sent home. Those too young or too old for military service started the Cape Municipal Band, playing weekly during the war at the Courthouse Park.

Dr. Clarence E. Schuchert was director of the Schuchert Band from 1918–1922. Dr. Schuchert moved his dental practice to St. Louis in 1922. Professor Harry Albert, former Director of the Southeast Missouri State Normal School Band, reorganized the Schuchert Band in his absence and directed from 1922–1927. During this time the band was supported by private funds, the Chamber of Commerce, and by some revenue from the City of Cape Girardeau.

In 1924–25, Dr. Clarence E. Schuchert returned to Cape Girardeau and directed the band, but left in 1926 for a salaried position as band director in Red Bud, Illinois.

The Municipal Band was reorganized in 1927 with the aid of the Missouri Band Tax Law and was adopted by the Cape Girardeau City Council in that same year (29).

In an undated document titled *History of the Band* (from a concert program) there were seven members who had been in the band for over fifty years and one member, Homer Gilbert, retired after playing in the band for 73 years (30).

Cape Girardeau Municipal Band directors:

1900–1910	Captain John F. Schuchert
1911–1921	Dr. Clarence E. Schuchert
1922–1927	Professor Harry Albert
1928–1931	Thomas Danks, Jr.
1932–1949	William Adam Shivelbine
1950–1966	O. Louis Wilcox
1967–1977	Edward T. Adams
1978–1992	Jon Kent Fisher
1993–2008	Ronald Nall

Cass County

County Seat: Harrisonville

The first town band in Harrisonville was formed in May, 1885, under the direction of Prof. J. N. Darlington as leader. All members wore uniforms and the band purchased 13 instruments at a total cost of $345.30. The instruments arrived on June 11, 1885. There was still $100 due on the instruments when they arrived, to be liquidated by public subscription.

A second band known as the Harrisonville Citizens Cornet Band was formed in 1887. Members played only cornets and similar instruments. There was no July 4th celebration scheduled in Harrisonville that year, so the band signed a contract to play at Merriam Park in Kansas City.

By 1898, a third band was founded and called the Harrisonville Cornet Band, a forerunner of John L. White's Concert Band of Harrisonville. This band had one woodwind instrument, a clarinet. John White, a cashier at the Allen Bank Company and an excellent cornet player, tutored and directed bands in Harrisonville for more than 30 years. The band frequently gave open air concerts in Harrisonville and other nearby cities. After about 20 years, "old" band members had become scarce and membership was declining. In response to the problem, White organized the Junior Concert Band in 1921. The original band had 42 members.

On Easter Sunday, 1922, several veteran musicians "sat in" with the young group when they made their initial public appearance on the west side of the square. The band continued to make public appearances and was one of the first live groups to be aired on Kansas City radio when they gave an hour–long program on WDAF.

The band ceased to function in 1930, and White died in 1938 (31).

Harrisonville Cornet Band – 1898
Cass County Historical Society photo

White's Concert Band
Cass County Historical Society photo

White's Concert Band
Harrisonville
Cass County Historical Society photo

Cedar

County Seat: Stockton

El Dorado Springs Municipal Band

The El Dorado Springs Municipal Band was founded in 1881. In the early years, two-hour concerts were held five nights a week and the town paid its band members $100 per month (32).

Around 1885 or 1886, a group of men headed by C. V. Mickey reorganized the original band and formed a band called the Wonder City Rube Band. Thus began what has become a 100 plus year tradition of concerts in Spring Park. Those concerts continue today after 124 years.

The healing qualities of the spring water of El Dorado Springs brought hotels, churches, and businesses as the town incorporated in 1881. An opera house, skating rink, and swimming pool were developed later for the recreation of tourists and residents. But the earliest entertainment revolved around Spring Park. Five years after the city's founding, $3,000 was approved by the voters for park improvements, including the first bandstand. A square two-story structure with elaborate lattice work was built and was first used in 1887.

The length of the band season and length and number of concerts changed many times. In 1895 the band played four months, three times a week, with two-hour concerts; and members were paid fifty dollars a month. All money came from public donations.

A.M. Henry was conductor from 1897–1901, then again in 1903. He was called "Professor Henry" and the band became known as "Henry's Park Band." On the off-season the "Professor" manufactured cigars. George Woodruff was director in 1895 and in 1901. Charles Neff served as conductor of the park band from 1904–1911.

The band was called on numerous times when special events were scheduled, such as greeting the first train to arrive in El Dorado Springs in 1898 and the first automobile through town in 1908.

Women first played in the band in 1919. In 1925, director D. I. Netherow formed a women's band called the American Maiden's Band. In 1929, the community began to support the band financially. A two mill (.002 cents) band tax was approved by the voters after El Dorado Springs' own Senator Snodgrass introduced a bill before the Missouri Legislature to allow towns and cities to levy a special "band tax."

Soon after the band turned 50, a new bandstand was built. It was a round structure constructed in order to save the surrounding trees. The bandstand's foundation of stone became a community project. People were invited to contribute rocks for the foundation of the new bandstand. Pieces of broken pottery from China, petrified wood, children's marbles, and large quartz rocks—all donated by the community—provided the foundation for the new structure.

In 1940, the band concerts were reduced from five to four, and then to three per week, because of the war. In 1959, the city band tax was lowered to 1.5 mills, and just a year later some citizens opposed the band tax altogether. However, the band tax was saved by people like Bess Dove who wrote: "El Dorado without a band would be like December without Christmas" (33).

In 1960 the mayor of El Dorado Springs wanted to abolish the band and turn the city park into a parking lot. Through the work of W. W. Sunderwirth, the band's director, and the city attorney, the plan was not implemented.

El Dorado Municipal Band Directors

1887	C. V. Mickey	1931	Dr. D. I. Netherow
1895	George Woodruff	1932–1933	W. W. Wick
1896	C. V. Mickey	1934–1943	John Davis
1897–1898	A. M. Henry	1944	Mr. Vernon
1901	George Woodruff	1945–1946	Kenneth Allen
1902	Charles Neff	1947	Bill Laws
1903	A. M. Henry	1948–1950	Joe D. Andrea
1904–1911	Charles Neff	1951–1957	Vernon Wade
1912	Everett Suggs	1958–1959	Carl Schecker
1913–1917	Unknown	1960–1961	Mr. Hathway
1918–1925	Dr. D. I. Netherow	1962–1965	Tom Glascock
1926–1927	Mr. Gray	1966–1979	W. W. Sunderwirth
1928	Lendon Enloe	1980–1983	Gary Hardison
1929	Emil Crawford	1984–1985	Ruth Koca
1930	Lendon Enloe	1986	Gary Hardison

American Maiden Band – 1925
El Dorado Springs
D.I. Netherow, Director
Preserve Our Past Society photo

El Dorado Springs Municipal Band – 1925
D.I. Netherow, Director
Preserve Our Past Society photo

Chariton County

County Seat: Keytesville

Forest Green Band

The Forest Green band was organized by August Renne in 1888, and was called the Forks of the Chariton Silver Cornet Band. It was a seven–piece organization at that time with three cornets, one tenor, two altos, and one drum. Later, a bass horn and another drum were added. When the band was first organized all attended the Salem Congregational Church, and many were related; this held true for 50 years.

In the early years, the band played for most of the social events in the congregation. This included wedding receptions, school picnics, mission festivals, and family reunions.

Music played by the band was written by Professor G. F. Kimmel of Glasgow. After the retirement of August Renne the band was led by William H. Kottman until 1897. Alfred H. Renne became the leader in 1897 and served for 39 years. In 1908, the band was reorganized into a 12-piece group and the name changed to "Forest Green Concert Band."

On New Year's Eve, the band would be invited to homes in the community to play a couple of selections in exchange for a "drink." At the last home visited, there would be a big supper and a party ending sometime between midnight and morning. Grandpa William Kottman said he decided to end his musical career on New Year's Eve, 1897. While walking home from the party at 3:00 a.m. in the bitter cold, he became lost and spent the night in a neighbor's barn. Later, he retired from the band but returned to play with the band at the Keytesville Fair. After that concert he quit again, saying all the members were all Democrats and no one could speak German. He never played again (34).

An article in the Salisbury County News of 1986 gave the history of the Forest Green Band as it celebrated 100 years of music. Marvin Kottman wrote, "The Forest Green Band was known far and wide for their volume. Many of them developed a hearing problem at an early age" (35).

Brunswick Silver Cornet Band – 1908
Chariton County Historical Society photo

Christian County

County Seat: Ozark

The Hopedale Band is shown in a 1902 photo with twelve uniformed members.
All that remains of the town today is the Hopedale Baptist Church on county highway CC south of Springfield and north of Nixa.

Nixa had a band in 1905, although the population was only around 200 people.

Hopedale Band – 1902
Missouri State Historical Society photo

Nixa Band – 1905
Greene County Historical Society photo

Clinton County

County Seat: Plattsburg

Chautauqua

Plattsburg had Chautauqua every year from 1906–1930 (36), writes historian Helen Russell of Plattsburg. This celebration was based on the New York Chautauqua, which was founded in 1874 in Chautauqua, New York, located in the southwest part of the state near the Pennsylvania state line. It began as an educational, recreational, and cultural experiment in an out-of-school environment. The concept became very successful and was copied by many communities offering opportunities in art, music, dance, theatre, writing skills, and inspirational lectures. George Gershwin composed his *Concerto in F* at the New York Chautauqua in 1925.

The Plattsburg Chautauqua was designed for the entire family and was first started in 1906. Families rented tents on three acres that was "nicely set with blue grass, full of forest trees making for fine shade. A beautiful stream of water runs through the ground, furnishing an abundance of water for horses" (37). The first Plattsburg Chautauqua was held from August 25 to September 2, 1906, at Birch Grove. The location had a large tent seating 5,000 people.

The Plattsburg Chautauqua of 1906 ran for nine days in late August and promoted three band concerts each day along with inspirational lectures, Bible study, moving pictures, and the Chicago Ladies Orchestra. Band concerts were held daily at 9:00 a.m., 1:30 p.m., and 7:00 p.m. Season tickets were two dollars and daily admission was twenty-five cents. The Santa Fe, Rock Island, and Q.O. and K.C. railroads offered half price fares to the Plattsburg Chautauqua from Leavenworth, Kansas, and from Cameron, Trenton, Richmond, and St. Joseph, Missouri.

Plattsburg Chautauqua Band

From the program: "The band, which for two years past has distinguished itself at our Chautauqua, is booked for several Chautauquas under the name of 'Central Chautauqua Band.' It is made up entirely of Plattsburg young men who have submitted to careful training and are ready for the finest of work, and several are special artists in different lines of music" (38).

The Cameron Municipal Band

The city of Cameron is in both Clinton and DeKalb counties

The band was first organized in 1866 as the Cameron Silver Cornet Band, with George Bissell as its director. Charter members included George Stokes, W. D. Corn, M. McPhetridge, Everett Ford, Dr. J. F. King, M. L. Helwig, Mr. Gibhart, George Shirts, John Britain, H. E. Ford,

Dr. D. B. Adams, H. Powers, Erstine King, and Russ Bing, with E. F. Darby as drum major. He served through 1884. The band's first engagement was in Mirable, Mo. They received $125.

In 1884, director Bissell was succeeded by W. E. Steck, who served for ten years and introduced military drill to the performances. The name was changed to the Cameron Military Band. The drum major, E. F. Darby, was replaced in 1885 by Jake Stoner, who led the band in their marching maneuvers in a uniform presented to him by John Philip Sousa.

With their outstanding precision drills and musical excellence, the band took part in many competitions. In 1883 they won first place at the Kansas State Soldiers reunion in Leavenworth. In1884 the band represented the Grand Army of the Republic at their National Encampment in Minneapolis. In competition with 80 other bands, the Cameron Military Band "carried off all the honors." In the reviewing stand was Gen. W. T. Sherman, who remarked that he had never seen a drill team with more precision while at the same time furnishing their own music. In 1888 the band traveled to the Republican Convention in Chicago and to the Triennial Conclave for the Masonic organization in Washington, D.C.

C. L. Rutherford directed the band from 1896–1899 and again from 1901–1906. During his tenure he organized a "Kid Band," which became well-known in Chicago and Kansas City. This band, while in Kansas City, joined with other bands to play in a massed concert under the baton of John Philip Sousa. Craig Sloan, being the only drum major present, was given the honor of leading the bands on parade.

In 1922 the band was reorganized under the direction of W. E. Tracy, whose wife, Mrs. Jessie Tracy, became the band's first female member. The band's new name was the Cameron Community Concert Band. They met their expenses through donations from local merchants and by holding benefit concerts and hiring out to other towns. In 1927 the young ensemble became the Rotary Boys Band, and for the next 25 years Cameron had two band concerts each week: the Boys Band on Saturday and the Concert Band on Thursday. In 1929 the State of Missouri enacted the Band Fund Tax Statute, which allowed towns to tax themselves for the purpose of providing free band concerts. The people of Cameron voted that same year to impose a band tax. The bands, in accordance with the new law, became the Cameron Municipal Band and the Cameron Junior Municipal Band. The Junior Band was disbanded in 1955.

In a 1934 *Kansas City Star* editorial, clarinetist D. K. Harper was praised for community service in playing for 58 consecutive years in Cameron's bands, from 1876–1934. Mr. Harper, a former buffalo hunter and member of the famous Patrick S. Gilmore Band, continued playing into his 60th season. Other musicians who have logged 50 or more years with Cameron's bands are Bernard Althouse, Dordie Bowen (grandson of D. K. Harper), Albert Hamlet, George O. Harris, and Thomas J. Price.

Thomas J. Price took over leadership of the band in 1962 and continued as its director through the summer of 1986. Mr. Price built the ensemble into a group noted throughout Missouri for the high quality of its performances, an attribute that continues to this day. In the summer of 1987 the band was directed by Joe Finnegan. Anne Goodwin took over in the summer of 1988, and Shawn Abel was conductor from 1989–1992. Dr. Michael Mathews has been the leader of the band since 1993.

Rotary Boys Band – 1927

In 1927 the Rotary Boys Band was created, and for the next 25 years Cameron had two concerts each week: The Boys Band on Saturday and the Concert Band on Thursday.

Cameron Military Band – 1867
Photo courtesy Cindy Price Svehla

Plattsburg Chautauqua Band – 1898
Photo courtesy Helen Russell

Cooper County

County Seat: Boonville

The popularity and importance of a town band was evident in this picture of the Otterville Silver Cornet Band taken in 1910. Otterville, a town of less than 500, supported a band of 15 fully-uniformed members.

Otterville Silver Cornet Band – 1910
Jefferson City *News Tribune* photo

Dade County

County Seat: Greenfield

The concert program of November 15, 1901, by the Greenfield Concert Band (39), indicates a variety of music styles centered around the classics. The Sousa influence is evident: the band performed two marches, an operatic selection, waltzes, and program music to complete the concert.

Dadeville Concert Band – ca 1901
History Museum of Springfield – Greene County photo

Greenfield Concert Band

PROGRAM

November 15, 1901

Part One

1.	March – *The Belle of the Season*	Bratton
2.	Sextette – From *Lucia*	Donizetti
3.	Operatic Selections – *Crème de la Crème*	Laurendeau
4.	Zenda Waltzes	Whitmark
5.	Concert March — *Willow Grove*	Sorrentino

Made famous by Sorrentino's celebrated Banda Rosa

Part Two

6.	*Village Life in Ye Olden Times*	Charles LeThiere

Synopsis:

Andante – Night: with incidental solo for tuba

L'istesso tempo – Sunrise: with incidental solo for clarinet

Moderato – Astir in the village: with incidental solo for clarinet

Allegro Con Spirito – Children going to school: Ensemble

Grandioso – The crowning of the May Queen: clarinet solo

Con Spirito – The May Pole Dance

Andante – The Village Choir: brass quartette

Andante Grandioso – Moonlight: The Lover's Serenade

Allegro Con Spirito – Finale

7.	Intermezzo – *Salome*	Loraine
8.	*Mill in the Forest* – Descriptive: The Murmuring Brook	Eilenberg
9.	*Concert Polonaise*	Kiesler
10.	*Good Bye Dolly Gray*	Chattaway

DeKalb County

County seat: Maysville

Fairport Cornet Band – 1896
Missouri State Archives photo

Dent County

County seat: Salem

Stone Hill Band – 1893
Missouri State Archives photo

Franklin County

County Seat: Union

Washington, Missouri has had nine different town bands since 1874. They've performed for fairs, riverfront functions, building dedications, picnics, celebrations, parties, parades, and a variety of civic functions.

"Washington's rich musical background didn't just happen. It came quite naturally with the Germans, and the town band in those early days was as much a part of the life of Washington as was the taste of beer. In fact, the two—bands and beer—were all they needed in those days for entertainment. You couldn't have a picnic without either of them" (40).

The first Washington Town Band was organized in 1874 with William Lange, a cornet player, as the director. The band was later known as the William Lang Silver Cornet Band, which played for the dedication of Eads Bridge in St. Louis on July 4, 1874. In July of 1894, a band contest was held at the Washington Fair Grounds. The Washington Cornet Band and other bands from towns around the area participated. In 1907, Edwin Spaunhorst was the director of the Washington Cornet Band when they performed for the dedication of the International Shoe Factory in Washington. In 1918 the Washington Cornet Band became the Washington Concert Band.

Another band, the Washington Philharmonic Reed Band, performed in Union, Missouri, in 1881.

On July 22, 1894, a band tournament was held in Washington with bands meeting at Turner Hall, then marching to the fairgrounds for concerts and a "music fest." Participating were bands from Forest Rose, Emmanuel, Augusta, Marthasville, Campbellton, New Haven, and Washington.

The International Shoe Company sponsored a company band from about 1907 through the 1920s. The band was composed of employees of the shoe company.

The Washington Concert Band, which evolved from the Washington Cornet Band, was organized in 1918. John J. Ernst, Washington's mayor from 1918–1926, was an ardent champion of the Cornet Band, and it was he who provided the rehearsal space in the city hall basement by the jail. In 1937, the director was Edwin G. Spaunhorst, a Washington police officer. Emil Boehmer, a trumpet player, directed this band during the 1939 Washington Centennial Celebration. However, Edwin G. Spaunhorst continued to direct the band in the 1940s and 1950s. In the later 1940s and 1950s, on July 4 the band played a sunrise concert from the top of the Nieburg-Vitt building located at the corner of Fourth and Elm Streets in downtown Washington. This band also played for many church picnics. They usually charged one dollar an hour to be paid to each band member. Henry Filla, a trumpet player, was the last director of this band. The five Filla brothers and their father had formed the nucleus of this band from 1918–

1964. In 1964 the band had approximately 15 members. Since the band members were getting older and they couldn't find younger players it was disbanded and the band music was donated to the city library.

The Washington Golden Rod Concert Band was believed to be in existence from the early 1920s until the mid-1930s. This band bridges the span between the end of the International Shoe Company Band and the beginning of the Washington Elks Band.

The Washington Elks Band was organized in the early 1930s. The band usually numbered 25 to 30 members and was directed by Otto Wilmersherr, a trombone player and employee of the International Shoe Company. Louis Semon, a trumpet player and also an employee of the shoe company, directed the band during the Washington Centennial Celebration in 1939. However, the Elks Band disbanded approximately two years after the Washington Concert Band.

Another band organized at the same time was the Washington Boys' Band. Fred Mauntel, owner of the Washington General Store, was the director. In 1936 the band was directed by Ed Reeves, who it is believed worked for the Army Corps of Engineers during the building of the bridge across the Missouri River in Washington. (The bridge was new in 1936.) In 1939, Charles R. Smith, the Washington High School band director, directed the Boys Band during the 1939 Centennial Celebration, but World War II forced the group to disband.

The Washington VFW Band was in existence from 1950–1962. Leo Holzem, an insurance agent, started the band and was the leader for 10 years. The last two years a Mr. Jones, manager of the Calvin Theatre in Washington, directed the band. The band consisted of about 25 members who were mostly young people in the community.

The Washington Brass Band was started in the late 1960s. Many of the members of the former Elks Band became members of this group. The Brass Band inherited the Washington Concert Band's music from the city library. They also purchased the music library and some instruments from the Elks Club Band. Their membership was usually 20 to 25 members. Don Hahne, a trumpet player and cashier at the Bank of Washington, was the first director. Elmer Schmidt, a trombone player and owner of the Washington Jewelry Store, was also a director of the band.

William Lang's Silver Cornet Band – 1874
Franklin County Historical Society photo

Washington Cornet Band – 1894
Franklin County Historical Society photo

Washington Boys' Band – 1935
Franklin County Historical Society photo

Gasconade County

County Seat: Hermann

Since the arrival of the first music-loving German settlers, Hermann has always had a band. The *Music-Chor Blech Instrumenten* (choral group with band instruments) was formed in 1839. Later groups included the Apostle Band and the Enterprise Military Band (41).

The Hermann Municipal Band can trace its origins back to the Enterprise Military Band organized in 1919. The band was reformed many times until B. A. Wagner organized the Hermann Municipal Band in 1946 with 30 members. Wagner acknowledged some disagreement when the band was formed. "It was a young group, and I got some criticism from some of the older members. But I discovered a long time ago, you don't live forever and you have to bring in the youth to keep the band going," he said (42).

Hermann was one of the communities in Missouri that received revenue from a city band tax. The tax was collected until 1973 when the band ceased to perform due to a lack of interest. The band was reactivated in 1987.

Hermann Apostle Band – 1882
State Historical Society of Missouri photo

Bay Brass Band – 1890
Missouri State Historical Society photo

Enterprise Military Band – 1919
Missouri State Historical Society photo

Gentry County

County Seat: Albany

The Albany Municipal Band

During the early years of the 1900s there was usually a municipal band in Albany. A picture from 1927 included band members who were merchants, teachers, a dentist, and county employees. Virgil Patton, the director, is standing at the front right. He was the assistant postmaster and led the band until his death in 1936.

Band concerts were performed on Saturday nights on the city bandstand located on the courthouse grounds. People came to town early so they could park their cars around the square to listen to the band. The stores stayed open sometimes as late as 11:00 p.m. Bill Jack's popcorn stand was open right next to the courthouse, and he did a big business. Later on, the high school band played the Saturday night concerts, sometimes augmented by adults in the community (43).

Albany Municipal Band – 1927
Gentry County Historical Association

Greene County

County Seat: Springfield

"The Springfield Military Band was most likely directed by Henry Gehrs. The original leader of the Springfield band had been Charles Dumars, who skipped out on Springfield, ending up in rival Carthage. Gehrs was born in Carlisle, Illinois in 1847. He married Jane Adams at St. Genevieve, Missouri in 1870 and moved his young family to Springfield in 1883. Within a year Gehrs had founded the Hobart Band which was a 'brass' group used to promote the business interests of a local merchant named Hobart. Gehrs also directed the Second Regiment military band for several years" (44).

Herbert Lee Hoover was in charge of the cadet band at Drury College in 1907. To augment the cadets, Hoover allowed others to join the band by special arrangement and audition. When musicians in the area formed the Springfield Association of Musicians, they selected Hoover as the director of the union band. He continued to lead bands in the Springfield area for 30 years, and because of his small physical stature, his performing groups were billed: "Little Hoover and his Big Band." Later he formed a music company with Charles Martin, of Martin Brothers Piano Company, that later became Hoover Music. The store remains in operation today.

World's Largest Boy Scout Band

R. Ritchie Robertson directed several different music groups in Springfield, but his most acclaimed achievement was in 1920 when he organized a band for Boy Scouts in the area. From a band of 50, Robertson's group of scouts grew to 400 young musicians and was known as the World's Largest Boy Scout Band (45).

World's Largest Boy Scout Band – 1928
Springfield
R. Ritchie Robertson, Director
History Museum for Springfield – Greene County photo

Ash Grove Concert Band – 1920
History Museum for Springfield
– Greene County photo

Howard County

County Seat: Fayette

The Fayette Town Band was formed in 1910 by dentist E. M. Blakey. The city built a bandstand for the band on the courthouse square a few years earlier. The bandstand fell into disrepair until recently restored by members of the Central Methodist University band and community patrons.

Roanoke Military Band – Salisbury – 1915
Missouri State Archives photo

Jasper County

County Seat: Carthage

The Carthage Light Guard Band was organized in 1878 by J. Henry Doyle. The band's name was taken from the Carthage Light Guard, a National Guard unit. Doyle left the Carthage area in 1885 and the leadership was given to C. R. Dumars. He was the conductor until 1919. The band, under Dumars, took first prize at a band contest in Springfield in 1886, winning $300 for their performance. Two weeks later the same honor was won at a contest of bands in Fort Smith, Arkansas, this time winning $400.

In June 1889, at the Fireman's Band Tournament in Clinton, Missouri, the band took first prize of $100, with the celebrated Pickwick band of Springfield receiving second place and fifty dollars. The Carthage Light Guard Band was given the highest review by the *Musical Times* that indicated, "This band is an exceptionally fine one, playing a splendid grade of music in a truly artistic style. Their exhibition drill received much favorable comment" (46).

In similar manner *The Metronome* (1889) wrote:

> The music played was of a high order, and both bands, Springfield's Pickwick and the Carthage Light Guard, showed skill in their renditions that speak well for the musical cultivation of the performers. The Light Guard band gave a fancy drill, which is unsurpassed by anything in that line. The large audience on the tournament grounds in Clinton applauded the band vociferously as each unique movement was successfully executed (47).

During his leadership, Dumars' Carthage Light Guard Band played for one week engagements in Denver (1892), Boston (1895), Pittsburgh (1898), and Louisville (1901).

The band under Dumars "…has come gradually up from a very insignificant affair to its present magnificent proportions, in membership, equipment, ability and attainments. It has filled many important engagements and everywhere been the recipient of high compliments. In five contests entered the first prize has been won each time, and the premium money thus obtained aggregates the neat sum of $1,100" (48).

In 1895 the *Carthage Weekly Press* reported in an article entitled: "The Band's trip to Boston":

> The trip to Boston via St. Louis will be made in a special car on the Frisco, leaving here Friday evening next (September 20, 1895). In St. Louis the band will be given a sleeping car which leaves Union Station Saturday afternoon, taking breakfast at Detroit then dinner at Niagara Falls.

The band is drilling and rehearsing every night this week and is getting in fine condition. Large banners will be placed on the sides of the band's private car and will attract attention to Carthage throughout the pilgrimage (49).

Carthage was such a haven for band music that even the Sousa Band, with 60 musicians, played at the Carthage Grand Opera House on November 8, 1911.

In 1919, Dumars resigned his position as leader of the famous Carthage Light Guard Band and moved to California. He died in 1925 at the age of 64 while living in California. The band was then led by Ray Clark until 1921. A concert program of September 1, 1921, credits R. D. Toutz, Jr. as being director of the band.

The State Normal School #4 in Springfield, later to become Missouri State University, indicated in their yearbook, *Ozarko,* that the band from the Normal School appeared at a conclave of bands in Carthage, which is the Mecca of bands in southwest Missouri. High praise for any town.

Band member George Stump wrote of the band in an undated, unpublished document called *A Short Historical Melange*, an article entitled, "Here Comes the Band." He observes the following:

> The members are, without exception, gentlemanly in conduct, absolutely temperate, and thorough musicians. The music played is of the highest grade, such as is handled by the best professional band in the cities, no 'trashy' music finds a place in the repertoire of the Light Guard Band. A feature which has elicited much favorable comment, and which has been mastered within the last year, is a unique fancy drill under the direction of the drum major, in which the band forms all varieties of grotesque figures, changing from each at the sound of the whistle, and finally ending the drill, with each member in the same position in which he started—the band playing a heavy march all the while the drill is in progress.

Reviews of the Carthage Light Guard Band, as compiled by band member George Stump, speak of the quality of the group:

"The Carthage Light Guard Band sustained its reputation as one of the very best musical organizations in the state," *Joplin Journal* (50).

Carthage Light Guard Band – 1880
Jasper County Historical Society photo

Jefferson County

County Seat: Hillsboro

DeSoto Concert Band – 1903
Photo courtesy Blane Olson

DeSoto Veterans Drum and Bugle Corps – 1940
Photo courtesy Blane Olson

Lafayette County

County Seat: Lexington

The Concordia Band

The Lafayette Raconteur reported that:

According to the records of the *Concordian,* our weekly newspaper, the first Concordia Band was organized by Otto Walkenhorst and some of his associates. In 1882 a band was organized and it was called the Concordia Cornet Band and a Wilhelm Wilk was its conductor. He led the band until sometime in the 1890s when he decided to quit, and J. J. Bredehoeft, who had studied music in Germany and was playing solo clarinet in the band, was then elected conductor of the band.

As years passed on, Wilhelm Wilk again decided to start another band, and this time it was called the Wilks Band. So Concordia at that time had two bands, the Concordia Cornet Band and the Wilks Band. But in a few years Mr. Wilk was aging, and he again decided to lay down the baton for good, and Mr. Julius Sagehorn was elected conductor of the Wilks Band. Still two bands in Concordia. Later it was decided to combine the two bands, and the name of the new organization was the Concordia Band. Mr. J. J. Bredehoeft was elected to direct the newly-formed band (51).

In 1910 the Concordia Band won the grand prize of $250 for amateur bands at the Missouri State Fair. Their winning musical selections were the march *Colonel Minor* and the *Overture to Lustspiel.* In 1914 the band represented the Elks Club at their state convention in Sedalia and won $100 for the best marching and the best band in regulation uniform.

In the early days there were no electric lights. The Concordia Band would play at night on the streets lighted by torches or under the coal oil lamps that hung on the street corners. A number of members played for 50 years or more in the Concordia Band. Drummer August "Secco" Brackman played in the band for 72 years before retiring in 1959.

Band member Harry R. Voight, writing in an unpublished *Centennial History of Concordia, Missouri*, recalls:

In 1917 when the United States entered World War I, quite a number of us young men had been called into the service of Uncle Sam's great army, and so in 1918 Mr. Bredeheft decided with so many men missing and the war going on, he would drop the band during the war. Well, again Mr. Kircheis took over, and he brought in his daughter who played the alto horn, his sister-in-law, Miss Edna Grotefend, who played the valve trombone, and his son and he played the trumpets. At two different times when I was home on furlough, I attended their rehearsals, and it really seemed strange because that was the first and only time in the 77-year history of the Concordia Band that we ever had any lady members in the band (52).

A 1890 photograph of the Mayview Cornet Band shows nine members playing for an outdoor celebration. Three of the band members were named Strasburg.

In 1910, the Odessa Band is shown in a formal picture indicating they not only played for civic events but for social gatherings and dances. Fourteen members were in the Odessa Band.

The Emma, Missouri, Cornet Band numbered 14 members and are shown in a photo with military-style uniforms. Three members of the Wehrs family were members.

The Lafayette Military Band of Higginsville was organized to serve and entertain the community as well as social gatherings for families in the largely German community. In 1915 there were 20 members, all in military uniforms with family names of Woltemath, Mollenkamp, Bergschneider, Schowengerdt, and Meinershagen.

African American musicians living in Lexington formed the Elmer Radd's Cotton Club Orchestra in the 1930s. This dance orchestra, complete with banjo and Sousaphone, traveled throughout the state playing mainly in "white only" ballrooms, which were popular at the time. Some of the members of the orchestra played with circus bands during the summer, returning to the dance orchestra after the summer circus season.

Mayview Cornet Band – 1890
Lexington Museum photo

Lawrence County

County Seat: Mount Vernon

From Wayne Glenn's *Ozarks' Greatest Hits* (2005), a picture of the Lawrenceburg, Missouri village band is shown. "On July 4, 1892 they will go over to Miller for the first Miller Picnic. The whole band went in a band wagon pulled by 4 horses and driven by Joe Woody. Members of the band were Jud Howard (leader of the group), Walter Hood, Buddy Adamson, 'Little Bill' Callison, Norm Moore, Frank Arnett, Elliot Fletcher, Jim Ginn, Jim Moore, Jim Callison, and Rube Snyde" (53).

Also from the same publication appears a comment on the Mt. Vernon Fireman's Band: "What normal lady could resist a second look at men wearing this type of dress (band uniform), especially if he can play an instrument" (54)?

The *Lawrence County Record,* on April 4, 1907, printed the following:

How About Our Band

The question is being ask (sic) "will we have a band this season?" Here's the answer, 'that depends upon how badly we want one.' The Fireman's Band is confronted with a situation it never had to deal with before. We have no resident Director. Let's get one. Our band is better equipped possibly than any amateur organization of its kind in the Southwest. Our entire outlay belongs to the city, is paid for and under direct control of the City Council. We are submitting a proposition to the citizens this week asking for enough money to employ a competent director and give concerts the entire summer. The band is not a charity organization, neither is it a money making venture. We feel that every dollar given is fully repaid by free concerts. Mt. Vernon is the best band town comparing size in this state. The writer has handled all moneys received by the band since a short time after its organization and would like to add right here. The business man has always given his part and large part of the other fellows as well. We like to have everyone come to the concerts. We also like any money that private citizens may hand us. Treat the boy kindly when he comes around with the paper and, better still, give something. We ask only a small amount from anyone (55).

The Mount Vernon Fireman's Band

Claude Kendall, Manager

Rotary Boys' Band, Aurora – 1929
Lt. Gene Loy, Director
Hinchey Photo courtesy Mary Strickrodt

Linn County

County Seat: Linneus

Bucklin Concert Band – 1898
State Historical Society of Missouri photo

Marceline Town Band – 1902
State Historical Society of Missouri photo

Moniteau County

County Seat: California

A well-documented history of bands in Moniteau County is described in *The Band Story* by an unknown author as part of the county's 100th year anniversary.

The Centennial history of the Moniteau County Fair would not be complete without telling the "Band Story." Indeed there is a band story, a story revealing the dedication of local musicians in giving of their time and their talents to help make the Fairs successful through the years.

A small band, the California Brass Band, was organized in 1867 under the leadership of L. L. Routen. In 1870 the Brass Band gave way to the California (County Seat) Silver Cornet Band led by Fred Hert, Sr. In 1871 this band carried off the first premium of $200 at the Kansas City Exposition. This was an honor to win first place in a state contest, and the highlight of the band's career.

At the 50th anniversary of the Moniteau County Fair in 1916 the Silver Cornet Band was honored, for the band had played continuously since 1870. The band played *Dixie* to a large crowd in front of the amphitheatre. They had played *Dixie* every year since 1870.

At times through the years other bands from surrounding towns would play with the Silver Cornet Band. At one time the Princess Stock Company Band and the Carnival Band also played with Mr. Hert's Band.

In 1921 the Silver Cornet Band did not organize. A McGirk Band was organized and this band played for several years. Later a California Band consisting of McGirk Band members, other local musicians, and high school students played at the fairs. In 1935 the California High School Band and the California (town) Band played together with Mary Hert as Drum Major for the California Band, and Mary Lee Breninger, Drum Major for the high school band.

High school bands led by Richard Kemm, Tom Lawrence, and Dean Douglas led the combined bands until 1947, when Melvin Peterman's High School Band joined the group. They have played continuously since.

This is the "Band Story." Imagine a fair without a band! Moniteau County has certainly been fortunate in having such fine bands throughout the last 100 years (56).

The McGirk Band

Neil Newton provides additional band history for Moniteau County in an unpublished 1966 account of the McGirk Band.

The McGirk Band in Moniteau County was organized by Ned S. Newton in 1921, with Neil L. Newton serving as assistant director.

After several seasons of regular rehearsals the McGirk Band began making public appearances. Rehearsals were held weekly in the McGirk school building.

After, the band began making public appearances, various plays, minstrels, and for the Moniteau County Fair for several years, and on one occasion was hired by the Missouri Pacific Railroad to play for the Booster's Club on a trip to Lexington, Missouri (57).

A Band Member Remembers

In an unpublished work entitled *A Band Member Remembers* (1966), Lawrence B. Hert writes:

It's a long time since the 50th anniversary of the Moniteau County Fair when the California Band was engaged to play five days instead of the usual four to celebrate the Golden Event, but I started with the band two years before as my "Music Satchel" has the date—1914—indelibly inscribed.

My uncle, Fred Hert, the leader and my father, Ben Hert, were the two stalwarts of the band. I played alto horn.

Possibly a year or two before my joining the band, I "got lost" after band practice, and when my father came home he was surprised that I was not home in bed. He went back to the courthouse and found me asleep on one of the benches.

The band held concerts those days too. Ones I especially remember were those held next to Dr. Burke's office uptown and across the street from Sperber's restaurant. At intermission Mr. Sperber always served big delicious ice cream sodas to each member of the band. It wasn't all roses though, as the green grass on the lawn was full of chiggers, and they had a few bites.

About fifty years ago, Ed Ward of the Princess Stock Company sat in with the band and played trombone. He said he had never taken any lessons but it became so necessary that he play an instrument in his show that he picked up the trombone and played by ear until he pretty well mastered the art.

Dr. Joe Taylor, a dentist and former band member from Eldon, furnished the band with a treat of "pop" for all the players on a regular basis.

During the war years, either in 1917 or 1918, as the fair was in progress a squadron in V formation of airplanes flew over the fair grounds. They flew low and amazed the crowd. Just think the "Big Thursday" had a feature of airplanes nearly 50 years ago through the courtesy of the federal government. It undoubtedly was my first chance to see a plane, and likewise for many others.

While the main purpose of the band was to play for the fair, they furnished the music at the High Point picnic, Prairie Home Fair, Bunceton Fair, and for political rallies in California (Mo.) as well as Jefferson City.

After the death of the Hert founders, the band remained dormant for a few years. Upon the insistence of Neil Newton the organization took on new life under the leadership of Tom Lawrence, Dean Douglas, and Richard Kemm, in turn. Then with new blood in the ranks, Neil Newton took over the directorship and the band flourished as never before. The band's extensive music library was quite extensive. World War II took its toll in more ways than one and the band folded as a town band and was ably taken over by Melvin Peterman and the California High School Band (58).

California Silver Cornet Band – 1870
Moniteau County Historical Society photo

McGirk Band – 1921
Moniteau County Historical Society photo

Newton County

County Seat: Neosho

Information provided from the Newton County Museum indicates several town bands in Newton County in the late 1800s and early 1900s. The *Granby News Herald* (1950) reports the following:

Over the years the town of Diamond has had numerous town bands. The first organization mentioned is the Diamond String Band in June 1892. A Diamond Cornet Band was organized in July, 1894. A. P. Hill was director. There were eleven members.

An undated photo shows members of the Stella "clown" band. All eleven members wore different clown costumes and are pictured in front of the Matt Atkinson General Store. The store sign indicates that Atkinson sold furniture, suit cases, trunks, picture frames, and was the undertaker.

The Newtonian Band is pictured in their own band wagon pulled by a pair of horses or mules. Caption on the picture reads: "Newtonian's Famous Band, is shown here with its picturesque conveyance (band wagon), which made possible the band's appearance in public programs throughout the area in the early 80s."

The best remembered band from the early days was the Neosho Hayseed band, which was formed around 1892 with Tom Jennings as their leader. By 1895, the band had grown to twenty-one members, with Jennings being the leader much of that time. Many times they wore the costume of a "hayseed," but in 1896 new white uniforms were purchased. This may well have been for their performance at Kansas City.

The Granby Silver Cornet Band was organized in 1880 by C. C. Ball. In 1907, Jess was director, and the name of the band was changed to The Granby Miner Band. Jesse Wells, a member of the band, composed "The Colonel Kingston March" for the Granby Band, in honor of Colonel Kingston, Superintendent of the Granby Mining and Smelting Company (59).

Oregon County

County seat: Alton

Alton Brass Band – 1910
State Historical Society of Missouri photo

Perry County

County seat: Perryville

An unpublished *Pictorial History of Perry County* indicates:

When Perry County was sparsely settled, people got together to help each other raise a house or barn or harvest crops. At the end of the activity, they would have a play—party or a dance. Each Lutheran church congregation had its own *Blaskapelle.* Bands were organized as early as the 1860s in Perry County and were always favorite entertainment. They played at parades, serenaded people on special occasions, played at dances and at picnics. There were cornet bands, brass bands, and string bands. By the turn of the century, some of the bands had their own band wagon.

The band history of East Perry County, Missouri is extensive. Each of the regional communities had a band which was affiliated with the local church, such as: Altenburg Band, Uniontown Band, and Wittenberg Band. The East Perry Band was organized on September 30, 1947 from the remnants of the Frohna Concert Band and the Altenburg Cornet Band. The leader of the original group was teacher M. H. Wunderlich. The East Perry Band had a constitution and a board of directors, and dues were 25 cents monthly. New uniforms were first worn on September 24, 1948.

The band played for the annual Community Fair, Mission Festivals, picnics, political rallies, and special concerts. When the Uniontown Band folded in 1953, some of the members joined the East Perry Band. In 1993, the East Perry Band voted to dissolve. However, they played for the Moniteau County Fair for several years, and on one occasion they were hired by the Missouri Pacific Railroad to play for the Booster's Club on a trip to Lexington, Missouri (57).
The band spirit was revived in the 1990s as the Saxony Hills Regional Band (60).

Wittenberg Band (date unknown)
Photo at a wedding celebration
Perry County Lutheran Historical Society photo

Altenburg Band – 1900
Perry County Lutheran Historical Society photo

Uniontown Band – 1929
Perry County Lutheran Historical Society photo

Phelps County

County Seat: Rolla

Rolla Town Band

John W. Scott (1870–1950) was a Rolla businessman who founded and directed the Rolla town band and many other local ensembles. Scott attended the Missouri School of Mines in 1886 and 1887 and worked as a clerk in Duby's Drug Store in Rolla. After serving as an apprentice, he became a registered pharmacist in 1890. In addition to the pharmacy, Scott handled textbooks and school supplies for students at MSM and expanded into the sales of musical instruments and sheet music.

Scott organized the Missouri School of Mines Reserve Officers Training Corps band in 1926 and directed it free of charge. He left that position in 1946 after serving for 20 years. The Rolla High School's band was organized and directed by Scott in addition to his running a drug store full-time. For nearly sixty years there was scarcely a concert or musical entertainment in Rolla in which John W. Scott did not have a hand. Most of the concerts took place in Rolla, but the venues also included performances in schools, churches, and halls in Newburg, St. James, Salem, and Steelville.

Expenditures, overseen by Scott of the Rolla Town Band, included:

October 24, 1905	Rent for rehearsal space (4 months @ $2.00 per month)	$ 8.00
October 24, 1905	Repair on horns	$ .40
July 5, 1905	Payment to 12 band members for Richland Concert	$79.80
	($6.65 each for transportation, food, and concert)	
July 25, 1905	Purchase of Conn five valve double-bell euphonium	
	with leather case and extra low-pitch equipment	$75.00
October 24, 1905	New SP mouthpiece for Steelville concert	$ 2.00

Russell Brothers Circus

The Russell Brothers Circus was headquartered in Rolla during the 1930s and 1940s on grounds near the site of Civil War Fort Wyman. John W. Scott was a friend of the circus owner, Charles W. Webb, and he looked after the troupe's musical instruments. During the years the circus wintered in Rolla, they would mail out many postcards in late spring, giving that year's itinerary for the circus. Scott would leave Rolla during the summer and travel with the circus, playing slide trombone in the circus band. In 1938, Scott took his thirteen-year-old Grandson, John Morris, along. Morris played clarinet and traveled as far as Downers Grove, Illinois, near Chicago, before returning home to Rolla. Because the performance stops were less than fifty miles apart, the Russell Brothers Circus was able to travel by truck and automobile.

Rolla Town Band cash expenditure journal – 1905
John Scott, Director
Western Historical Manuscript Collection photo

Polk County

County Seat: Bolivar

The Humansville Band in the picture below shows the group in cowboy garb in front of N.A. Robertson's dry goods store. Note the band member on the right—the bass drummer with both bass drum and cymbal beater. The group may have been featured at the performance of the "Cattle Rustlers" locally playing with admission prices of fifteen and twenty-five cents.

Advertising on the back wall of the department store is for Old Virginia cigars: three for five cents. The building also housed a grocery store and W. W. Mack's tin shop.

Humansville Band – 1915
Missouri State Archives photo

Randolph County

County Seat: Huntsville

Huntsville Knights of Honor Band – 1874
Missouri State Archives photo

Higbee Silver Cornet Band – 1891
Photo courtesy Wendell E. Doyle

Saline County

County Seat: Marshall

The Marshall Municipal Band

A concert program of July 4, 1993, indicates that organized band music in Marshall dates back to 1871, shortly after the Civil War.

The Marshall Municipal Band was organized in 1921 and the first director was Ray Hillings. The first band had twenty members. Hillings was the director of music at what is now known as the Marshall Habilitation Center. The first band had twenty members.

When the band was first organized, members purchased their own music and instrument. There was no salary paid for rehearsals or concerts, and there were no uniforms. Through the efforts of C. B. Balthis and Edward Flake, $800 was collected for the purchase of uniforms in 1924. In 1934 a half—mill tax was approved by voters to operate the band. This authorization placed the band under the supervision and control of the City of Marshall. In 1948 the city purchased new uniforms and instruments for $2,800.

Hillings, who founded the band, was followed by Cecil Hough, Royal Claycomb, Mr. DeArvill, E. J. Eckles, Michael Waters, Stanley Westbrook, and Charles Ferguson. E. J Eckles had the longest tenure of 32 years as director. After service in World War I, Eckles entered the Army Band School in Washington D.C. and was assigned to the US Army Band. When he returned to Marshall, he was employed for a number of years at the Auditorium Theatre as a member of the orchestra, playing both saxophone and drums, during the days of silent films.

In 1959, Howard Bell, director of the band at Marshall High School, was appointed assistant to Mr. Eckles, and held that position until he left Marshall in 1962. In 1963 Michael Waters was assistant director replacing Bell. He became director of the band after Eckles passed away in June of 1965. Mr. Eckles' request to have a band march from the church to the cemetery was honored.

The Missouri Band Tax provided funds for the erection of a bandstand in 1935 at a cost of $1,000. In 1971 the original bandstand was removed and a new stand erected costing $7,000. The new bandstand was paid for from funds accumulated through the years from the half-cent mill tax.

The Marshall Municipal Band played an annual concert at Arrow Rock State Park. The tradition began when a band member who lived in Arrow Rock could no longer travel to Marshall for rehearsals and concerts. It was decided to take the band to Arrow Rock, and a tradition was started (61).

Shannon County

County Seat: Eminence

In the records of the Western Historical Manuscript Collection, at the University of Science and Technology – Rolla, is a photograph of the Ozark Land and Lumber Company in Fishertown, Shannon County. Fishertown is no longer listed as a town in Missouri. The photograph is from the collection of Lon Hogan of Winona, Missouri, and shows the Ozark Land and Lumber Company Band with fifteen uniformed members (62).

Ozark Land and Lumber Company Band – 1900
Western Historical Manuscript Collection photo

Ste. Genevieve County

County Seat: Ste. Genevieve

Early Bands

The date of the first band in Ste. Genevieve County is unknown, but the Knights of Columbus Band was in existence until the 1930s. At that time it was replaced by the Lions Band, which remained in existence until the start of World War II. A town band was not organized during the war years, but emerged in 1946.

Ste. Genevieve Municipal Band

The Ste. Genevieve Municipal Band was organized in 1946. Returning servicemen from World War II who played in service bands wanted to continue performing, so the band began as an opportunity to get together once again. The city had a band tax, as provided by state statute, but in 1990 the Board of Aldermen wanted to dissolve the band and transfer the funds to the park department. In a vote by the community, 74 percent voted to retain the band and the band tax. (63).

Directors of the Ste. Genevieve Municipal Band:

Pete Lilley	1946–1958
Harvey Mueller	1959–1966
Bob Donze	1967–1970
Mark Caputo	1971–1984
John Wibbenmeyer	1985

St. Charles County

County Seat: St. Charles,

Missouri's First Capital 1821–1826

Missouri was granted statehood in 1821. A decision was made to build a "City of Jefferson" for the state capital, in the center of the state. Since the land was undeveloped a temporary capital was needed. St. Charles, the second oldest city west of the Mississippi, beat eight other cities to house the temporary capital, and free space was donated over a hardware store that still stands today. The new Missouri state capital was ready in 1826.

The La Frenier Chauvin family first established the St. Charles, Missouri music tradition in 1819, when they presented free concerts in the small park at 624 South Main Street. This may be credited as the first town band in the state.

Records show that in 1830 the "Town Band played on the steps of the Market House on Sunday afternoon." Since that time, there have been other bands that have carried on this tradition: The French Band, The German Band, and the St. Charles Brass Band.

The current (2007) St. Charles Municipal Band dates back to 1870. Their initial event was a Fourth of July celebration in 1870 in which a photo identifies the St. Charles Brass Band in an Independence Day Parade with Joseph Decker as the leader. The Brass Band continued to perform into the mid-1880s, at which time its name was changed to the St. Charles Cornet Band. In 1887, Harry Rummel began playing in the Cornet Band and became the leader in 1897. Concerts were held on Office Clerk's Hill in St. Charles.

In 1900, Harry Rummel changed the name of the band to Rummel's Military Band. This continued for 12 years until his leaving the band and moving his family to California. Rummel's musicians hired a new director in 1913 and changed the name to the St. Charles Military Band. In 1916, Professor D. G. LaBanca became the permanent director. The band was reorganized as the St. Charles Municipal Band in 1929. LaBanca stayed on until 1942. He was fondly known as the "Music Man of St. Charles." As a tribute to his many years of leadership, the band provided music and marched at the head of his funeral procession in 1942 (64).

Boys Drum Band
St. Peters Catholic Church – St. Charles – 1880
St. Charles Historical Society photo

St. Charles Cornet Band – 1880
St. Charles Historical Society photo

Rummel's Military Band – 1900
St. Charles Historical Society photo

Rummel's Military Band – 1926
St. Charles Historical Society photo

St. Clair County

County Seat: Osceola

Osceola Town Band – 1891
State Historical Society of Missouri photo

St. Louis County

County Seat: Clayton

Webster Groves Municipal Band – 1930

The director of the Webster Groves High School Band, Hans J. Lemcke, started the Webster Groves Municipal Band in 1930. Lemcke himself had been a member of the famous John Philip Sousa Band. The Lemcke family came to the United States from Germany in 1927, and Hans was engaged to teach both band and German in the high school.

The "town band" tradition was strong in smaller communities that did not enjoy the many entertainment opportunities offered in the city. Lemcke was an advocate of the evening or Sunday afternoon concerts in the park. He witnessed it first in Germany, then as a member of the Sousa band.

The first concerts were held on the lawn of the Masonic Temple in Webster. Later the band played at Webster College and Eden Seminary. The concerts were always held outdoors and were always free of charge.

Lemcke was a popular conductor and selected music that involved the audience singing, clapping, or whistling. He was a masterful showman and offered special selections designed especially for younger children. Lemke shared the conducting duties with his son, Henry, who was named after Lemcke's father, a professional band musician in Germany.

On July 24, 1957, the *St. Louis Globe Democrat* announced, "Webster Only St. Louis Community Continuing Band Concert Tradition" (65).

The early Webster Groves Municipal Band was composed of community members who played a musical instrument, and students were not allowed to participate with the adults. As the band grew older so did the band members. Students were becoming more accomplished, and the older band members were unable to play as they once had. The first high school students were allowed to perform as special ensembles, novelty numbers, or soloists. They were not permitted to be members of the brass, woodwind, or percussion sections. With time that changed, and because of the quality of the band, students from surrounding schools were accepted as members of the band.

Warren County

County Seat: Warrenton

Dutzow Cornet Band (undated)
Franklin County Historical Society photo

Washington County

County Seat: Potosi

Caledonia Band – 1908
Picture taken in front of "Skeeters" bar (written on back of photo)
Western Historical Collection Manuscript photo

Webster County

County Seat: Marshfield

The earliest band in Webster County was the Grand Army of the Republic Band. The organizational date of the GAR Band is not documented but it was replaced in 1888 by the Marshfield Cyclone Band, with many of the same band members (66).

According to Wayne Glenn's book *Ozarks' Greatest Hits*:

> Marshfield, Missouri, was hit by a major tornado on Sunday, April 18, 1880. The town was nearly demolished by what came to be known as the 'Marshfield Cyclone.' Best estimates at the time declared about 92 people were killed in the immediate Marshfield area. The town had to totally rebuild. The community musical aggregation became known as the 'Cyclone Band' when it was reorganized around 1888 (67).

The Cyclone Band was replaced with the Marshfield Concert Band in 1903 under the direction of Professor H. Blaine. The band was directed for 25 years by Theron Watters until his death in 1928.

Watters was born in Watseka, Illinois, February 25, 1874, and came to Webster County with his parents when a young boy. He married Mamie Candace Ballard of Marshfield in 1896. They had seven children, all of whom were taught to play one or more musical instruments. His earliest jobs were barbering and working as a telegraph operator for the Frisco Railroad.

In 1906 he bought *The Marshfield Mail* from Editor John H. Case in 1906. During his years as editor of the local newspaper he and his wife also operated the Universal Theater on the south side of the square, where silent movies were shown on Friday and Saturday nights. Watters was very involved in the civic activities of the county and community of Marshfield. He was on the City Council and the school board and later became postmaster.

Of particular interest was a bandwagon built especially to transport the early bands. It was drawn by four horses and also served as a bandstand until a permanent bandstand was built in 1909.

Cyclone City (Marshfield) Band – 1888
Webster County Historical Society Journal photo

Marshfield Concert Band – 1903
Webster County Historical Society Journal photo

The Missouri Town Band Tax
1922

State Senator Snodgrass, from El Dorado Springs in Cedar County, introduced a bill before the Missouri Legislature in 1922 to allow municipalities to levy a "band tax" to support the local community band. Arthur Harrison and Clarence Schuchert from Cape Girardeau helped implement the State Band Law of 1922.

Missouri State Statute 71.640
Authorization

Any city, village or town having a population of less than twenty-five thousand and any city having a population of more than thirty-five thousand located in any county of the first class contiguous to a county of the first class having a charter form of government and not containing any part of a city of over four hundred thousand, howsoever organized, and irrespective of its form of government, may by one of the two methods authorized in section 71.650, levy a tax for use in providing free band concerts, or equivalent musical service by the band upon occasions of public importance.

Missouri State Statute 71.650
Limitations

1. The mayor and council, board of aldermen or trustees may levy a tax of not more than one-half mill (1mill = .001 cents) on each one dollar assessed valuation on all property in such city, village or town, or, when initiated by a petition signed by at least ten percent of the voters, the question shall be submitted to the voters, and a majority of the voters thereon shall be sufficient to carry the provisions of this law into effect, and it shall become the duty of the mayor and council, board of aldermen or board of trustees to levy each year on all the property in such city, village or town a tax not to exceed two mills, or such part thereof as shall be petitioned for, on each one dollar assessed valuation.

2. The question shall be submitted in substantially the following form:

   Shall (name of city, town or village) levy a tax of ___ mills on each one dollar assessed valuation for the creation of a band fund?

3. The levy made under either of the options of sections 71.640 to 71.670 shall not increase the tax levy of any such political subdivision to exceed the limitations fixed and prescribed by the constitution and laws of the State Band Law of 1922.

Missouri State Statute 71.660

Discontinuance

A petition, signed by at least ten percent of the voters, may at any time be presented asking that the following question be submitted:

Shall the tax for the creation of a "band fund" be discontinued?

If a majority of the votes be cast in favor of said question, no further tax shall be made.

A study of "band taxes" made in 1995 by Kevin L. Lines, of Marshall, Mo. indicated:

Community	Band Organized	Band Tax per $100 evaluation
Cameron	1901	1 cent
El Dorado Springs	1881	1.5 cents
Hermann	1952	2 cents
Jackson	1920	1 cent
Marshall	1921	5 cents
Ste. Genevieve	1946	6 cents

The study acknowledged that many municipal bands receive funds generated by other sources, including tax supported parks and recreation departments. It included only those communities that received revenue from the state statue (68).

ST. LOUIS
WORLDS FAIR
1904

Chapter 4

THE LOUISIANA PURCHASE EXPOSITION OF 1904

St. Louis World's Fair

The Louisiana Purchase Exposition, informally known as The St. Louis World's Fair, opened on April 30, 1904, and closed on December 1st of the same year. Designed by George Kessler, the Exhibition was located on what is now the 1,200-acre Forest Park. There were over 1,500 buildings, connected by 75 miles of roads and walkways. Exhibits were staged by 62 foreign nations, and 43 of the 45 states were represented. The Palace of Agriculture alone covered some 20 acres. The Palace of Fine Arts, designed by architect Cass Gilbert, remains today on top of Art Hill and is home of the St. Louis Art Museum. The Administration Building for the fair is now Brookings Hall, the defining landmark on the campus of Washington University. The building was duplicated in Maryville, Missouri in 1905, with the founding of Missouri Normal School Number 5, now known as Northwest Missouri State University.

Bands at the Fair

The St. Louis World's Fair gathered an unprecedented number and variety of bands. John Philip Sousa and his band opened the fair on April 30, 1904, and combined with a 400-voice choir to perform *Hymn of the West*, the official hymn of the Exposition. Over the next six months there were 1,087 band concerts performed on the fair grounds.

This great assemblage of bands was planned by the Bureau of Music, appointed by the Board of Directors with the directive: "... to engage musicians for performances, planning the musical programs, organizing musical contests, and creating a successful series of concerts by following the musical policy of brass bands and popular music" (69). The majority of musical events planned for the fair were of a popular nature and the most numerous of these were band concerts. The Bureau of Music had a generous budget of $450,000 for musicians and commissions and 60 per cent, or $264,787.34, was allocated for military bands.

The list of professional bands appearing at the 1904 World's Fair constituted a "Who's Who" of bands. By contracting prestigious bands, the Bureau's stated intent of offering the public "the most celebrated bands in Europe and America" was certainly realized. Three to six bands were playing on the fairgrounds all of the time. (11:00 a.m. through 9:30 p.m.).

In addition to professional bands, there were a great number of state, regimental, university, and unique bands. The variety included The Cowboy Band, Milwaukee Band of the Boys' Charity School, Philippine Constabulary Band, and the Philippine Scout Band, which was said to be the most popular band at the fair after the Sousa Band.

The Sousa Band: The Most Popular Band at the Fair

The Sousa Band had gained fame and popularity prior to the 1904 World's Fair. Sousa was originally contracted to play for only four weeks at the Fair, from April 20–May 27, but the band was such a success that the engagement was extended one more week to June 4. The famous band performed 669 different band pieces during the engagement. The Sousa Band was the largest of the professional bands to play with 65 members. The band received $5,000 per week for their performances. It was the highest paid band at the Fair (70).

Musical Director

The Bureau of Music also had to choose a musical director. At the top of the list were John Philip Sousa and Frederick Innes. Jacob Kunkel, a St. Louis band leader and music publisher, was also considered, but the eventual choice was William Weil. Weil had a local following and was most popular in St. Louis. The only role of Director of Music appears to have been to conduct the "utility band." The entire musical programming for the fair was left up to the Master of Programs, Ernest Kroeger.

Master of Programs

Ernest Richard Kroeger (1862–1934), a St. Louis musician, was appointed Master of Programs for the Fair, giving him complete supervision of the musical programming. Kroeger, born in St. Louis on August 10, 1862, studied piano and violin—taught by his father. As Master of Programs he organized brass bands and band contests, which were the most popular form of concerts. But he also invited the world's greatest organists to give recitals, planned a series of great orchestral and choral concerts, and arranged for competitions in all forms for musical composition. The music at the 1904 fair was considered by many to be one of the outstanding attractions of the event, and for his work in that capacity Kroeger was elected an Officer of the French Academy. He was a founding member of the American Guild of Organists (71).

At the end of his official duties at the Fair he founded the Kroeger School of Music in 1904. He remained in charge of the school until the time of his death in 1934. His daughter, Louise Kroeger, succeeded him until the school was closed in 1975. The second floor location at the Musical Art Building at Olive and Boyle was, for a time, a very popular nightclub venue called Gaslight Square. Ernest Kroeger was also the Director of the Washington University Music Department from 1925 until 1934.

William Weil's Band

The Official Band of the St. Louis World's Fair

Weil formed his band in 1898 and played at many St. Louis venues prior to the fair, including the Olympic Theatre, Pompeii Gardens, and the Tower Grove Park. The Weil Band played at the fair for 31 weeks, two concerts per day, and six days a week. The band was paid $2,000 per week and played from the opening day to the closing of the fair.

The following appears in *The Official History of the Fair:*

> William Weil, the St. Louis bandmaster, had a band, the official band of the exposition. Additionally, Weil won some fame by falling out of favor with the musicians union over his world's fair contract. He paid a $1,000 fine to the union and afterward was required to play *The Union Forever* march at every concert (72).

A Question of Pitch

The Bureau of Music also dictated policy by announcing that the official pitch for brass bands will be the standard, or French low-pitch, otherwise known as international pitch. This decree was unusual, as the international pitch was acknowledged to be about a half-tone lower than that used by most of the bands at the fair.

Concert (French) Low Pitch	A – 440	C – 523.2
High Concert Pitch	A – 450	C - 535.1
Philharmonic Pitch	A – 454	C – 539.9
American High Pitch	A – 461.6	C – 548.9

The pitch policy was blamed for the failure of the highly promoted band contest. Thirty thousand dollars was offered as money for bands in the contest, but only two bands participated. Many withdrew because of the disagreement regarding the pitch ruling. The winning band received fifty dollars in prize money. The choral contest, unencumbered by such stipulations, yielded prizes totaling $16,000 (73).

Bands at the World's Fair

1st US Cavalry Band, Fort Clark, Texas

24th US Band, Fort Harrison, Montana

26th US Cavalry Band, Fort Sam Houston, Texas

2nd US Infantry Band, Fort Logan, Colorado

5th Regiment Canadian Artillery Band

6th US Infantry Band

Banda Rossa Band

Boston Band

Contorno's Band

Ellery's Band

Fanciulli's Band

Ferris Wheel Band

First Royal Marine Band of Germany

Garde Republicaine Band

Government Indian Band

Grenadier Guard

Haskell Indian Band

Innes' Band

Ireland's Own Band

Kilties' Band

Knights of Pythias Band

Mexican Artillery Band

Philippine Police Band.

Philippine Scouts Band

Phinney's Band

Sousa and His Band

US Army Band, D.C.

US Marine Band, D.C.

Victoria Band of Vancouver

Weber's Band

Weil's Band

Missouri Bands at the World's Fair

Centerville, Missouri, Volunteer Fireman's Band

First Regiment Missouri National Guard Band

Fourth Regiment Missouri National Guard Band

Second Regiment Missouri National Guard Band

St. Charles Volunteer Fire Department Band

University of Missouri Cadet Band, Columbia

The Ferris Wheel Band

The 1904 Ferris Wheel was the same one used in the 1893 Columbian Exposition in Chicago. It afforded an incredible view of the entire fair, being the largest vertical structure at the event. The wheel had 36 cars that carried 60 passengers in each car. It was transported from Chicago to St. Louis on 175 flatbed railroad cars. Don Essig was the conductor of a band that played on the Ferris Wheel. It is not documented if the band played on a daily basis or only special occasions.

Essig was originally from Plattsburg, north of Kansas City, in Clinton County. He attended the Chicago Conservatory of Music (now Roosevelt University), graduating in 1900. Besides being a professional musician he appeared on the vaudeville and Chautauqua circuit performing on rare and unique instruments that he developed himself. After conducting his own band at the fair he continued to perform and direct circus bands and in vaudeville theatres. In 1920 he became the director of the band at Central Missouri State Teachers College in Warrensburg. He remained in this position for 21 years and retired in 1941. Essig was in poor health when he left the university and died in 1943. His collection of unusual instruments is now on display in the library and music department at the University of Central Missouri (74).

First Royal Marine Band of Germany

Bandsman Henry Lemcke was a member of the First Royal Marine Band of Germany that played at the 1904 fair. His son Hans was born in Germany and started studying the violin at the age of eight. Later the family moved from Germany and settled in St. Louis. Hans J. Lemcke played cornet in the Sousa band during the 1923 season.

In 1925, Hans J. Lemcke was engaged by the Webster Groves School District in suburban St. Louis to teach German and direct the high school band. His teaching of the German language ended with the start of World War II. Lemcke went on to build a very successful band program at Webster Groves and was the founder of the St. Louis County Bandmasters Association. That organization became the foundation for the St. Louis Suburban Music Educators Association.

1904 World's Fair
Louisiana Purchase Exposition
Ferris Wheel
Avery Library – Columbia University photo

1904 World's Fair
The Louisiana Purchase Exposition
St. Louis, Missouri

Dedication of
THE FRENCH NATIONAL PAVILION
Monday, May 16, 1904   4 to 6 pm

GRAND CONCERT BY SOUSA AND HIS BAND
Mr. John Philip Sousa, Conductor Mr. Franz Helle,
Flugelhorn Soloist

PROGRAMME

1.	Fantasie from "Carmen"	Bizet
2.	"Scenes Pittoresques"	Massenet
3.	Suite de Ballet from "Sylvia"	Delibes
4.	"Serenade"	Gounod
	Flugelhorn Solo – Mr. Franz Helle	
5.	Scenes from "Faust"	Gounod
6.	Overture, "Fra Diavolo"	Auber
7.	Excerpts from "Samson et Dalila"	Saint-Saens
8.	Valse, "Rose Moussa"	Bose
9.	March, "Hail to the Spirit of Liberty"	Sousa

Dedicated to the memory of the Marquis de Lafayette. Written expressly for the Exposition Universelle de 1900, Paris, France, and played there by Sousa and his Band.

10.	Airs from "Les Cloches de Corneville"	Planquette (75)

PIONEERS

PIONEERS

Keith K. Anderson
Fayette

Clarence Best
Webster Groves

Keith Collins
Sikeston

J.M. Dillinger
Hannibal

Charles Emmons
Columbia

Marie Turner Harvey
Kirksville

J.R. Huckstep
Raytown

Hans J. Lemcke
Webster Groves

Martin A. Lewis
Hannibal

LeRoy Mason
Cape Girardeau

Arthur Pryor
St. Joseph

R. Ritchie Robertson
Springfield

John Scott
Rolla

Claude T. Smith
Kansas City

Chapter 5

PIONEERS

———◆‹❄›◆———

Keith K. Anderson (1900–1967)   Fayette

Organized one of the first college bands (Central College) to tour annually with three concerts daily. Established the first band camp in 1939.

Clarence Best (dates unknown)   Maplewood

Co-founder and first president of Missouri School Band and Orchestra Director's Association, which was the forerunner of the MMEA (Missouri Music Educators Association).

Keith Collins (1916–1974)   Sikeston

Provided instruments and free instruction to any students interested in playing in the band. Served as President of Missouri Music Educators Association, 1954–1956.

Early organizer, along with others, of the Southeast Missouri Bandmasters Association.

T. Frank Coulter (1893–1977)   Joplin

Wrote the first constitution (along with Clarence Best) for the Missouri Band and Orchestra Directors Association, later to become MMEA.

James Dillinger (1895–1969)   Hannibal

Organized the Mark Twain Bandmasters Association. Served as President of MMEA, 1940.

Charles R. Dumars (1861–1925)   Carthage

Organized 14 different town bands in southwest Missouri. Directed the Carthage Light Guard Band, which was considered one of the finest town bands during the late 1800s and early 1900s.

Charles Emmons (1917–2000)   Columbia

    Brought a new dimension to the quality of bands in Missouri. Founded the Lambda Chapter of Phi Beta Mu, National Bandmaster's Fraternity in1959.

Marie Turner Harvey (1895–1952)   Kirksville

    Taught in the rural Porter School, nine miles from Kirksville. Organized a boys' band in 1915 then a second band in 1919, which included girls.

J. Roy Huckstep (1890–1980)   Raytown

    Taught in Bowling Green, Chillicothe, Raytown. Served as President of MMEA (Missouri Music Educators), 1945. Received first Missouri Bandmasters Association Hall of Fame Award.

Hans J. Lemcke (1893–1977)   Webster Groves

    Was a member of the Sousa's band (cornet). Organized one of the earliest band directors' associations in the state: the St. Louis County Band Directors Association.

Martin A. Lewis (1872–1945)   Hannibal

    Served as band director and principal of Douglass School. The school served a two-county area for African American children. He took the Douglass High School band to the first National Band Contest in Chicago in 1923. Douglass High School was the only Missouri band to compete in the National the National Band Contest.

LeRoy Mason (1912–1976)   Cape Girardeau

    Organized one of the first marching band festivals in state. President of MMEA— 1952–1954. Directed first band (Southeast Missouri State University) to play at a National Football League Superbowl, 1971.

Arthur Pryor (1870–1942)   St. Joseph

    Was a member of the Sousa Band for 12 years. Considered by Sousa to be the "World's greatest trombone player." Traveled the world with Sousa and his own band, but always considered St. Joseph his home.

Richie T. Robertson (1870–1939)   Springfield

    Established the music program in the Springfield Public Schools. Organized World's Largest Boy Scout Band in Springfield in 1920.

John W. Scott (1870–1950)   Rolla

Trained and worked as a pharmacist but had a lifelong love of music. He established the first town band in Rolla, started the band program at Missouri School of Mines, and started the band program in the Rolla Public Schools.

Claude T. Smith (1932–1987)   Kansas City

Brought international recognition to Missouri through his compositions. President of MMEA, 1976–1978.

Keith K. Anderson

(1900–1967)

Central College

Fayette, Missouri

Keith King Anderson was born in Coin, Iowa, the son of a local merchant. His route to Central College in Fayette, Missouri was told by E. E. Rich, the College's Director of Admissions for fifty years.

While recruiting new students, Rich noticed a picture of a "sharp-looking band" in the store owned by Anderson's father. After inquiring about the picture, he learned that the young director was the owner's son and had not completed college. Rich then outlined a plan in which the younger Anderson could complete his education at Central and also direct the college band. If he proved to be acceptable, it was agreed that he would be employed after graduation to continue as the band instructor. An interview with the college president was arranged and the man destined to be one of the most influential directors in the history of Central College bands was hired.

K. K. Anderson joined the Central faculty in the fall of 1925, having studied trumpet and directed the band at Simpson College, Indianola, Iowa. He also had conducted bands in Clarinda, Northboro, Coin, and College Springs, Iowa. After completion of his degree at Central in 1927, he continued his studies during the summer at Vandercook School of Music in Chicago, receiving a master of music degree in 1936.

Anderson's first marching band, with 25 members, was quick to gain popularity by performing at all possible college functions and traveling with the football team to games in nearby towns. The following spring, 1926, he revived the annual tours that had been so successful a decade earlier. According to Ulysses Clatworthy, a member of Anderson's first band, they traveled by train and flat-bed truck through northern Missouri and southern Iowa. The twenty-member unit was billed as "A Million and Nineteen Member Band," a title made possible because of the oboist's name, Marion Million.

Membership grew quickly in the following years as the band's reputation spread throughout the state. As the band enrollment increased, Anderson formed a second marching unit, which paraded separately but was combined with the first band when marching on the football field. After the marching season, auditions were held from both bands to determine those chosen for the Concert Band that toured during the spring. Membership in the concert group was limited to the size of the bus used for touring.

Soon known as "the finest college band in the state of Missouri," the Central Band became known as Anderson's Army and extended its tours to include over one thousand miles of travel each spring. In 1928 the band was invited to perform at the political rally for Democratic candidate for president, Al Smith. A special 11-coach train carried the band and party supporters to Sedalia, Missouri, where the musicians performed for over 1,500 people.

In 1928, student body president William Lesley paid tribute to the band in *The Central Collegian* newspaper, writing:

> … to be a bandsman requires more work than any extra-curricular activity on the campus. Absolute and unflagging attention during practice and hours of lonely woodsheding (personal practice) in the privacy of one's room are required. The band is always there to go anyplace, to do anything. The credit for the perfection of the bands and their spirit is due primarily to Keith Anderson, the director, whose efforts to improve the band are unceasing.

Seventy-five members were enrolled in the band in 1929, prompting Anderson to divide the group into three different musical ensembles. The first band dressed in blue uniforms, the second in black sweaters with a green emblem, and the "only one of its kind" girls' band wearing dark skirts and many-hued sweaters. The Concert Band was still selected from the best personnel of the three groups and limited to 28 members. The "Best Band in Missouri" set a goal to be the "Best Band in the Midwest."

Anderson loved competition and introduced incentives to the band members for their participation. An insignia pin was awarded to the members of the tour band and proudly worn by the group. Also, a contest was held in which the band member who enlisted the most new members was awarded a prize. Innovation and showmanship were part of Anderson's style. In 1932, he established a short-lived drum and bugle corps that rehearsed daily. For his concerts, Anderson used footlights and special lighting effects to highlight the mood of the music. The lights were controlled by the timpanist who often had many measures of rests.

Anderson organized the first summer band camp in Missouri in 1939. Students slept in tents provided by the local Boy Scouts and rehearsed in the Fayette city park. Only three summer camps were held due to the start of World War II in late1941.

Innovations displayed by the marching bands were also new in Missouri and were equaled by few bands in the country at the time. Besides the girls' band, Anderson was one of the first to employ a separate 25-piece girls' baton twirling corps. For night games, flashlights were affixed to the hats of each bandsman and used to spell out words in the darkness. A fire baton developed by Drum Major Robert Stepp and a three-way twirling act in 1938 provided a program that was unmatched in other Missouri colleges and duplicated by only the larger universities in the Midwest. So overwhelming was their performance that the radio announcer during a game at Rockhurst College in Kansas City seemed amazed at the spectacle of the band's performance and stated that he could find no words to describe it. The *Kansas City Times* carried a front-page story in the sports section the following morning. A few years later, Parke Carroll of the *Kansas City Journal* wrote:

> If it is color you are seeking, no university presents a prettier sight than the well-drilled band of Central College parading between halves of all games played at Fayette. Central takes pride in its musicians, both guys and gals, drilled with military precision.

The *Kansas City Star* noted that a "football game was played at intermission of the band concert."

In 1937, the Central band was named the official inaugural band for Governor Lloyd C. Stark. A sixty-piece band performed a one-hour concert before the inauguration and also played during the ceremony and reception afterward. The cost of the trip to Jefferson City was paid by the citizens of Fayette, who have always been generous in their support of the College and its activities.

Anderson's success was not limited to the marching bands. For two years, beginning in 1944, he also served as the Director of Athletics for the college. In both years his basketball teams won the MCAU championship. The success of the bands and athletics at Central during the 1940's created a friendly feud between Anderson and head football coach, C. A. Clingenpeel. The two competed for students who were talented in both music and athletics. It is reported that Clingenpeel, in talking to his athletes, informed them, "See that man over there…that's the band director. Take one good look at him and have nothing to do with him again."

The feud was reported in the sports section of *The Philadelphia Inquirer* in 1948:

> At Central College in Fayette, Missouri, the band is a subject of intense school pride. The football team may win or lose, but the band always goes undefeated. This year more than one-fifth of the college's students tried out for the band. Football coach Clingenpeel and Maestro Anderson have a rivalry for the services of a 200-pound freshman enrolling at Central. The band director invariably is on hand at the first football practice of the school year and Coach Clingenpeel has a routine paragraph in his initial pep talk warning his squad against the lure of the band.

By 1950, only Central College and the University of Illinois could boast of a marching band with tympani.

Author's note:

I wanted to attend the University of Illinois because of their marching tympani and giant bass drum. My parents thought a smaller school would be better for me and chose Central. In my second year at Central, my grandfather helped me build a platform with bicycle wheels to which I attached two old kettledrums found in the Central band room. The cart was unbalanced and each time it was pulled from a stopped position the front end came off the ground. That was the least of the "marching tympani" problems. To find someone to pull the tympani cart was not easy. A piano major who played cymbals in the marching band suggested her roommate. Sally Stabenow, joined the Central College Marching Band as the tympani puller. Stabenow was a physical education major and one hour of PE credit was given to members of the marching band. Professor Anderson gave her a "C" in marching band for pulling the cart and it was recorded as her grade in physical education. She was so upset that she asked that the marching band grade be deleted from her college record since she was an "A" student in all other academic studies. The grade was removed. This author and the "tympani puller" were married in 1952.

CHD

In the early 1950's, the National Association of Intercollegiate Basketball Athletic Association (NAIB) held its championship basketball tournament in Kansas City. Central's basketball team qualified for the tournament in 1950–51, and the band also made the journey. The following year the basketball team failed to qualify; however, the band received a special invitation to perform. Never before had a band been invited when the team from that school was not playing in the tournament. Bill Moore of the *Kansas City Times* wrote that, "You've never heard band music until you've heard the Central aggregation." Anderson referred to these entertainment specialties for the fans as "dog and pony shows." Whatever term he might use to describe them, they were immensely popular programs.

During the 1948–1949 academic year, Anderson suffered a heart attack that decreased his activities only temporarily. By this time, the marching band had been combined into one unit and two concert groups were formed in the spring. The Varsity Band, or "3:30 band," named after its hour of rehearsal, was student-directed and open to all students. The "4:30 band" was the Concert Band of distinction under Anderson's direction.

Despite his health, Anderson followed the marching band in his Model A Ford, maintaining his military discipline and rigorous rehearsal schedules. Anderson would follow the band as it marched around the square or to and from the football rehearsal field. He was always on the lookout for those who marched out of step or were caught talking in ranks. He devised the use of a radio transmitter in the shako of the drum major to give directions and corrections.

Donald Panhorst, Chairman of the Department of Music and Drama at Edinboro State College, Pennsylvania, recalls the rehearsal demands of Professor Anderson:

For two weeks prior to the annual spring band tour, we would practice in the Assembly Hall for at least two hours in the evening, Monday through Friday, in addition to our regular one-hour afternoon rehearsals. On Saturday and Sunday we would sometimes rehearse as long as four hours each day. In most cases we would have our entire tour program practically memorized.

The band's memorization ability was tested during one concert as the special lighting system overloaded the electrical system. The resulting darkness did not hinder the band as they continued to play without a flaw. Some in the audience thought the blackout was part of the show.

"Prof" Anderson held a special place of distinction as a member of the faculty at Central, a distinction that was not appreciated by some of the teaching staff. All members of the music faculty were required, either by decree or faculty understanding, to present a recital on their major instrument each year. There is no evidence that Anderson, a trumpet player, ever performed a recital during his tenure at Central. In addition, each faculty member was required to attend the weekly chapel and assembly programs with students at the school. Again, there is no record that he attended either. It was well-known by his students that during the weekly chapel and assembly time he could be found at the local drug store drinking coffee and visiting with friends.

Anderson's final year as Director of Bands at Central College was 1952. He had directed the band for 27 years. An unfortunate conflict of personalities and styles of performance existed between Anderson and the director of the A Cappella Choir, Luther T. Spayde. It was after Spayde had been appointed the new Dean of the Sweeny Conservatory of Music that Anderson left his position at Central and accepted the directorship of the band program at Boonville High School. He taught at Boonville for one year, and then returned in 1953 as an admissions counselor at Central College.

Keith K. Anderson died in 1967 and was recognized in 1973 with the Hall of Fame Award presented by the Missouri Bandmasters Association for his many achievements as Director of Bands at Central College (76). The school was later named Central Methodist University.

Clarence Best

Co-Founder of MMEA

Clarence Best played in the Joplin High School band under the direction of Frank T. Coulter. He was a graduate of Kansas State Teachers College in Pittsburg, Kansas, and Washington University in St. Louis.

After teaching in Wichita, Best came to Webster Groves High School in suburban St. Louis in 1931 as orchestra director. He left in the 1936–37 school year to take a similar position at neighboring Maplewood High School. During his six years at Webster he developed a symphonic-size orchestra numbering 77 members in his last year. The orchestra included 14 first violins, 10 seconds, 9 violas, 6 cellos, 6 bass, one concert harp, and a full complement of winds and percussion.

Best came to Maplewood High School from Webster Groves as orchestra director. In 1940 he replaced Eugene Van Meter, who had organized the first band program in 1930. Best became both the band and orchestra director at Maplewood. At the time, Maplewood was one of a number of suburban school districts in the St. Louis area, including Clayton, Jennings, Fairview (later incorporated into the Jennings district), Wellston, Ferguson, Kirkwood, Webster Groves, University City, and Normandy.

Leaders in school band programs in the late 1930s were Webster Groves and University City. The Webster band was directed by Hans J. Lemcke, a former member of the Sousa band. The University City band was under the baton of Norman Falkenhaner, formerly the Assistant Director of the University of Missouri band where he attended as a student. The size of the larger county bands numbered 60 to 80 members. In 1944 the Maplewood High School Band, under Clarence Best's direction, numbered an impressive 70 members with five tubas and one concert harp. In 1944 Best was also listed as the school's trigonometry teacher. (World War II reduced the number of teachers and it may be assumed that he filled in as trigonometry teacher during that shortage.)

According to the minutes of the first Missouri Music Educators Association, Clarence Best was one of the two founding directors of the soon-to-be-formed state music organization. It is reported that: "Clarence Best of Webster Groves and James Robertson of Springfield decided to take positive action toward the formation of a state music educator's organization" (77). The discussion was during a golf game in Joplin, Missouri in 1934.

After the Joplin golf game with Robertson, Best presented the idea at a meeting of the St. Louis County music directors, and sent invitations state-wide for an organizational meeting in Columbia. The Missouri Band and Orchestra Directors' Association was formed at that meeting in Columbia on November 25, 1934. Clarence J. Best was elected the first president of the organization, later to become the Missouri Music Educators Association (MMEA) (78).

Keith Collins

(1916–1974)

Keith Collins was born on July 3, 1916 in Jefferson City, Missouri, but grew up in Higginsville and graduated from Higginsville High School. After graduation, he attended the Swinney Conservatory of Music at Central (Methodist) College in Fayette, Missouri. During his college days he played in the Charlie Armstead Orchestra, a popular dance band in central Missouri. At Central he was a pupil of Keith K. Anderson, the Director of Bands. He graduated from Central in 1938 with a Bachelor of Arts in Music Education, later receiving his master's degree from the University of Missouri. He did further graduate study at the University of Iowa.

From 1938–1940, Collins taught in Marceline, Missouri. In 1939, he married Miss Jean Smith of Fayette, the daughter of a Central College professor.

His son, Robert Collins, related that his father was offered $1,500 to leave Marceline and teach at Sikeston. In 1940 he accepted the position of Director of Bands and Supervisor of Music there. He was the second band director at Sikeston High School; the program had been started by Reid Jann in 1934. Collins remained at Sikeston until 1970, but took time away to serve in the US Marine Corps from August 1943 until May 1946. During his military service he directed the West Coast Marine Air Corps Band in San Diego, California.

While at Sikeston, Collins taught both band and choir, and by 1949 the band had 76 members. In 1955 the school expanded the music program, starting an orchestra under the direction of James Butler, and employing Betty Cooper to take over the high school choir. She later married Warren E. Hearnes, who was the governor of Missouri from 1965–1973. She sang at many public and civic events as First Lady of the state.

By 1956 the Sikeston band had grown to 105 members, and in 1958 new band uniforms were needed. The district did not have funds for uniforms due to the planned construction of a new high school. Collins turned to the community for help. Because of the respect he had gained as band director, generous donations were received to purchase new uniforms in 1959. The new Sikeston High School campus opened in the middle of the 1960–1961 school year. Collins helped design the band building, which is still in use. Collins' band uniform, cap, and baton are on display at the school as a tribute to his leadership.

In 1961 the band program had become so large that it was divided into an "early" band (7:30 a.m.) and a "late" band (8:30 a.m.). Ed Carson, teaching in Jackson and a Central College graduate, was hired to assist Collins and taught the beginning students, 8th grade band, and the "late" band.

In 1962, students decided to honor their director and asked for assistance from Carson. Unknown to Collins, the students rehearsed on Sunday afternoon and changed the coming half-time show. The planned show, titled "America on Parade," was changed to pay tribute to Collins on his 25th year anniversary at Sikeston High School. The band formed "K"–"C" on the field then played *Semper Fidelis* March (Always Faithful) in recognition of his service in the US Marine Corps.

After the show was over, Collins was heard saying, "This is the greatest honor a band could have bestowed upon its director, but one thing really has me confused—how could so many women keep a secret for so long and so well?"

Collins was very passionate about his teaching career. His first innovation was to introduce free music instruction into the public school system. Anyone who wanted to learn to play an instrument could. In his early years at Sikeston he did not have a place to teach, so he used the stage of the gymnasium to hold classes.

Collins, along with LeRoy Mason of Jackson High School, formed the Southeast Missouri High School Band Association. Later he served as president of that organization, and in 1954 he was elected president for a two-year term of the Missouri Music Educators Association. He served as state chairman for the American School Band Directors Association, and several of his articles on music were published in national music magazines.

In 1947 he opened the Collins Piano Company in Sikeston, later branching into a full-service music store with band instruments, music, and accessories. His primary instrument was the clarinet.

After retirement in 1969, Collins began working in his store full-time. In 1974, following a March vacation trip, he developed colon cancer and died in June at the age of 57. His wife, Jean Smith Collins, survived her husband by 33 years and died in 2007 at the age of 94. They had two sons, Robert and Michael (79).

T. Frank Coulter

(1893–1977)

Born in Joplin in 1893, Frank Coulter graduated from Olivet College in Olivet, Michigan in 1916 at the age of 23. Upon graduation, he returned to Joplin and taught mathematics at Joplin High School, his alma mater. When he arrived at Joplin High School, he found that there was no band program and only a makeshift orchestra.

He taught his first orchestra in 1916 and organized the first Joplin High School band in 1919 and a glee club soon after. His success in winning orchestra contests in the early '20s began to awaken the Joplin community to the value of music, and in 1923 music classes began to earn regular school credit.

In 1922 one of his students dubbed his enthusiastic director with the nickname "Chief," and for the next four decades his thousands of students would also affectionately refer to him as "Chief." The student body highly respected him and the parents and local citizens appreciated his love and respect for his students, as well as enjoying the cultural aspects of attending the operas, orchestra, and band concerts that he masterfully directed.

In 1926 he started the Joplin Boy's Band, which included 219 grade school boys.

The ever-entrepreneurial Coulter chartered trains and later buses to transport his students all over the United States for competitions while never spending any school district funds. It is said by one person that he would start on one end of Main Street and by the time he had finished at First and Main, he would have gained enough donations from businesses and individuals to pay for the music trips.

In the 1930's, Coulter's orchestras received Division 1 ratings in National competitions in places like Chicago, Madison, Wisconsin, Columbus, Ohio, Mason City, Iowa, and Topeka, Kansas. Included in this was an appearance by the Joplin High School Orchestra at the National Music Educator's National Conference Annual Convention in Chicago in 1938. In that same year, he became the first conductor of the Joplin Junior College orchestra—later to become Missouri Southern State University.

In December 1934, Coulter, along with Clarence Best from Webster Groves and James Robertson from Springfield, met in Joplin to write a constitution and by-laws for the organization, which would eventually become the Missouri Music Educators Association— MMEA. In 1934 he was elected the First Vice President of the newly organized state band-orchestra directors association.

"Chief" retired in 1962 after 45 years of teaching instrumental and vocal music at Joplin High School. It was the only school in which he taught. His long tenure at Joplin was rewarded in 1991 with the naming of the Joplin High School auditorium after the creative and caring individual who had influenced so many students.

T. Frank Coulter died in 1977 at the age of 84. He is buried in Mount Hope Cemetery in Joplin. Jim Norman succeeded Coulter as band director at Joplin High School (80).

James M. Dillinger, Jr.

(1895–1969)

James Dillinger was born in Humphreys, Missouri, and received his early education in a rural school near his home. He attended Milan High School, and then received his BS and MA degrees from Northeast Missouri State College (later Truman State University) at Kirksville. During his career he continued with advanced studies at the University of Colorado, New York University, and DePaul University.

His first teaching assignment was in the rural areas of north central Missouri. He later served as superintendent of schools at Edina. His first music position was as supervisor of music at Bethany, Missouri. He then taught music at Chillicothe and Lebanon before going to Hannibal in 1936. He served as director of instrumental music in the Hannibal schools until his retirement in 1965. He taught briefly at Hannibal-LaGrange College after his retirement from public schools.

Dillinger was widely known in music circles throughout the Midwest. He was active as an adjudicator and clinician. He organized the Mark Twain Bandmasters Association, which sponsored the annual marching band festival in Hannibal. He was active in church and civic activities, serving as Lieutenant Governor of the first district Missouri-Arkansas Kiwanis International.

Dillinger was an active member of the Missouri Music Educators Association and was among those who founded the organization in 1934. He was elected vice president in 1939 and the president in 1940. Even after retirement from music education, Dillinger remained active in the affairs of the MMEA and attended all meetings of the Council of Past Presidents.

Dillinger died in March 1969 at the age of 74.

Charles R. Dumars

(1861–1925)

Charles R. Dumars was born in Ohio in 1861 and received his education in Missouri. During his career as a band director he organized many community bands in southwest Missouri.

In 1885, at age 24, Dumars became the leader of the Carthage Light Guard Band. Through his careful training the band became one of the premier town bands, which traveled extensively to perform for civic events. Included in the band's travel itinerary were excursions to St. Louis, Kansas City, Little Rock, Boston, Denver, and Pittsburgh. Travel was always by train, and the *Carthage Weekly Press* wrote about the director in 1891:

> It is a fact now well-known and conceded through the west that Carthage has one of the best bands in the country. That the success of the organization is in large measure due to the energy and tact of Mr. C. R. Dumars, its director, is also a recognized fact.

Mr. Dumars commenced his career as a musician in 1874 in Bolivar, Missouri. A year later he went to Springfield, taking a prominent part in the old band there. In 1877 he organized Dumars Springfield Band of which he was the leader, and for the next three years he put in his time organizing and teaching bands through the Southwest. In that time he started some twelve to fourteen bands on the high road to success. In the fall of 1880 he joined the Golden Dramatic Company band, playing with that organization for two years, after which he led the Agnes Villa combination, resigning his position in 1884 to go to Joplin. He led the Joplin band two years and during the time he was at its head attaining quite a reputation, winning several band contests. In November 1885 he came to Carthage and reorganized the defunct Light Guard band. He was made its leader and has held that position until his retirement in 1922.

The *Carthage Weekly Express* in the August 27, 1891 publication stated:

> The band has come gradually up from a very insignificant affair to its present magnificent proportions, in membership, equipment, ability and attainments. It has filled many important engagements and everywhere been the recipient of high compliments. In five contests entered the first prize has been won each time, and the premium money, thus obtained aggregates the neat sum of $1,100 (81).

In 1899, Dumars established the Dumars' Music Company in Carthage. The business had grown to such proportions by 1908 that a new store was opened on the east side of the town square.

Dumars died in 1925 at the age of 65 while living in California.

Charles Emmons

(1917–2000)

Charles Emmons was born May 19, 1917 in Lipscomb County, Texas and began his musical career in Kingfisher, Oklahoma in 1937, teaching elementary music and high school band and orchestra. He moved to the position of band and orchestra director at Cushing, Oklahoma in 1941. From 1943–1946 he served as a saxophone, clarinet, and violin player in the US Army in the Pacific, performing with Bob Hope and other nationally known entertainers. He later became a supply sergeant with the 353rd Engineer Construction Battalion.

After the war years, Emmons returned to teaching in Chickasha, Oklahoma, where he also taught at the Oklahoma College for Women. In 1949 he moved to Amarillo, Texas, and developed a public school band and orchestra program of extraordinary quality. From 1949–1957 the Amarillo High School Band received successive Sweepstake Awards at the Tri-State Band Festival in Enid, Oklahoma, one of the renowned festivals of the time. In addition, he served as head of the music department and coordinator of secondary instrumental music at Amarillo High School. During the summers he held a position at West Texas State University in Canyon, Texas, where he received his master's degree.

Emmons was interviewed for the position of Director of Bands at Missouri University – Columbia, in the summer of 1957 by Rogers Whitmore, the Chairman of the Music Department. He joined the University of Missouri music department faculty in September 1957. Although never authenticated it was said he was hired on his strength as a builder of fine bands and orchestras, plus he played viola, an instrument needed to complete the university string quartet.

During his tenure as Band and Orchestra Director, the instrumental music program made monumental progress, appearing at state, regional, and combined regional conventions of the Music Education National Conference and the national convention of the Music Teachers National Association. The Symphonic Band appeared at the regional convention of the College Band Directors National Association and regional and national conventions of the Music Educators National Conference. With Emmons as director, Marching Mizzou received national recognition with performances at bowl games on national television. He introduced new marching band techniques, and the floating MIZZOU–TIGERS formation became a tradition at all half-time football performances. It was Emmons who first allowed women to perform on the field as members of the university marching band.

Emmons served as College Vice President of the Missouri Music Educators Association, President of the Southwestern Division of MENC President and founding member of Lambda Chapter of Phi Beta Mu. He was the Southwestern Division chairman of the National Band Association and a 1980 inductee to the Missouri Bandmasters Association Hall of Fame.

Professor Emmons became chairman of the music department at the University of Missouri – Columbia in 1966 and served in that position for sixteen years until his retirement in 1982. Emmons remained in Columbia after his retirement, where he continued to be a judge and active participant in professional music organizations. He died in Columbia on November 21, 2000 at age 83 (82).

Professor Emmons
Charting band show for Marching Mizzou
1967

Marie Turner Harvey

(1869–1952)

Marie Turner had begun teaching in the rural St. Louis area before coming to Kirksville, where she married H. Clay Harvey, a teacher at the First District Normal School (Truman State University). Because she herself had attended a rural school she believed that the school could become the center of the community both educationally and culturally. Acting on her belief, in 1912 she went to L. B. Sipple, the Adair County Superintendent of Schools, and requested that he give her the worst school district in the county. He assigned her to the Porter School. She accepted the assignment with the understanding that she would stay three years and would be allowed to teach without interference from others. She also would have a residence of her own within the community.

Porter Schools

The first Porter School had been founded in 1843 by Sarah Porter in Farmington, Connecticut. A preparatory school for girls, its purpose was to educate the elite young women of the Eastern seaboard. The school was the preparatory school attended by such distinguished women as Jacqueline Kennedy Onassis (1947), actresses Gene Tierney (1938), and Barbara Hutton, as well as socialite Gloria Vanderbilt.

Built on the philosophy of a "progressive school education," additional Porter Schools were established in the United States. Advocates of progressive education were searching for ways to address the new problems in society created by the rapid industrial expansion of the late 19th century. Progressive programs shared the common belief that environment is the primary influence on behavior.

In Missouri, the Porter school district was a nine-mile square district, three miles west of Kirksville in Benton Township, Adair County. The school was built in 1882 at a cost of $600 with land donated for the education of rural children. Although it was built on some of the richest land in the area, the Porter school had gained the reputation of being the worst district in the county. It was devoid of community spirit, involvement, and interest in education. This was caused in part by the lack of a permanent teacher. The district often had two teachers a year: one for the winter session and one for the summer. The people of Porter district also felt that if people were looking for involvement they looked to the church, not the school. Before Harvey's arrival the people of the district had never considered using the school for community events.

The schoolhouse was badly in need of repair, but with the help of six or seven core community families the Porter School was made ready for Harvey's first class. A new furnace was installed together with a new water system, including a drinking fountain paid for by Harvey.

The curriculum that was taught was more than just the basics and was not confined to the traditional classroom methods. Frances Wright, a former student of Porter School, remembered how the school day started. "Every morning we said the Pledge to the Flag and then we opened all the windows and marched around the room to *Washington Post March,* no matter how cold it was. That was the morning ritual" (83). The day ended when the students went home in the wagon Harvey had purchased to transport the children from outlying farms. The wagon was driven by patrons and pulled by their horses. All of these activities were done to promote a sense of community patriotism.

Not everything taught at Porter was directed toward the goal of improving the community. Some subjects were taught to improve the person or the family. For example, art, music, and penmanship were included in the curriculum to help increase the students' sense of self-worth.

Marie Turner Harvey advocated music "...as the one thing that would organize, harmonize, and stabilize a community" (84) and in 1915 put this theory into practice at Porter with the creation of the Porter Community Band, originally made up of the senior boys in the school. By 1917, women were included and a professional musician was engaged as director. The inclusion of women in a band was often looked upon as "unladylike." Later, a Junior Band was organized as well. Through the years the Porter Community Band became one of the best known ambassadors for the Porter School. Included among its accomplishments were appearances at the State Fair in Sedalia in 1920 and a contract with the City of Kirksville for regular Saturday night concerts during the summer.

"Mrs. Harvey's work at Porter School has long been remembered. It touched the hearts and lives of many people. She made the residents proud to be a part of the Porter District even after she left there to teach at Kirksville State Teachers College" (85).

The Porter School was closed in May 1967, when it was incorporated as part of the Kirksville School District. The Porter School building was sold at public auction for $450. The new owner used it as a shed for his farm equipment (86).

Porter School Senior Band – 1915
Adair County Historical Society photo

Porter School Junior Band
Adair County Historical Society photo

J. R. Huckstep

(1890–1980)

Jesse Roy Huckstep was born June 5, 1890 in Whiteside, Missouri, south of Bowling Green, into a family whose musical talent could be traced back five generations. His grandfather, Jacob Edward Huckstep, founded a singing school in Bowling Green. His father was a violinist, directed church choirs, and formed a 100-voice male chorus. His uncle Jesse C. Huckstep founded the Huckstep Concert Band, which eventually became the Bowling Green Concert Band. J. R. Huckstep would later become director.

In 1908 Huckstep completed high school in Bowling Green and worked as a telegrapher at the local depot that served the Chicago-Alton Railroad. During that time he remained very active in his avocation as a band member and director. In 1912 he traveled to Holland, Michigan to study piano tuning. In 1913 he married Linnie Pool in Centralia, Missouri.

The Bowling Green High School Band was organized by Huckstep in 1921, and in 1925 he began leading bands in Eolia, Clarksville, Paynesville, and Elsberry. In 1929 he lived in Kirksville, studying music at the college. While pursuing his bachelor's degree he taught in Greene City and other towns nearby. After completing his degree he taught two years in Greene City and one year in Brunswick.

Huckstep accepted the position of director of instrumental and vocal music in the Chillicothe schools in 1936. His band grew to 90 members by 1945 and was the outstanding band in the area. He remained at Chillicothe until 1945.

At the age of 55 "Huck," as he was sometimes called, was selected from several candidates to build a music program in Raytown, a small, unincorporated town east of Kansas City. Outdated capes and dilapidated military hats were replaced in a few months with new band uniforms. The emphasis on excellence was apparent. There was a big interest in the spring music contest, and Huckstep and Jack Overbey from nearby Ruskin High School worked together to develop the contest movement in the area.

In 1946 he was one of the founders of the Raytown Kiwanis Club and served as president in 1955.

J. R. Huckstep retired with honors at the age of 69 from the Raytown School District. In 1961 the Hucksteps were invited to return to Raytown for the annual high school band banquet held in May. The event was hosted by Carroll Lewis and Bob Schupp. During the event Mrs. Huckstep, who suffered from angina, collapsed at the banquet and could not be revived.

In 1980, J. R. Huckstep became the first bandmaster inducted into the Missouri Bandmasters Association Hall of Fame. He died on January 25, 1980, five months before his 90th birthday. He was a 50-year Mason and had 13 years' perfect attendance in the Raytown Kiwanis Club. In January 2005, the Missouri Music Educators Association honored J. R. Huckstep with the Hall of Fame Award (87).

Hans J. Lemcke

(1893–1977)

Born in 1893 in Germany into a musical family, Hans J. Lemcke began his musical education at the age of six playing the violin and piano. His musical ability was hereditary, for his father was leader of one of the German naval bands chosen to accompany Prince Henry of Prussia, brother of the Kaiser, on a tour around the world in 1900. In 1904 the band was invited to the St. Louis World's Fair. The C. G. Conn instrument manufacturing company described the German band in their trade publication, *Truth*:

> The First Royal Marine Band of Germany, which has been commissioned by the Emperor to come to the United States as part of the German exhibit at the St. Louis Exposition, sailed on March 10. After a short engagement in St. Louis the band will make a tour of the United States and Canada. Every man in the band is a musician, and they are all equally expert on string instruments as they are on wind instruments. All men are nearly six feet in height, broad-shouldered, robust and perfect specimens of the strong, ruddy German type. The leader measures six feet three and one-half inches, and is a veritable giant. The repertoire of the band includes 1500 compositions by the most famous musicians (88).

After studying the violin and piano, young Hans Lemcke took up the trumpet and started composing light marches when he was 14 years old. Talking about his schooling, Lemcke recalled:

> I had a German teacher in college—Professor Hohn—a wonderful man. When he entered the classroom in the morning he would open the class by saying, 'Guten morgen, Meine schulerin'. Then he would go into a song with the class. We each had a German songbook. This put everyone in a good mood, and so the class would begin. He was a teacher who understood the humanities of life (89).

The Lemcke family moved to St. Louis after the World's Fair and Hans played trumpet in the famous John Philip Sousa Band in 1923.

In 1927, Lemcke was hired in the middle of the school year by the Webster Groves school district to teach German and direct the band. The band and orchestra program was one of the first in St. Louis County, having been organized in 1925 by W. A. Gore, who was replaced the following year by William B. Heyne. John Philip Sousa visited the Webster Groves Band during Lemcke's first year. He recalled that visit from the "March King":

> Our band was still in its infancy in 1927. I remember Sousa trying to evoke some accents from the band, but they would not come. The band did not respond to his wishes. I was standing behind the scenes and looked at Mr. Sousa and smiled, and he smiled back at me, and went on and finished the march, with much applause.

In Lemcke's first year as director, five students from Missouri were selected to be members of the National High School Orchestra. Two were from Webster. The symphonic group represented all 48 states and played for the National Education Association annual meeting in Dallas.

The Webster Groves 1926 yearbook, *Echo*, described the band before and after Lemcke's mid-term arrival.

> This year our band had a gloomy outlook. Our instrumentation was bad. We lacked organization. About the middle of the year, a new director was secured, a man of great ability to whom the band owes its greatest progress. Mr. H. J. Lemcke was our new director. Mr. Lemcke worked hard on our instrumentation problem and soon the outlook was bright (90).

In 1931 Lemcke became the orchestra director at Webster Groves for a short period of time. The size of the band and orchestra at Webster Groves in the mid-1930s is a tribute to the director's enthusiasm and organizational skill. The band of 1933 had 66 players, which included 21 clarinets, 7 French horns, 6 basses, and one concert harp. The orchestra was a full size symphonic ensemble with 14 first violins, 10 seconds, 9 violas, 6 cellos, and 6 basses, plus the full complement of wind and percussion players. The yearbook indicates that the band practiced during the summer, entered the Greater St. Louis Band Contest, and took first place, receiving a loving cup for their award.

Hans Lemcke was a graduate of Berlin University and also taught German at Webster. Due to the growing anti-German sentiment in the US, he chose to delete the Berlin University acknowledgement from his faculty picture in the 1933 Webster Groves yearbook. Instead, his 1941 entry lists a Bachelor of Music degree from Illinois Wesleyan University.

Upon his retirement in 1963 from the Webster Groves School District, his son, Henry, succeeded him as the director of the high school band.

Hans J. Lemcke died in 1977 in Webster Groves at the age of 84.

Webster Groves High School Band – 1927
Hans J. Lemcke, Director
John Philip Sousa visits Webster band
Lemcke played cornet in the Sousa Band
Yearbook photo

Martin Lewis

(1872–1945)

Martin Lewis was born in Louisiana, Missouri in 1872. He graduated from high school in 1893, and then began teaching in a colored school in his hometown. He saved all of his earnings from teaching to go to Washington D.C. to attend Howard University. After teaching two more years at Louisiana, he came to Hannibal to teach at Douglass, the only high school in Marion and Ralls County for African American children. At Douglass he taught science, Latin, mathematics, manual training, and directed the high school band.

In 1921, Douglass became a first-class high school with high standards. It was that same year that Lewis organized the first Douglass High School Band. A bond issue provided for two new school buildings in Hannibal along with improvements to others. Douglass was awarded $23,000 for indoor toilets.

The National Band Contest was organized in Chicago in 1923. The contest was sponsored by the Music Industries Chamber of Commerce, which represented publishers, manufacturer, and retail dealers. Thirty-five bands participated in the first contest, and Douglass was included in the historic event. The Hannibal School District provided eighty-five dollars for the Douglass band to participate. Hannibal merchants were so impressed with the discipline and quality of the band that they raised an additional $400 to help defray the cost of the trip.

The band traveled from Hannibal to Chicago on the Wabash Railroad and was met by a welcoming committee upon arrival. The contest concluded on June 7th with a massed band concert and parade through the Loop area led by the Chicago Police Band and mounted police.

Douglass High School placed last in the contest but received $100 for their participation.

To show their appreciation for the community support, the band presented a concert in the Hannibal City Park on May 29, 1923. The program included:

Billboard March

Wabash Blues

Overture, *The Sky Pilot*

General Pershing March

Waltz, *Three O'clock in the Morning*

Fox Trot, *The Shiek*

National Emblem March

Songs from *The Old Folks*

Fox Trot, *Broken Hearted Blues*

Overture, *Land of Liberty*

Martin Lewis resigned from Douglass High School in 1944 at the age of 72. He died one year later.

LeRoy F. Mason

(1912–1976)

LeRoy Mason was born on December 5, 1912 in Salisbury, Missouri, and graduated from Salisbury High School. He earned both his bachelor's and master's degree at Northeast Missouri State Teachers College [Truman State University] in Kirksville. He did additional graduate work at Northwestern University and the University of Colorado in Boulder.

His early teaching included schools in Mendon, Triplett, Sumner, and LaGrange, Missouri. In 1936 he went to Riverview Gardens to start the band and choral program in that suburban St. Louis district. Three years later he accepted a position with the Jackson R–2 School District in southeast Missouri. In addition to his schoolwork he directed the Jackson Municipal Band and Choral Club. Under his leadership women were invited for the first time to participate in the municipal band. In 1944 he started a band festival, which led to the formation of the Southeast Missouri High School Band Association the following year.

Mason joined the music department at Southeast Missouri State College in Cape Girardeau in 1957 after serving as director of music for the public schools in Jackson. Ed Carson was appointed to replace Mason at Jackson High School.

An early innovation for the university marching band was the "marching marquee," developed by Mason. The idea for the moving formation of words came after he had seen lighted letters moving across an advertising display in a local jewelry store. He perfected the marquee to the point the band could include the current football score as part of the bands half-time performance.

Mason began with 37 band members in 1957 and built it to 150 members, constantly improving its performance. From 1957 until his retirement, more than 1,150 students marched in his band. The Golden Eagles entertained during televised professional football games 23 times, including 16 performances for the St. Louis Football Cardinals and the 1971 Super Bowl in Miami. The band was the first from Missouri to perform on national television for the National Football League. The Golden Eagles were unique among college bands in the fact that their official colors were blue and gold, making both their name and colors different from those of the University.

The summer music camps at the university were organized by Mason. The first camp in 1958 had a total of 170 high school students. By 1985 the camp had grown to attract over 2,000 during several sessions.

Mason became department head and chairman of the Division of Music at Southeast Missouri State College in 1959 and was made professor emeritus of music upon his retirement in

April of 1977. During his tenure, the Golden Eagles claimed more national television time than any other band in the country.

Mason was president of the Missouri Music Educators Association in1952 through 1954. He was a charter member of Lambda Chapter of Phi Beta Mu, the International Bandmasters Fraternity.

He was married in May of 1941 to Miss Frances Hardy, who died in 1961. On July 19, 1963, he and Lola Schuette were married in New Madrid, Missouri. Mason died on July 14, 1976 at the age of 64 at Missouri Baptist Hospital in suburban St. Louis. He devoted 42 years to music education in Missouri (91).

Arthur Pryor

(1870–1942)

"The World's Greatest Trombone Player"
Sousa

Pryor was born on the second floor of the Lyceum Theatre in St. Joseph, Missouri on September 22, 1870. His father, Samuel, was the town bandmaster and his mother gave piano lessons in their home (92).

At age six he started to study several instruments with his father as teacher. His mother gave him piano lessons. The valve trombone was his special love, and his astonishing skill caused him to be billed as "The Boy Wonder" when he performed with a Chicago band at age 11.

Although the valve trombone was the popular instrument of the time, young Arthur Pryor was fascinated with a slide trombone left to his father as payment for a debt. The slide trombone was the only one of its kind in St. Joseph. For some time Arthur tried to master the instrument without using any slide oil, and he played using only two positions. Later, he learned quite accidentally that there might be as many as seven positions on the instrument. He found these, though his lack of opportunity to study with a good professional player apparently resulted in his forcing some tones with the slide in the wrong position. Later, in the heyday of his performing fame, he made great use of these alternate or "false" positions (93).

His innovative expressiveness and phenomenally fast slide technique would earn him the title of "Paganini of the Trombone." In 1889 he joined the celebrated Alessandro Liberati band and toured the West. Shortly after, he became director of the Stanley Opera Company in Denver where his skill on piano and his vast repertoire earned him additional recognition (94).

In 1892, John Philip Sousa, the nation's premier bandmaster, heard of Pryor and asked him to audition. Young Pryor was not interested but later agreed to audition for the popular Sousa. His audition was at a rehearsal in New York with the full Sousa Band in attendance.

During the audition, a particular difficult trombone part was given to young Arthur by Frank Holton, the first-chair trombonist. After hearing him play Holton offered to step down and gave Pryor his seat in the band. A year later Holton retired from the Sousa Band to start his own instrument manufacturing company. Pryor played his first solo with Sousa's band at age 22. He continued for twelve years as a featured soloist and later as Assistant Conductor with the Sousa Band. Many of the Sousa recordings were conducted by Pryor.

Pryor played concerts with Sousa throughout America as well as before the crowns of Europe, among them King Edward II and Kaiser Wilhelm of Prussia.

In 1903, Pryor formed his own band. It premiered at the Majestic Theater in New York and would go on to make six coast-to-coast tours. In his international travels he always listed his hometown as St. Joseph, Missouri. The Arthur Pryor Band was booked for numerous important exhibitions; but Pryor disliked the pace of touring, and in 1904 he settled in Asbury Park, New Jersey, where his band played weekly concerts on the boardwalk. To start the summer concert season he would parade through the town, ending with a concert at the boardwalk bandstand (95).

Pryor composed over 300 compositions, including his most famous, *The Whistler and His Dog,* published in 1905. He used his prominent position with the Sousa Band, and later his own band and orchestra, to promote the emerging ragtime style of music.

In the 1920s and '30s, Pryor was a pioneer in recording for the Victor Company with his band. While in retirement on a New Jersey farm he was elected to the Monmouth County Board of Freeholders.

In the summer of 1942, he and former band members played an engagement in Asbury, after which he suffered a fatal stroke. Pryor died at age 72 (96).

R. Ritchie Robertson

(1870–1939)

Born in Burnt Island, Scotland in 1870, Ritchie Robertson was the son of a shoemaker and the village choir director. Young Ritchie sang tenor in his father's choir and learned to play almost every instrument except the bagpipes.

At the age of 30, Robertson's health was failing, and he was advised to move to a drier and milder climate. In 1900 he came to the US and lived in Iowa, Louisiana, and Kansas. He remained in Paola, Kansas for 15 years while working as a grocery clerk and department store salesman. His musical accomplishments were well-known and in 1916 he moved to Springfield, Missouri to teach music at Springfield High School, which later became Springfield Central High School (97).

World's Largest Boy Scout Band

In November 1920 Robertson organized a Boy Scout Band, with nearly 40 boys showing interest in participating. Within three months Robertson invited parents to a concert of the new scout band, which had grown to a 60-member band. The band's first public concert was on February 22, 1921 for the Rotary Club in the Colonial Hotel. After hearing the band, the club voted to raise funds to take the band to their Missouri-Kansas District Convention in April. The convention required the band to march so Robertson had the band rehearse each Saturday on the football field at Drury College. The Rotary Club raised $6,000 for the band to attend the district convention in 1922.

Band rehearsals were held in various Springfield churches and public buildings until 1926 when the third floor of the Greene County Court House became a training school for the Boy Scout band (98).

Vaudeville was on its last leg in 1926, but the Boy Scout Band went on stage at Loew's State Theatre in St. Louis for nine days in July, playing four concerts each day. While in St. Louis, the 110-piece concert band made three phonograph records for the Brunswick Record Company. At the same time the band was featured in a film made by the C. G. Conn Band Instrument Company to be used to promote the sale of their instruments.

The Kilties Drum Corps.

It was in this same year [1926] that Robertson organized the "Scotch Lassies" [later renamed "Kilties Drum Corps"] at Springfield High School. The Kilties were organized by Robertson to honor his Scottish heritage and to give girls an opportunity to participate in a performing group. It was the first girls' kilties drum corps organized in America with bagpipes, bugles, and drums (99).

In 1933 the Springfield Boy Scout Band was picked as Missouri's representative to the Chicago World's Fair. By that time over 200 scouts were in the band program and 103 were selected to attend the fair. In later years, several of the former band members "admitted" to attending the popular Sally Rand striptease show in Chicago. It was on that same trip that three members were caught smoking and immediately discharged from the band. Robertson relented some months later, allowing all three to graduate from the Scout Band.

Robertson was known as a strict musical disciplinarian, but he was also keenly aware of the type of music enjoyed by his audience. His programming was modeled after that of John Philip Sousa. He programmed classical and operatic music, marches, and novelty favorites. *The Farmer and His Dog* was especially entertaining because of the various sounds provided by the percussion section...not on traditional percussion instruments.

In his later years, "The Star Spangled Scotsman" turned many of his conducting duties over to James, his son, who was a graduate of Drury College in Springfield and the famous Juilliard School of Music in New York. On August 27, 1938 Richie Robertson was honored at a Western Association Springfield Cardinal baseball game. As he stood at home plate a new red sedan was presented to him by community admirers.

On Sunday morning, November 5, 1939, Robert Ritchie Robertson died at his home. The route of the funeral procession from Calvary Presbyterian Church to Greenlawn Cemetery was lined on both sides of the street with scouts, all in uniform. After the death of his father, James became the director of the "World's Largest Boy Scout Band."

During the late 1930s there were over 400 members in the Springfield Boy Scout Band.

The year 1949 was the last for the band. Music in the public schools was expanding so much that the Boy Scout Band had outlived its usefulness. For many years national Boy Scout executives had been dubious of the band, expressing the fear that boys joined the scouts as a means to membership in the band rather than for the total scouting experience. Ozark Council Scout Executive Allen Foster fought attempts to disband the group until his death in 1947. However, succeeding Ozark Council Executive Mel Tudor was not in sympathy with the band. The news of its dissolution shocked Springfield. The end of the "World's Largest Boy Scout Band" was a disappointment to the community and to all who remembered Robertson's leadership and inspiration. The following year, 1950, James P. Robertson left Springfield to become the conductor of the Wichita Symphony Orchestra, a position he held for 20 years (100).

The World's Largest Boy Scout Band – 1926
Springfield, Missouri
Richie Robertson Founder and Director
Photo taken in St. Louis Union Station

Springfield Boy Scout Band

R. Ritchie Robertson, Director

PROGRAM
July – 1926

Lowe's State Theatre, St. Louis, Missouri
One week only

Opening Overture, "The Fall of Jericho"	Mailochand
Piccolo Solo, "The Skylark"	Cox
Soloist, Elgin Swineford	
New Smile Song, "Mr. Worry"	Evans / James
Words by Ada Evans, music by Bill James Dedicated to the Boy Scout Band	
Novelty, "The Whistling Farmer Boy"	Fillmore
Featuring Charles Huey, the world's greatest boy whistler. Barnyard effects by the boys.	
Patrol, "The Blue and the Gray"	Dalbey
Organ Recital by Mr. Tom Terry, organist of Lowe's State Theatre, St. Louis, Mo.	
Demonstration of records made by the band for the Brunswick Phonograph Company.	
Descriptive Overture, "William Tell"	Rossini
Baritone Solo, "Maggie"	Butterfield
Finale, "The Stars and Stripes Forever, March"	Sousa

John W. Scott

(1870–1950)

John W. Scott was the youngest of five children. His family moved to the Rolla area from Galesburg, Illinois in 1875. He attended the Missouri School of Mines and Metallurgy from 1887–1889 and became an apprentice pharmacist, later passing the examination to become a registered pharmacist. While managing Duby Drugs in Rolla before becoming the owner, Mr. Scott met and married Stella Sappenfield, who had been a student at the School of Mines in 1891–1892.

Scott came from a musical family. His father, James H. Scott, was a Methodist minister but also built reed organs. His brother, Ephraim, founded the Western Conservatory of Music in Rolla in 1883. In the early 1900s Ephraim moved the Conservatory to the Kimball Building in Chicago and established another branch in Kansas City. Both conservatories were accredited to issue certificates, diplomas, and degrees in music.

John Scott's instrument was the trombone, which he played as a member of the First Artillery Band in 1898 during the Spanish-American War.

During the late 1800s he formed and directed several local bands and orchestras. The book, "A History of Rolla, Missouri," written by Dr. and Mrs. Clair Mann, tells about Rolla's cultural life around the turn of the century and called John Scott the "Man of Music" in Rolla (102). For years Scott enlisted townspeople and the university students who played an instrument to perform at fairs, picnics, commencement, and baccalaureate exercises. He formed the Rolla Imperial Band and the Rolla Silver Cornet Band. Both of these groups played the accompaniment to silent films at the only motion picture theatre in Rolla.

A cash book from the Rolla Town Band dated June 1905 shows a seventy-five dollar expenditure for the purchase of a new Conn five-valve, double-bell euphonium with leather case and extra low-pitch equipment. Another entry lists payments to 12 band members for their performance and transportation for the "Richland Concert." Each band member received six dollars and sixty-five cents (103).

In 1926, John Scott organized the first official band program at the Missouri School of Mines. It was given the nickname "The Miners' Band." In its first year, most performances were for local football games, but the band did travel with the team to St. Louis to play both Washington University and St. Louis University.

Funds for instruments and music were limited, and Scott often purchased what was needed for the band from his own resources. As become available from the university he insisted that it be used for student scholarships rather than music or equipment for the band. Through the years Scott and his wife provided their extra bedroom for band members needing housing while attending the university. This was always done without charge.

In 1930 the Army Reserve Officers Training Corps (ROTC) became a co-sponsor of the band, and army uniforms were issued. In 1933 the band had 34 members, and from it a concert band was organized. This group presented formal concerts throughout the winter and spring semesters, all directed by John Scott, the pharmacist. About this time a financial grant was established by the university to cover fees and tuition for any student playing in the band.

Dr. Tom Beveridge, a member of the MSM–ROTC band in the 1930s, wrote an article in the MSM Alumni Magazine about its director. "Scott had the tradition of one non-traditional ensemble per concert. This ensemble sometimes consisted of an ocarina band, which had the full complement of bass through soprano." At another concert, Scott presented his group playing antique band instruments collected by Scott and stored in his basement. He had a matched set of handmade French clarinets among his various personal instruments (104).

In the early 1930s Scott bought a Theremin from its inventor in New York. It was a very unusual electronic instrument and was used for several musical effects in motion pictures. Scott learned to play it and performed at several concerts. Robert Moog built Theremins at one time and later invented the synthesizer, which sounds very much like the Theremin but has more range and versatility. Scott spent years putting a piano and reed organ together so that both instruments could be played from one keyboard.

John Scott was the only piano tuner in the southern part of Missouri. He much preferred this activity to working in the pharmacy. In addition to his years of service to the MSM–UMR band program he organized the first band at Rolla High School.

The Miners' Band or volunteer groups often gave concerts in surrounding towns. According to Dr. Beveridge, one such trip, on a freezing night, "marked the final trip of Mr. Scott with the band to which he had devoted decades of his time, hundreds of dollars of his money, and infinite patience." In February of 1950 he took the band to Salem for a concert. The heater system on the bus failed, aggravating a cold and leading to Scott's death (105).

John W. Scott was first to organize the Rolla Town Band, the Rolla High School Band, and the Missouri School of Mines Band, along with many other musical ensembles in the community. He was a pharmacist by profession but a musician at heart. He never received any compensation or salary for the work he loved best (106).

Author's note:
Scott is listed as a member of the Carthage Light Guard Band, playing E-flat alto horn. The Light Guard Band was one of the most popular and highly regarded bands in southwest Missouri. Under the direction of Charles R. Dumars it traveled extensively by train to cities in the Midwest and East. The quality of the Carthage Light Guard Band may have been an incentive for Scott to travel the long distance from Rolla to be a member.
CHD

June 22nd, 1912

Mr. Jno. W. Scott,

     Rolla, Mo.,

My dear Sir: —

     I am in receipt of your favor of the 20th and beg to advise that I will allow you a cash discount of 10% on the instrument you desire. I trust this will be sufficient inducement for you to place your order at an early date.

     Assuring you the instrument represents full falue for the money and that you will not be disappointed in same, I beg to remain,

     Yours very truly,

     C. G. Conn

Letter to John W. Scott
from C. G. Conn
Courtesy of Susan Miller family collection

Claude T. Smith

(1932–1987)

A Daughter's Tribute
Pam Smith Kelly

Claude Smith was born in Monroe City, Missouri, on March 14, 1932. He grew up loving music, mainly due to the early influence of his grandmother, Nina Thomas, who played the piano. With her guidance and the encouragement of his mother and father, Harriet L [Thomas] Smith and Claude M. Smith, he took piano lessons and began his journey into the world of music. He and his parents moved to Carrollton, Missouri when Dad was two years old. During his junior high years, he really began to look forward to his piano lessons. Part of this enjoyment might have been due to the fact that his piano lessons were close to the same time as the lessons of a young classmate, Maureen Fay Morrison, who later became his wife.

Claude T. Smith, known during the early part of his life as "Tommy," began band instruction playing the trumpet under the direction of Harold Arehart. Arehart was responsible for helping Dad truly love music and later helped him find his first teaching job in Cozad, Nebraska. It is interesting to note that Maureen, his piano companion, had now joined the band playing timpani. Tommy also had the pleasure of having many close friends during his years in Carrollton. Two of Tommy's closest friends were brothers, Bob and Bill Maupin. Bob and Tommy were very close, and Bill, the younger brother, usually hung around them. Even though Bob and Tommy used to play tricks on Bill, he became one of Dad's closest friends, and they later taught together for ten years in Chillicothe.

After high school, in 1950, Dad began his college career at Central College (Central Methodist University) in Fayette, Missouri. It was during this time that he changed to French Horn as his main instrument. It was Ed Carson, a member of the Central horn section, who suggested that Smith switch instruments since "he didn't have a chance to make the Concert Band on trumpet." Members of the trumpet section included Keith House, Gene Henderson,

Joe Labuta, Kenneth Seward, and Harry Hoffson.

My father loved his college days at Central under the direction of Keith K. Anderson. In later years he was commissioned to write several pieces for the Central music department.

Upon getting married in 1952 to his childhood sweetheart, Maureen, Dad was assigned to the 371st Army Band at Ft. Leavenworth, Kansas. He was stationed there until 1955. While he was in the army band he began writing music for enjoyment and as a creative outlet. He never had any formal lessons or classes in composition and never thought he would become heavily involved in composition. He did enter one composition in a contest while in the army:

World Freedom, his first composition, written in 1954. It took third place. First and second place were won by the warrant officer and conductor of the 371st Army Band, Claude's commanding officer.

After Dad completed his active duty, the family moved to Lawrence, Kansas, where he completed his Bachelor's of Music Education Degree at the University of Kansas. While at the University of Kansas, he met many talented and dear friends. Some of his closest friends were Herb Duncan; a fellow musician from Central College, Phyllis Glass, who would later tell Dad that I would play the bassoon; Gary Foster, a life-time professional musician in Los Angeles; Charlie Molina, a great humorist and instrumentalist; and Johnny Woody, a freshman horn player who took first chair horn from him, moving him to second chair in the KU Band and Orchestra. Johnny and Dad remained great friends through the years. Johnny became the principal horn for the US Air Force Band [Washington, D.C.], and when Dad wrote *Festival Variations* it always became a joke that "those horn licks were written to make Johnny practice." When he attended KU, Dad's teachers thought he had natural ability in composition, and received many opportunities to play and write for full band, soloists, orchestral accompaniments, and ensembles.

In 1963, our family moved to Kansas City, where Dad taught high school band in the Center School District. It was during this time that Dad began searching for a publisher for a piece he composed for that band. This work, entitled *Overture for Winds and Percussion*, contained a few unique time signatures, and many publishers were too timid to take a risk with such unfamiliar rhythm patterns. As fate would have it, Dad found a Kansas City-based print music company who was willing to take a chance with this young composer. His colleagues at Wingert-Jones Music included owners Merrill Jones and George Wingert. Frank Fendorf, Joyce Pinnell Martin, Ron Allen, and Gerry Fuchs were employees of the company who, along with the owners, became his life-long friends.

Joyce Pinnell Martin and Frank Fendorf reflect on the friendship they had with Dad: "Our small young print music store saw exceptional talent in this young composer and therefore developed a publication division for the company. We purchased a booth at the prestigious Midwest Band Clinic held in Chicago to share our 'single' publication, *Emperata,* with the national band community." Considerable thought and discussion took place regarding changing the title of *Overture for Winds and Percussion* to *Emperata*. Suggestions for the title included that it must begin with a letter early in the alphabet and that the title should be unique and describe the power of the piece. It was Kay Wingert and Merrill Jones who helped Dad finalize the title, suggested from the word "emperor."

Our family moved to Chillicothe, Missouri in 1966. It was there that Dad's writing began to flourish. He was teaching elementary, junior high, and high school band with his childhood friend, Bill Maupin. While in Chillicothe, our family was members of a small Presbyterian Church. It was here that I witnessed my parents' faith in God and developed the beliefs which became an integral part of my life. Dad was the choir director at church and my mom and I sang in the soprano section. Along with other members of the choir we laughed, cried, and poured our souls into the lyrics of so many beloved hymns. Dad was very private about his faith, but shared his faith through his music. In 1974, Dad arranged the hymn *God of Our Fathers* for the Henderson, Nebraska schools. For its third performance, Dad's high school band performed the work at the 1975 Missouri Music Educators Association Convention. As the bassoon soloist, I was thrilled and honored to perform this work for so many of his close friends. That experience was one of those magical moments that will never leave my memory.

On March 4, 1975, our family had another magical experience. Dad had become good friends with the alto saxophonist with the US Navy Band, Dale Underwood. Dale and Dad often talked until the wee hours of the morning. They had a unique bond of friendship and musicianship. It was during this year that Dad was commissioned by the US Navy Band to arrange *Eternal Father, Strong to Save* for the Navy Band's 50th Anniversary. This was Dad's first work commissioned by one of the premier service bands, which then added another dimension to his career.

In the spring of 1976, he accepted a teaching position at Southwest Missouri State University in Springfield, Missouri. During the next two years, Dad taught theory, composition, arranging, and also conducted the SMSU orchestra. He also began accepting many commissions from bands and orchestras throughout the United States.

Two years after arriving at SMSU, my dad and mom relocated to the Kansas City area so he could compose full-time. In 1978, Dad became a publishing consultant for Wingert-Jones Music in Kansas City. He continued writing for them and also became a staff composer for a new publishing company, Jenson Publications. This led to his becoming a nationally renowned conductor and clinician.

He was the recipient of many awards and honors:

> National Band Association Award
>
> President of Missouri Music Educators Association – 1976–1978
>
> Academy of Wind and Percussion Arts award – 1988
>
> Honorary Doctorate of Humane Letters from Central Methodist College – 1988
>
> Hall of Fame Award from the Missouri Bandmasters Association – 1988
>
> Kappa Kappa Psi Distinguished Service to Music Award – 1989
>
> Hall of Fame Award from the Missouri Music Educators Association – 1992
>
> School Director of the Year from the Christian Instrumental Directors – 1994

On Sunday, December 13, 1987, Dad returned home from church and died that afternoon at the age of 55. Word of Dad's death reached Dale Underwood, his friend in the US Navy Band. At their Midwest Clinic concert the next week in Chicago the Navy Band performed Dad's arrangement of *Eternal Father, Strong to Save*. In his memory it was performed without a conductor (107). That year, in his honor, the Wingert-Jones Music Company's booth at the Midwest Clinic had a single picture of Smith, a floral tribute and the conductors score of *Emperata* on display in his honor.

World Freedom, Smith's first composition, was lost among his many manuscripts and was not found until 1998. It was published at that time, 44 years after it had been written and 11 years after his death. The family dedicated it to his long-time friend, Dr. Russell Coleman, Director of Bands at Central Missouri State University in Warrensburg, now The University of Central Missouri (107).

Author's note:

> "Anyway, it's not very good"
> (Memories of a hot summer in Kansas)

Summers in Kansas are always hot. Claude asked Russell Wiley, Director of Bands at the University of Kansas, to let members of the summer high school band camp sight-read a composition he had written. Claude was the camp librarian.

The band assembled on the stage of Hoch Auditorium—a combination theatre, rehearsal hall, and basketball arena. The auditorium held the heat well. Claude asked that I assist in the percussion section. All parts were in manuscript form. Assistant Band Director Kenneth Bloomquist was watching from the wings. Professor Wiley started the opening bars of *Emperata*. Wiley came upon the first multi-meter section without preparing in advance. He conducted the 7/8 meter change incorrectly as if it were 7/4. The second time was no better. Claude, always a gentleman, offered his suggestion on conducting the multi-meter measures. It was not well received by Wiley, who was also Claude's employer for the summer. On the third try, the band carried the director through to the end of the composition, which included more unfamiliar meter changes. Handing over the conductor's score, Professor Wiley said to Claude: "Anyway, it's not a very good composition."
CHD

Through the years, *Emperata* has sold more copies than any of Smith's 100 plus compositions.

Photo courtesy of Pam Smith Kelly

Emperata Overture Copyright 1964
by Wingert-Jones Music, Kansas City
Used by permission

BAND
ASSOCIATIONS

Chapter 6

BAND ASSOCIATIONS

———————

Regional Band Associations

	Founded
Southwestern Band Association	1886
St. Louis County Band Directors Association	1930
Southeast Missouri High School Band Association	1945
Mark Twain Bandmasters Association	1949
North Central Bandmasters Association	1951

State Band Associations

Phi Beta Mu / Lambda (Missouri) Chapter	1959
Missouri Bandmasters Association	1968
National Association of Jazz Educators – Missouri	1969

Regional Band Associations
Southwestern Band Association
1886

The Aurora Historical Society in Lawrence County has on display a quilt with several lapel ribbons sewn into it as pieces. One reads: "Sixth Annual Meeting of the Southwestern Band Association, Springfield, Mo., May 9, 10, 11, 1892."

A printed program from May 21, 1889 lists seven bands participating in a concert in Sicher's Park [possibly Rolla, Mo.] including town bands from: California, Warrensburg, Carthage, Concordia, Hermann, Clinton, and Springfield, and sponsored by the Southwestern Band Association.

Quilt announcing the annual meeting
of the Southwestern Band Association
May 9, 10, 11, 1892
Photo courtesy Mary Strickrodt

PROGRAMME

Southwestern Band Association

SICHER'S PARK

Tuesday Afternoon, May 21st, 1889
Rolla, Missouri

Quickstep, (Fire Brigade)   Phil S. Rose
                        All Bands

Pearls, (Baritone Solo)   Geo. Southwell
                        California Band

Fantasia, (Fairies Moonlight Revels)   Phillip Goetz
                        Warrensburg Band

Overture, The Turner's Motto   Thomas Kiesler
                  Light Guard Band of Carthage

Concert Selection   L. Pette
                  Concordia Cornet Band

Fancy Drill   By the Light Guard Band of Carthage

Kuknk Polka   William Reine
                  Apostle Band of Hermann

Overture, (Little Beauty)   Paul Ripley
                  Eclipse Military Band of Clinton

Tuba Oblegato, "Dicapolis"   Chas. Dalby
                  Hobart Military Band of Springfield

Serenade, (Bell Air)   G. Southwell
                        All Bands

St. Louis County Band Directors Association

ca 1930

The St. Louis County Band Directors Association was organized by Hans J. Lemcke, from Webster Groves, along with other area band directors. The first All-County Band was formed in the same year. The Webster Groves High School yearbook of 1933 records that the band practiced all summer and entered the Greater St. Louis Band Contest. Webster was the winner of the first place cup (trophy). In later years, the St. Louis County Band Directors Association merged into the St. Louis Suburban Music Educators Association, a division of the Missouri Music Educators Association.

Southeast Missouri High School Band Association

1945

The Southeast Missouri High School Band Association was an outgrowth of a band festival in 1944 organized by LeRoy F. Mason of Jackson. Mason, W. L. Giddens (Lilbourn), and Keith Collins (Sikeston), were founding members of the SEMO Band Association.

Mark Twain Bandmasters Association

1949

The Mark Twain Bandmasters Association was established in 1949 by Hannibal High School band director, J. M. Dillinger. The organization sponsored the Northeast Missouri Marching Band Festival.

North Central Bandmasters Association

1951

The North Central Bandmasters Association was organized in the fall of 1951 in Chillicothe by Frank W. Fendorf, band director at Chillicothe High School, Harold Linton of Linton Music Company, and area band directors. A photograph of the 1957 North Central Bandmasters Association shows 27 directors meeting at Pershing State Park near Chillicothe.

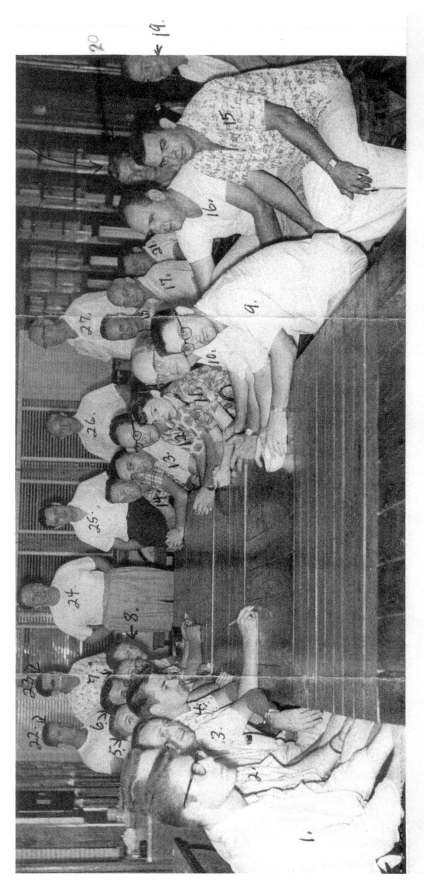

1. Unknown
2. Unknown
3. Elmer Pundman
4. Frank Fendorf
5. Dick Perkins
6. Brad Moore
7. O. O. Humo
8. Gene Henerson
9. Jim Fetters
10. Kenneth Crawford
11. Nancy Seward
12. Kenneth Seward
13. Keith House
14. Bill Mack
15. Tom Price
16. Jack Overbey
17. Elford Horn
18. Earl Dillinger
19. Addison Webber
20. Walt Lovejoy
21. Jim Adair
22. Gerald Sandbothe
23. Charles Emmons
24. Harold Linton
25. Paul Strub
26. Unklnown
27. Bill Schrader

North Central Missouri Bandmasters Association (date unknown)

State Band Associations

Phi Beta Mu
National Bandmasters Fraternity
Lambda (Missouri) Chapter

Minutes of the organizational meeting
January 8, 1959

On the night of January 8, 1959, the Lambda Chapter of Phi Beta Mu was formed in Columbia, Missouri, with Milburn E. Carey, National President, presiding. The following charter members were initiated:

James Adair	Marceline
Howard Bell	Marshall
Tom Birch	Fayette
Lowell E. Brunner	Odessa
Keith Collins	Sikeston
J. M. Dillinger	Hannibal
C. Herbert Duncan	Normandy
Charles Emmons	Columbia [transfer from Alpha / Texas]
Frank Fendorf	Chillicothe
Jon Ferguson	Rich Hill
James O. Fetter	Windsor
Harold L. Hillyer	University City
Keith House	Lee's Summit
O. O. Humo	Grandview
N. Orville Johnson	Independence
Don Verne Joseph	Jefferson City
Joe Labuta	Lexington
Gerald McCollum	Boonville
Ben E. Markley	Kansas City
LeRoy F. Mason	Cape Girardeau
Leland E. Muller	Butler
Wilby A. Rice	Camdenton
Gerald Sandbothe	Macon

Kenneth Seward	Kansas City
Lee T. Schneider	Maryville
Bill Tetley	Rolla
John Willer	Mexico

Lambda Chapter officers – 1959:

President	Charles Emmons	University of Missouri
Vice President	Tom Birch	Central College
Secretary-Treasurer	Jon S. Ferguson	Rich Hill
Board Member	Orville Johnson	Independence
Board Member	Howard Bell	Marshall

Lambda (Missouri) Chapter
Phi Beta Mu

Minutes of the organizational meeting – January 9, 1959

The first regular business meeting of Lambda Chapter of Phi Beta Mu was held on January 9, 1959 in room 320, Lathrop Hall, on the campus of the University of Missouri at Columbia, newly elected president Charles Emmons, presiding. The following business was transacted:

A motion was made by James Adair (Marceline) that the annual fraternity dues be five dollars per person (two dollars national dues, three dollars chapter dues). The motion was seconded and carried.

It was agreed that the president and secretary-treasurer were to arrange for the annual luncheon or dinner with the business meeting on the next day during the Missouri Music Educators Association yearly conference.

It was thought that a smoker should be held the first day to decide on the prospective members and the installation should be on the second day. If the next meeting is a two-day meeting, it will be necessary to have a luncheon meeting.

John Willer [Mexico] made the motion that the secretary-treasurer be allowed the necessary amount of postage, etc., to properly function. Don Verne Joseph [Jefferson City] seconded this motion and the motion carried.

A motion was made by Ben Markley [Kansas City] and seconded by M. O.

Johnson [Independence] that the persons indicating their desire earlier by mail that they wished to become members but for some reason were unable to attend the installation meeting, be given membership in Phi Beta Mu. This motion carried. Those persons affected are: Frank Fendorf, Keith Collins, Bill Tetley, Gerald Sandbothe, and Herbert Duncan. These members are approved and will be notified that they will be installed next year.

The membership committee consists of: Vice President Tom Birch, Keith House, Ben Markley, and Kenneth Seward.

At the dinner meeting the previous evening, there was a 26-person guarantee with 24 persons present. President Charles Emmons was required to pay for two persons. It was moved by M. O. Johnson and seconded by John Willer that we reimburse President Emmons for this amount. This motion carried.

Jon S. Ferguson, Secretary Treasurer
January 9, 1959 – Rich Hill

(108)

Band of the Year Award

In 1971 the fraternity established an award to recognize individuals for their contribution to the profession. College and university band directors provided the adjudication for the Band of the Year Award.

1971	Raytown	Robert Schupp
1972	Park Hill	Bill Mack
1973	Chillicothe	Claude T. Smith
1974	Maryville	Lee T. Schneider
1975	Hickman	John Patterson
1976	Jefferson City	Jerry Hoover
1978	Marshfield	F. D. Lewis
1978–1982	No Award	
1983	Savannah	Mark Mitchell

Award changed to

Charles Emmons Outstanding Band Director Award

1986	Robert J. Boedges	Normandy
1987	John Patterson	Hickman
1988	No Award	

1989	John Baker	Parkway West
1990	Robert Drummond	Grandview
1991	Jim Oliver	Lee's Summit
1992	Gene Hunt	Washington
1993	Wendell Doyle	Platte City
1994	John Bell	Park Hill
1995	Larry Bennett	Macon
1996	Nick Leist	Jackson
1997	Russell Coleman	Warrensburg
1998	Bob Hanson	Wentzville
1999	Chris Becker	Parkway South
2000	Mary Lightfoot	Kansas City
2001	Keith Ruether	Lebanon
2002	Paul Warnex	Liberty
2003	No Award	
2004	Todd Reinhardt	Independence
2005	Paul Swofford	St. Clair
2006	Rob Nichols	Columbia
2007	F. D. Lewis	Marshfield
2008	Gary Anders	Grandview
2009	Bob Spiegelman	Lindbergh
2010	Tim Allshouse	Blue Springs
2011	Diana Williams	Webb City

Claude T. Smith Memorial Band Composition Contest

Under the leadership of prominent band composer Claude T. Smith, the fraternity established a contest for young composers in 1982. The contest is offered every three years with a cash prize to the winning composer.

The first contest was awarded to David Gorham in 1985. Following the untimely death of Claude T. Smith in 1987, the contest was renamed in his honor. The Claude T. Smith Memorial Band Composition Contest encourages young composers to write original music for the band. Composers must be 26 years of age or younger and the composition must be grade III or IV in difficulty.

The winning compositions include:

1985	*There Shall Only Be Silence*	David Gorham
1989	Variations on *A Mighty Fortress Is Our God*	Darren Jenkins
1992	*I Am*	Andy Boysen, Jr.
1995	*Ovations*	Andy Boysen, Jr.
1998	*Sal ya Tanzania*	Ken Hakoda
2001	*Prestidigitato*	Kyle Kindred
2004	*Twilight in the Wilderness*	Christopher Tucker
2007	*Play*	Carl Holmquist
2010	*Robinson Suite*	Joseph Earp

(109)

Lambda Chapter / Phi Beta Mu
50th Anniversary photo – 2009

Missouri Bandmasters Association

by
Robert Scott, Founding Member
First President of MBA

I was stationed with a Navy Band in Corpus Christi, Texas for a number of years and became familiar with the fine Texas high school band movement. Also, I had a brother-in-law that was a high school band director in Texas, and he introduced me to the Texas Bandmasters Association. I began attending their conventions in San Antonio.

After leaving the Navy and returning to the Kansas/Missouri area, we would return each year to San Antonio for the TBA. It is a huge convention, and the clinics were nothing short of amazing. While at Ruskin [suburban Kansas City] High School, I annually attended TBA to attempt to keep growing as a band director. In the mid-to late-1960's, and there were a few good bands in Missouri, but for the most part the majority of the high school bands were mediocre or worse. Clifton Williams was visiting in Kansas City and I remember him making the statement, "How many good bands do you have in Missouri, five or six?" He continued, "In Texas there is a good band every six miles."

I kept thinking that we need an organization to strengthen high school bands. MMEA [Missouri Music Educators Association] was fine, but I thought we needed more. So I began talking about the formation of a Missouri Bandmasters organization. Finally, after a Wingert-Jones reading clinic, we decided to meet and discuss the possibilities of such an organization. We met at a park at Lake Jacomo [Kansas City area] in August of 1968.

I remember Carroll Lewis was there and provided from his garden fresh tomatoes for the picnic lunch. Hot dogs were the main course. Those who were there were Charles Emmons, Jess Cole, Carroll and Ellie Lewis, Frank Erickson, Merrill Jones, Clifton Williams, and Alice and myself. It was agreed that we should proceed with the planning of the first clinic. It was also decided that the convention was to be a family affair and that the Lake of the Ozark was probably the best and most central location for the convention.

Several months later Jess Cole, Alice, and I drove to the lake to find a place for the first convention. After several trips it was decided that the Millstone Lodge was the best and most affordable of the many resorts we visited (110).

During this inaugural period a logo for the new organization was designed by Zelia and Romaine Bell of Kansas City.

The Beginning of MBA

1968

Transcribed from handwritten notes by Carroll Lewis on file in the archives of the Missouri Music Educators Association.

August 23, 1968	Organizational meeting of Missouri Bandmasters Association. In attendance were Clifton Williams and Frank Erickson, composers, and Missouri Bandmasters and their families. Bob Scott was elected Chairman for the first clinic. A Charter Committee, a Clinic Site Committee, and a Service Band Selection Committee were appointed.
August 25, 1968	The Charter Committee met and prepared the document to be presented to the Missouri Music Educators Association Board in September. Members are: George Alter, Howard Bell, Charles Emmons, Carroll Lewis, Tom Price, and Don Welborn.
September 7, 1968	Representatives from MBA met with the MMEA Board. The MMEA Board went on record as favoring the affiliation with MBA.
September 8, 1968	A preliminary visit to Lake of the Ozarks for a site inspection was made by the Site Selection committee [Jess Cole, Alice and Bob Scott].
September 29, 1968	A contract was signed with Millstone Lodge, Gravois Mills, Missouri. The resort will be the headquarters for the First Annual MBA Clinic, July 13–15, 1969.
October 4, 1968	Confirmation was received from Nilo Hovey, Educational Director, H & A Selmer, that he will present his outstanding Clarinet Clinic and a session on 'Rehearsal Psychology' at MBA.
October 14, 1968	Confirmation was received from Dean Killion, Texas Tech University, Lubbock, Texas, that he will present a session on, 'The Texas System' for marching bands. Mr. Killion's clinics will include, films, printed formations, etc.
Submitted by:	Carroll Lewis, Charter Member (111)

Missouri Bandmasters Association

Founding Members
Lake Jacomo, Kansas City, Missouri

August 1968

Jess Cole	Kansas City
Charles Emmons	Columbia
Frank Erickson [guest]	Composer
Merrill Jones	Kansas City
Carroll Lewis	Raytown South
Robert Scott	Ruskin
Clifton Williams [guest]	University of Miami

Charter Members

Millstone Lodge...Lake of the Ozarks

July 13, 1969

George Alter	Kansas City
Howard Bell	Raytown
William Bodanske	Springfield
Jess Cole	Kansas City
C. Herbert Duncan	Normandy
Frank Fendorf	Chillicothe
W. L. Giddings	Lilbourn
Jack Janes	Smithton
Russell Kormeier	Ruskin
Nick Leist	Jackson
Arch Martin	Kansas City
Paul Montemurro	Fayette
Dick Perkins	Centralia
Willis Pettigrew	Raytown

Tom Price	Cameron
DeRoy Rogge	Ruskin
Jim Rothwell	Kansas City
Claude Smith	Kansas City
Bob Stanfield	Carthage
Harold Turner	St. Louis
Don Welborn	Independence

Missouri Bandmasters Association

Year	President	All-State Band Conductor	Hall of Fame Award
1969	Robert Scott		
1970	Robert Scott		Roy Huckstep
1971	John Patterson		James Dillinger
1972	John Patterson		Keith K. Anderson
1973	John Willer		T. Frank Coulter
1974	John Willer		
1975	Herman Rekittke		Paul Strub
1976	Herman Rekittke		Robert Scott
1977	Larry Pohlman	Dean Killion	Robert Schupp
1978	Larry Pohlman	John Paynter	Ed Downs
1979	Mary Lightfoot	Arnald Gabriel	Tom Price
1980	Mary Lightfoot	Harry Begian	Charles Emmons
1981	David Taylor	Robert Reynolds	Ken Seward
1982	David Taylor	Don Wilcox	Charles Wells
1983	Jim Oliver	John Bourgeois	John Willer
1984	Jim Oliver	Francis MacBeth	Mary Lightfoot
1985	Mike Everman	Claude T. Smith	Carroll Lewis
1986	Mike Everman	Joseph Phillips	Keith House
1987	David Goodwin	James Bankhead	William Mack
1988	David Goodwin	Ken Bloomquist	Claude T. Smith
1989	Kent Summers	Frank Wickes	Russ Chambers
1990	Kent Summers	Larry Rachleff	Merrill Jones
1991	Ed Roberts	Arnald Gabriel	Lowell Brunner
1992	Ed Roberts	Mark Kelly	John Patterson
1993	Paul Copenhaver	Ray Cramer	Nancy Seward

1994	Paul Copenhaver	Bryan Shelburne	Lee Schneider
1995	Skip Vandelicht	Francis MacBeth	Bill Maupin
1996	Skip Vandelicht	Paula Crider	Russell Coleman
1997	Steve Litwiller	Timothy Mahr	Wendell Doyle
1998	Steve Litwiller	Anthony Maiello	Robert M. Smith
1999	Jim Cunningham	Allan McMurray	David Taylor
2000	Jim Cunningham	James Croft	Robert Hansen
2001	Kurt Bauche	Anthony Maiello	Frank Fendorf
2002	Kurt Bauche	John Locke	Larry Bennett
2003	Paul Swofford	Craig Kirchoff	Larry Pohlman
2004	Paul Swofford	David Holsinger	Gerald Fuchs
2005	Ann Goodwin Clark	Ray Cramer	Ron Curtis
2006	Ann Goodwin Clark	John Bourgeois	Gene Hunt
2007	Rob Nichols	John Whitwell	Mike Everman
2008	Rob Nichols	Timothy Mahr	Dan Peterson
2009	Keith Ruether	Anthony Maiello	Jerry Hoover & C. Herbert Duncan
2010	Keith Ruether	Andrew Boysen	Paul Copenhaver
2011	Linda Huck	Lowell Graham	Jim Oliver

The Missouri All-State Band

Research in the archives of the Missouri Music Educators Association indicates the formation of an all-state band, orchestra, and chorus in 1941, for the purpose of concerts and clinics at their annual conference. Because of the limitations of travel during World War II, the All-State Band was terminated. There is no indication of all-state groups until 1976.

The formation of an all-state band was the topic of discussion on Friday, January 23, 1976 at the Ramada Inn in Jefferson City during the annual Missouri Music Educators Conference and Clinic. Mr. Robert Scott, Southwest Missouri State University band director, presided over the 11:30 am session in Theatre # 4. Many band directors attended because of the high interest in forming an all-state group.

The all-state band idea had been talked about for years. Unfortunately, nothing had ever materialized out of all the talk. It seemed there were insurmountable obstacles to be overcome and myriad impossibilities. Yet many states had such an organization, including every state which bordered Missouri. As the session came to a close, it was apparent that the majority of those in attendance wished to see the formation of a Missouri all-state high school band.

Larry Pohlman, Missouri Bandmasters Association president-elect, assumed responsibility for the project, indicating that this would be an opportunity for the MBA to promote its motto—"Building Better Bands." The next eleven months would involve a tremendous amount of time, correspondence, meetings, research, organization, and salesmanship—all in an effort to see the reality of an all-state high school band. Through his persistence and personal commitment to the project, Mr. Pohlman saw the idea reach fruition, as he introduced the first Missouri All-State High School Band on January 22, 1977, as part of the annual meeting of the Missouri Music Educators Association. The concert was held in the Ramada Inn in Jefferson City.

Approval for the activity was quickly received from the Missouri Music Educators Association with the aid of its president, Claude T. Smith. The MMEA Executive Committee adjusted the conference program, allowing for a grand finale concert which would feature the Missouri ACDA All-State High School Choir and the Missouri MBA All-State High School Band.

Next, approval of the Missouri State High School Activities Association was received, although not without problems. All aspects of the activity met with the approval of this body, except for a membership requirement. The MBA believed a band director should be a member of the MBA if his/her student was going to participate in the all-state band. The MSHSAA ruled that the MBA could not set a membership requirement for band directors. Final approval for the all-state band would not be granted until the MBA removed this requirement.

This situation posed a difficult problem for MBA. If enough students did not audition, expenses might not be met, and the organization could find itself bankrupt. It had been decided that the additional MBA memberships received from band directors would help meet the financial costs of the all-state band activity, along with a nominal audition fee for each student. This situation generated lengthy debate at the 1976 summer MBA meeting. The membership finally voted to proceed with the all-state band, adhering to the dictate of the MSHSAA. The

All-State Band Chairman and MBA officers were charged with the additional responsibility of seeing that the project met its expenses.

Officers of the MBA, MMEA, and representatives from each district proceeded to correspond and meet in an effort to work out the details involved at the district level. Most districts had an honor band. Some were by audition and some were not. The MBA pressed for each district to have an audition process for membership to their respective honor bands, and to have the honor bands perform. This would require individual students to prepare audition materials, which would improve their musicianship and technique. This would result in improved quality for high school bands resulting in a higher quality of district honor groups. After a great amount of debate the idea was approved and another hurdle had been cleared.

The next major problem centered on audition times. The districts would have to audition students in the fall. This would enable district membership rosters to be forwarded to the All-State Band Chairman in time for an all-state audition sometime in the late fall. Auditions for the all-state band would have to be held in December, to allow students ample time to prepare their music for the rehearsals and concert in January.

More debate followed as many districts auditioned students in late winter or early spring. It was argued that early fall would be too early—students would not have developed a good concert sound that early in the year and they would not have time to prepare audition materials. Again, after lengthy debate, the district representatives agreed to make the necessary changes. It was pointed out that some districts would require time to make the changes in audition and performance schedules. With this in mind, the MBA allowed "paper bands" for the first year only. After the first year, all students who auditioned for the all-state band would have to be members of a performing district honors band.

With the major obstacles overcome, there remained only the selection of an audition site, the selection of audition materials, and setting the instrumentation of the all-state band. John Patterson was approached with the idea of hosting the auditions at Hickman High School in Columbia. The central location of Columbia and the excellent school facilities at Hickman High School seemed to provide a logical site. Mr. Patterson convinced the school administration as to the value of this activity, and received approval to host the all-state band auditions on the first Saturday in December.

At the same time, Bob Scott and John Cheary requested all-state lists of audition materials and instrumentations from Arkansas and Texas. Both states were known to have outstanding all-state groups. After extensive review, the Texas audition material and instrumentation was selected.

The MBA membership approved a three dollar per student audition fee at its summer meeting in 1976. This three dollar fee would have to cover all the expenses of the all-state band. If enough students auditioned, it was determined that the all-state band would meet its expenses. It was a risk that few major corporations would have taken. Eleven years later, it is obvious that the MBA made the right decision.

Housing and meal arrangements for all-state band students were prepared at the Holiday Inn in Jefferson City. Those costs would be paid for by the all-state band members.

With everything finally in place, Wingert-Jones Music, Inc. supplied MBA with a statewide mailing list. In September of 1976 a list of audition materials and instructions was mailed to every high school in the state. The all-state band was going to be a reality.

As costs have increased, audition fees have been raised to offset the increased expenses. Each year brings more students to Columbia for all-state band auditions. In 1976 approximately

300 students auditioned for the first all-state band. Subsequently, each year more and more students have auditioned, finally justifying the selection of a second all-state band.

The Missouri MBA All-State Band has been praised by all of the distinguished directors who have conducted it. Several have indicated it to be one of the finest they have conducted. In addition, the quality of the student musicians improves each year.

The Missouri Bandmasters Association motto—"Building Better Bands"—stood behind the decisions made in formulating the all-state band. As a result of its commitment and foresight, the actions of the MBA have resulted in an all-state band of the highest quality. All-district bands have also improved, along with numerous local high school bands. It is believed that, to some degree, the all-state band idea has helped to nurture more and more young musicians with a desire to excel in their instrumental music studies.

"Building Better Bands" has been the cornerstone of the Missouri Bandmasters Association. The Missouri MBA All-State High School Band is living proof of that commitment. (112).

Missouri Association for Jazz Education

1969

The Missouri chapter of the National Association of Jazz Educators (NAJE) was organized in the summer of 1969 during the inaugural meeting of the Missouri Bandmasters Association conference at Millstone Lodge at the Lake of the Ozarks. Bob Scott from Ruskin High School, Kansas City was elected president.

Jess Cole was an early leader in jazz education and played saxophone professionally in the Kansas City area. Through his efforts, along with his friend Arch Martin, the NAJE chapter gained recognition throughout the state. Others who pioneered the jazz movement included Carroll Lewis, (Raytown), Jerry Hoover, (Jefferson City), Bob Scott, (Ruskin), Roger Cody, (Northeast Missouri State University / Kirksville); Leon Bradley, (School of the Ozarks), Don Verne Joseph, (Drury College / Springfield) and Ronald Stilwell, (Meramec Community College / Kirkwood). Bradley was secretary-treasurer for twenty-five years, from 1971–1996.

The first high school jazz contest in Missouri was hosted by Boonville High School in 1956. Gerry McCollum was the director of bands and the event was patterned after the Kansas City Jazz Contest, which allowed student and professional bands to participate. The Boonville Jazz Contest was won by Jefferson City High School, directed by Don Verne Joseph. Joseph was a talented arranger who later became the Director of Bands at Drury College in Springfield.

The University of Missouri at Columbia hosted the first MU Jazz Festival in March 1968. Participating schools included Lebanon (Jerry Hoover), Southwest Kansas City (George Alter),

Columbia Hickman (John Patterson), Hannibal (Terry Boone), Bolivar (Gordon Calame), Montgomery City (Vern Rolle), South Shelby (Mary Lightfoot), Raytown (Robert Schupp), and Marshfield (F. D. Lewis).

The Jess Cole Jazz Award was established in 1976 to honor the contribution Cole made to foster jazz in the total music education curriculum. He died in 1972 while attending the annual Missouri State Teachers Association conference in St. Louis. The motor home in which he was staying during the conference was destroyed by fire. He did not survive the accident.

Jess Cole Jazz Award

1976	Arch Martin	Kansas City
1977	Don Vern Joseph	Springfield
1978	Jerry Hoover	Jefferson City
1980	Carroll Lewis	Raytown
1981	No award	
1982	Roger Cody	Kirksville
1983	Ronald Stilwell	Kirkwood
1984	No award	
1985	Frank Haspiel	Overland
1986	John Brophy	University City
1987	No award	
1988	No award	
1989	No award	
1990	Jim Widner	Jefferson City
1991	Craig Buck	Hannibal
1992	Charles Meneese	St. Louis
1993	No award	
1994	Mary Lightfoot	Shelbina
1995	Gerry McCollum	Boonville
1996	Steve Lenhert	Kansas City
1997	No award	
1998	Terry Boone	Hannibal
1999	Warren Durrett	Kansas City
2000	Charles Loeber	Springfield
2001	Paul Smith	Kansas City
2002	Paul Drummond	Grandview

2003	Leon Bradley	Branson
2004	Robert Waggoner	St. Louis
2005	Mike Parkinson	Kansas City
2006	King Schollenberger	Springfield
2007	Robert Scott	Springfield
2008	Robert Boedges	St. Louis
2009	Gary Anders	Marshall (113)

MMEA
MISSOURI MUSIC
EDUCATORS
ASSOCIATION

Chapter 7

MISSOURI MUSIC EDUCATORS ASSOCIATION

M.M.E.A.

1930s

The idea of organizing Missouri school music directors had been casually discussed by music educators throughout the state. During a golf game in Joplin's Schifferdecker Park, Clarence Best of Webster Groves and James Robertson of Springfield decided to take positive action toward the formation of such a group. Best then presented the idea at a meeting of the St. Louis County music directors. With encouragement from the St. Louis directors, Best sent an invitation to all Missouri music educators to attend an organizational meeting. The meeting was held on November 25, 1934 at the Tiger Hotel in Columbia. At the time, Clarence Best was the orchestra director in Webster Groves but later moved to the Maplewood School District as Director of Bands and Orchestra.

First Organizational Meeting

Approximately fifty directors attended the organizational meeting in 1934. Wayne Sherrard, Superintendent of the Clayton School District, presided. James Robertson from Springfield acted as secretary. Clarence Best explained the purpose of the meeting was to establish by-laws and perfect an organization that would be in the interest of instrumental music directors in the state.

Organization

At that time there were few states that had state-wide music organizations; consequently, there were no models to consult.

Best distributed a letter containing the purposes of the National Band Association. A discussion then followed concerning the readiness of Missouri for a separate organization for instrumental music. Some suggested the idea that vocal directors also be included, since many music directors taught both vocal and instrumental music. It was argued that the instrumental field was large enough to require an organization of its own.

The point of separation of vocal and instrumental music organizations was discussed at length. A motion was made to establish the organization as a band and orchestra association, for the purpose of furthering instrumental music. The motion was amended to the effect that the organization links its efforts with the vocal music area and seeks recognition of the Music Department of the State Teachers' Association. The motion was voted upon and carried.

Whether to organize as individual teachers or by schools was discussed. The relationship of this new organization regarding contests played an important part in this discussion. In relation to contests, it would best serve the purpose to organize as schools. The question was raised by T. Frank Coulter of Joplin, as to whether this would be an organization to conduct contests or a group for sharing concerns of music education (113).

Temporary Officers

Temporary officers were then elected, their terms to last until the next meeting:

President	Clarence Best	Webster Groves
First Vice President	T. Frank Coulter	Joplin
Second Vice President	Lytton S. Davis	Monett
Secretary-Treasurer	James Robertson	Springfield

The executive committee, consisting of the temporary officers, was asked to form a constitution and by-laws and submit the documents for approval at the next meeting, which was scheduled for Sunday, January 13, 1935 in Jefferson City. After adjournment, the executive committee decided to change the January meeting to December 22, 1934 to consider the constitution and by-laws of the organization. The meeting site was changed to Joplin.

Second Organization Meeting

The second meeting of the new music educators' organization was held in the Senate Library of the State Capitol Building in Jefferson City on January 13, 1935. Adoption of the constitution and by-laws, drawn up by the executive committee in December was the first order of business.

President Best distributed copies of the constitution and read the entire document to the members, asking them to make notes in those areas where one needed clarification or desired to make recommendations for consideration. The same procedure took place in the presentation of the by-laws.

Contests

References to contests had been omitted from the constitution and by-laws, since there was some heated discussion of this topic at the first meeting, but no action was taken. Contest recommendations were dealt with after the constitution and by-laws were approved.

Though no official vote was taken at the first meeting in November, it was the feeling of the Executive Committee that many of the music directors in the state were dissatisfied with the manner in which District and State Music Contests had been handled in the past. In an effort to air these feelings in an organized manner and to effect changes in the contest structure that would make them better serve their purpose, the Executive Committee prepared a list of resolutions and recommendations concerning contests. This list was presented to the members for discussion and approval.

State Music Advisory Committee

One of the major recommendations was that a State Music Committee, made up of representatives of the Band and Orchestra Directors' Association, the Superintendents' organizations, and representatives from each teachers college and university, be formulated. A committee was appointed to devise such a plan and present it at the next meeting. This plan evolved into the State Music Advisory Committee, made up of two members of the Band and Orchestra Directors' Association, two members of the Choral Directors' Association, and two members of the Administrators' Association, and the Director of Music for the State of Missouri.

Officers Retained

The temporary officers elected at the first meeting in 1934 were retained for 1935.

Choral Directors Association

On April 6, 1935 the choral directors of the state met to organize the Missouri State Choral Directors' Association. Officers for the new association were:

President	T. Frank Coulter	Joplin
First Vice President	Sarah K. White	St. Joseph
Second Vice President	Verdis Mays	Columbia
Secretary	Lelia Mooney	Steelville
Treasurer	Jessie Smith	Independence

Missouri's music educators were now organized into professional associations and ready to focus their collective efforts on improving the quality and scope of music education in the state.

1935

First Conference and Clinic
Instrumental and Choral Associations Merge

As plans for the first conference/clinics were being made, it was recognized by both the instrumental and choral associations that a joint program would best serve both groups.

The two organizations met in joint conference on November 1–2, 1935 at Phelps School, Springfield, Missouri. Clinicians included Harold Bachman, Conductor of Bachman's Million Dollar Band, Charles Righter, Director of the University of Iowa Orchestra, and Max Krone, Choral Director at Northwestern University. Additional clinic sessions were presented by outstanding Missouri musicians.

"Granting of School Credits for Music" and "Cooperation between Vocal and Instrumental Music in the Schools" were delivered jointly by Bachman, Righter, and Krone, and were the two major addresses on the program. The latter probably helped give impetus to the idea that the two music educators associations merged. Within two years, the MSBODA and the MSCDA would merge into one organization to be known as the Missouri Music Educators Association, in order to concentrate their collective efforts for the benefit of music education in Missouri.

1935–1945

The major emphasis of band, orchestra, and choral clinic sessions from 1935–1945 was the performance of compositions from the National Contest Lists. Clinics on specific instrumental and vocal problems, including instrument repair, were also part of the program, and grew in number and diversity each year.

Elementary Music and Rural School Music

Though the elementary music field was not yet represented by an executive board officer, Mabelle Glenn of the Kansas City Public Schools presented a set of demonstrations in this area for grades one through six for the 1937 conference. The particular needs of rural school music educators were recognized and sessions on "Fine Arts in Rural Schools" were added as an annual feature.

First All-State Band, Orchestra, and Chorus

The first All-State High School Band, Orchestra, and Chorus were organized for the 1941 Conference. These organizations served as clinic groups and also presented a concert.

During World War II, the conference/clinic programs reflected the changes in school music programs that were made to meet the demands of the war. To enable as many members as possible to attend, the annual meetings were held in conjunction with the Missouri State Teachers Association meeting. The program was somewhat limited and clinic sessions were directed by Missouri music educators, rather than by out-of-state clinicians. The All-State High School organizations were discontinued for the duration. Instrumental repair clinics took on more meaning due to the circumstances, and dealt with the repair and salvage of instruments. Panel discussions on "Music Education in Wartime" and "Music and Art in the War Effort" showed the important role that music educators and music would play in our nation at that time. State level festival/contest activities, which were jointly coordinated by MMEA, the University of Missouri, and the state teacher colleges, were somewhat curtailed during this period.

1946–1959

Following World War II, the Missouri Music Educators Association began to expand its efforts on behalf of music education in the schools. An important element in this expanded effort was the publication of *Missouri School Music* magazine beginning in March 1946. Harlan Spring of Kansas City served as the first editor. The magazine continued to be an important sounding board for issues and information of interest to Missouri music educators.

Elementary music, which had long been recognized as a vital part of the music curriculum, was becoming even more important with the increase in the number of school systems now employing elementary music specialists. New and varied teaching methods and materials were being developed to broaden the scope of elementary music education. MMEA established the office of Vice President of Elementary Music in 1949, for the purpose of planning and providing elementary music sessions for the annual conference/clinic.

Missouri State High School Activities Association
MSHSAA

In 1946, appointed members of MMEA became involved with the new Missouri State High School Activities Association—formerly the State Athletic Association. In the following year, 1947, superintendents of Missouri requested that the Activities Association oversee all interscholastic events, including music, which had been previously coordinated by a state music committee. The role that MMEA would play was the topic of much debate and discussion in the *Missouri School Music* magazine. This resulted in the MMEA Executive Board becoming the Music Advisory Committee to the Activities Board. In 1951, music activities came under the auspices of the Missouri State High School Activities Association—MSHSAA.

The tenure of MMEA officers was changed in 1948 from one to two years, and the annual meeting moved from the fall to winter. To boost membership in the organization it was decided to hold the association meeting on the campus of the University of Missouri biennially and at one of the state teacher's colleges on alternate years.

Music educators had long recognized the importance of music in the curriculum of public schools. Through the efforts of MMEA and the State Director of Fine Arts, Alfred Bleckschmidt, new classification standards, requiring music to be included in the school curriculum, were adopted by the State Department of Education in 1950.

1960–1970

In the early 1960's, and largely as a result of the Russian launch of "Sputnik" in 1957, the emphasis on science, math, and foreign language greatly influenced the liberal and fine arts programs at all levels of education.

School music courses that were performance-based—band, orchestra, and chorus—received the brunt of this new educational emphasis. Before this time, the teaching of technical and musical skills toward a goal of quality performance could be justified by boards of education. Now music educators were being asked to justify these skills and goals as academic and necessary to the education of students. MMEA, along with the Music Educators National Conference, encouraged and developed "Pilot Programs for Development of High School Ensemble Music Classes" into "Courses Representing an Academic Discipline."

End of State Contest

In 1959, the member schools of the MSHSAA voted to terminate participation of large, conducted ensembles at the state contest level, starting with the school year 1960–1961. The reasons given for this action were that the cost exceeded the value and it interfered with the academic programs of the member schools. In addition to the time away from classes, the cost of transportation was another major factor for the decision.

The Missouri Music Educators Association was organized for the purpose of providing opportunities for professional growth by teachers of music in the state. Early clinic sessions focused on the preparation of music from the National Contest List. The National Band Contest, started in 1923, was duplicated in Missouri and continued until 1960.

The success of the Missouri Music Educators Association is due to many dedicated individuals who provided the leadership through the years to improve the quality of music education in the state, which included an annual conference and clinic, a state publication devoted to music education, the establishment of all-state performing groups, and in later years a research division of the association.

A golf game in Joplin in 1934 started the discussion between Clarence Best of Webster Groves and James Robertson of Springfield, which resulted in the formation of the Missouri School Band & Orchestra Directors Association, later to be known as the Missouri Music Educators Association—MMEA (114).

Missouri Music Educators Association
Presidents

1935–1936	Clarence Best, Instrumental	Webster Groves
1935–1936	T. Frank Coulter, Choral	Joplin
1937	Wilfred Schalger	Kansas City
1938	James P. Robertson	Springfield
1939	Roger Whitmore	Columbia
1940	James Dillinger	Hannibal
1941	Jewell T. Alexander	Sedalia
1942	Alfred W. Bleckschmidt	Warrensburg
1943	Arthur G. Harrell	Jefferson City
1944	Norman Falkenheiner	University City
1945	J. Roy Huckstep	Raytown
1946	Harling A. Spring	Kansas City
1947–1948	Paul A. VanBodegraven	Columbia
1948–1950	Lawrence Guenther	Normandy
1950–1952	George C. Wilson	Columbia
1952–1954	LeRoy F. Mason	Cape Girardeau
1954–1956	Keith Collins	Sikeston

1956–1958	M. O. Johnson	Independence
1959–1960	Paul Strub	Kirksville
1960–1962	John Willer	Mexico
1962–1964	Gerald Sandbothe	Macon
1964–1966	Robert Schupp	Kirksville
1966–1968	George M. Turmail	Ladue
1968 Deceased	Ben Markley	Kansas City
1968–1970	Don Anderson	Brentwood
1970–1972	William G. Mack	Park Hill
1972–1974	Gerald W. Fuchs	Savannah
1974–1976	Wynne J. Harrell	Florissant
1976–1978	Claude T. Smith	Kansas City
1978 – 1980	Ed Carson	Webster Groves
1980–1982	Charles W. Maupin	Chillicothe
1982–1984	Russell Coleman	Warrensburg
1984–1986	John Patterson	Columbia
1986–1988	Noel Fulkerson	Raytown
1988-1990	Robert M. Gifford	Cape Girardeau
1990–1992	Robert L. Meeks	Carthage
1992–1994	James C. Oliver	Lee's Summit
1994–1996	David B. Goodwin	Chillicothe
1996–1998	Charles "Bud" Clark	Joplin
1998–2000	Martin L. Hook	Columbia
2000–2002	Aurelia Hartenberger	Mehlville
2002–2004	Jeffrey Sandquist	Rolla
2004–2006	Kurt Bauche	Farmington
2006–2008	Paul Swofford	St. Clair
2008–2010	Paul Copenhaver	Moberly
2010–2012	Rob Nichols	Columbia

Missouri Music Educators Association
Hall of Fame Award

1985	Paul A. Van Bodegraven	University of Missouri – Columbia
	George C. Wilson	University of Missouri – Columbia
	O. Anderson Fuller	Lincoln University – Jefferson City
	Mabelle Glenn	Kansas City
1986	Clarence Best	Maplewood
	Alfred W. Bleckschmidt	State Department of Education – Jefferson City
1989	Harold C. Lickey	Marshall
1990	Lewis Hilton	Washington University – St. Louis
1991	Claude T. Smith,	Kansas City
	Tom Mills	University of Missouri – Columbia
	Jack Stephenson	University of Missouri – Kansas City
1993	John Willer	Mexico
1994	Charles Emmons	University of Missouri – Columbia
	Franklin D. Lewis	Marshfield
	Elmer W. Pundmann	Brookfield
1998	Ed Carson	Webster Groves
	T. Frank Coulter	Joplin
	Wynne J. Harrell	Missouri State University – Springfield
	Larry Hiltabidle	Waverly
	Keith House	Central Methodist University – Fayette
1999	Charles William Maupin	Chillicothe
	Hubey E. Moore	Jefferson College – Hillsboro

2000	Lowell Brunner	Lindbergh
	William G. Mack	Missouri Western State University – St. Joseph
	John G. Patterson	Columbia
2001	Mary Lightfoot	South Shelby
	Tom Price	Cameron
2002	Richard Weymuth	Maryville
	Lee T. Schneider	Maryville
	Douglas Turpin	Chesterfield
2003	Russell Coleman	University of Central Missouri – Warrensburg
	Jerry Hoover	Missouri State University – Springfield
2004	Nancy Seward	Richmond
2005	Roy Huckstep	Raytown
	Robert Scott	Missouri State University – Springfield
	David Larry McSpadden	Canton
2006	C. Herbert Duncan	Normandy
	William Grace	Gladstone
	Robert Gifford	Southeast Missouri State U. – Cape Girardeau
	Carroll Lewis	Raytown
2007	Gerald Fuchs	Savannah
	Sharon King	Sedalia
	Nick Leist	Jackson
	John C. Overby	Kansas City
	Luther T. Spayde	Central Methodist University – Fayette
2008	David L. Goodwin	Cameron
2009	Doyle Dumas	Southeast Missouri State U. – Cape Girardeau
2010	Aurelia Hartenberger	Mehlville

	Martin L. Hook	Columbia
	Kenneth Seward	Richmond
2011	Noel Fulkerson	Raytown
	Robert Nordman	University of Missouri – St. Louis

Missouri School Music Magazine Editors:

1946–1947	Harling Spring	Kansas City
1947–1949	Paul Van Bodegraven	Columbia
1949–1952	Harling Spring	Kansas City
1952–1955	Leon Karel	Kirksville
1955–1956	Karl E. Webb	Kirksville
1956–1957	Leon Karel	Kirksville
1957–1962	Paul Strub	Kirksville
1962–1965	Lansing W. Bulgin	Kirksville
1965–1966	Arthur Humphreys	Kirksville
1966–1969	Ira Schwarz	Kirksville
1968–1970	David C. Nichols	Kirksville
1970–1971	Elizabeth Topper	Kirksville
1971–1977	Ed Bostley	Kirksville
1977	Franklin Dee Lewis	Marshfield

COLLEGE
UNIVERSITY
BANDS

Chapter 8

COLLEGE AND UNIVERSITY BANDS

Central Methodist University
Fayette

Formerly
Central College
Central Methodist College

The College

Central College was formally granted a charter from the Missouri General Assembly in 1855 and opened officially in 1857. The College was sold in 1869 to Reverend Moses U. Payne, who deeded the property to the Methodist Episcopal Church, South. The school was renamed Howard-Payne College in 1892 as a two-year college for women. Howard-Payne College for Women of Fayette remained an independent college operating alongside with Central until 1922.

In 1925, the Southern Methodist schools in Missouri were centralized into one system located at Fayette. The establishment of Central College brought together Marvin College at Fredericktown (Madison County), Central College for Women at Lexington (Lafayette County), and Scarritt-Morrisville College at Morrisville (Polk County).

In 1961 the Board of Curators voted to name the institution Central Methodist College. The name was changed in 2004 to Central Methodist University.

The Swinney Conservatory of Music

Established in 1925, the Swinney Conservatory of Music, located on the Central campus,

207

was well-established in the training of piano and voice at Howard-Payne College before it became a field of study at Central. Edwin F. Swinney, a Kansas City banker, contributed $35,000 to the college and provided for the establishment of a music school at Central. The Swinney Conservatory of Music was dedicated on June 7, 1927. The first Dean of the Conservatory of Music was N. Louise Wright, a respected concert pianist and publisher of compositions for the piano. Wright was Swinney's niece. The Conservatory's mission as written in the *Central Methodist College Bulletin*, March 1977:

> To train professional musicians, critics, and teachers of music, and to prepare students for graduate study; and to offer to students who do not wish to major in music an opportunity to participate in band, orchestra, and choir; and to supply a good musical climate for the entire college and community (115).

The Swinney Conservatory of Music became a full member of the National Association of Schools of Music in November 1951. Central was the first church-related college in Missouri to receive this distinction.

The Central Bands

The bands at Central College were founded in January 1910 as an outgrowth of the Fayette Town Band, which was led by a young dentist, Dr. E. M. Blakey. The city had built a bandstand for the Town Band on the courthouse square a few years earlier. Music at Central was at first an extra-curricular activity. The student interested in the arts found it necessary to organize his or her own activities or enroll in music lessons at Howard-Payne College for Women.

Many of the band traditions were not formed until 1925 and the arrival of Keith King Anderson as Director of Bands. Although civic bands were organized in the early 1900's and served as incentive for similar college-related groups, the band did not become an established part of the curriculum of Central College until the merger of the two schools, Howard-Payne College for women and Central College. Early pictures in the yearbook from Marvin College at Fredericktown show the establishment of a band for that small school, which merged with other Methodist colleges to become Central College. The first bands at Central were student-organized and directed.

The initial idea of forming a band appeared in an editorial in the student newspaper, *The Central Collegian*, October 1908:

> Dr. Lee, in his chapel talk, suggested that we have a college band. We believe this to be a very wise suggestion. We are fortunate in having in school this year a number of boys

who play musical instruments of various kinds, and there is no reason why we should not have a band of our own. There is nothing that would develop college spirit and arouse a deeper interest in our contests, both local and inter-collegiate, than would a few stirring selections from a band. This would also prove quite a drawing card for these contest. Boys, let's have a band (116).

Norvill Brickey and Robert Carroll, Student Directors
1910–1913

The band did not become a reality until almost one and one-half years later when two students, Robert William Carroll and Norville Walcott Brickey, organized the first band to be associated with Central College. Carroll, a senior, directed the twenty-two member band for one year, and was also the first cornetist. N. W. Brickey assumed the leadership the following year and is responsible for building the early reputation of the band. Considered an excellent pianist and knowledgeable in band and orchestral work, Brickey was fortunate to have over forty interested musicians with well-balanced instrumentation.

An editorial in the November 1911 school newspaper, *The Central Collegian:*

> We doubt if a livelier set of musicians can be found in any college or university in the state.Mr. Brickey has shown himself in every way equal to his task of taking forty boys and transforming them into the best college band in the state (117).

Brickey's band not only performed for various college and civic functions, but was the first to embark upon a ten-day tour to cities in central Missouri. In March 1912, the band appeared in six cities, playing before three thousand people, and receiving acclaim in the *St. Louis Republic*:

> The Central College Concert Band, under the direction of N. W. Brickey, will make a concert tour through the state. Critics pronounce this to be one of the best bands among colleges and universities in the West (118).

Not all activities of the bands on tour were serious, as revealed in *The Collegian*, 1913, which contained a report of the "Beautiful, Bizarre, Baneful, Boneheads of Brickey's Band— Revised and Corrected Up-to-Date" (119). The report contained the daily account of the successes, misfortunes, and anecdotes encountered by thirty unsupervised college men.

Leonard Davis, Student Director

1913–1914

The graduation of Brickey, as well as several other band members, left the membership low because of the lack of replacements. Leonard Prewitt Davis became the next student to direct the band, which had nineteen members. Unfortunately, the popularity of the band diminished due to the lack of available musicians and adequate instrumentation. An appeal for more members was made through the school newspaper but resulted in few new members. Brickey's Band had set a high standard and was hard to duplicate, thus the band was in decline until 1915.

G. B. Lombardo, Director

1915–1916

Professor G. B. Lombardo directed the band for a short time in 1915, but his tenure was less than a year. The College began to search for a permanent director in the fall of 1916.

DeLos McCampbell, Director

1917–1919

DeLos McCampbell was appointed to revise and "have complete control" over the direction of a new music department in 1917. Thirty-five students were enrolled in the glee club and twenty in the band that year. McCampbell proved to be an able conductor and was described as "a hustler and believes in doing things properly or not at all," reported *The Central Collegian* in November 1917 (120). Following McCampbell, the band had four different directors until 1925. All were graduates of Central College. Directing the Central band during this time were Charles Orrin Ransford (1919–1921), Lendon A. Enloe (1921 1922), Warren Chandler Middleton (19221923), Edwin F. Peters (1923-1925).

Keith K. Anderson

1925–1952

In the fall of 1925, Keith K. Anderson joined the faculty as Director of Bands. Anderson was a native of Coin, Iowa and had studied trumpet at Simpson College in Indianola, Iowa. He had not completed his studies when approached by E. E. Rich, Admission Counselor at Central, to finish his degree at the college combined with directing the band. Anderson's tenure at Central lasted twenty-seven years until his resignation in 1952. Thomas E. Birch, Director 1952-1964

Thomas Erskine Birch, IV, who graduated from Central in 1937, followed Anderson in 1952. Birch had served as student assistant and as staff member at Anderson's summer band camps in the 1940's. He earned his Master of Music Education from the University of Missouri in 1948 and the Doctor of Education degree, also from Missouri, in 1962. He previously taught at Norborne High School, Boonville High School, and Kemper Military Academy in Boonville.

Through Birch's efforts, the musical facilities at Central were greatly expanded, including a new band room, nine practice rooms, three studios, an office, and library, all available for instrumental music. On May 1, 1964, while conducting the first selection on the home concert, Thomas Birch collapsed and died, having served the college for twelve years. The new band facilities, encouraged by Birch, were not ready until the following spring.

Kenneth & Nancy Seward, Co-Directors
1964–1966

Following Birch, Raymond Kenneth Seward and Nancy Heitmann Seward assumed duty of the band program. Both were Central College graduates. The Sewards had been directors at Ruskin High School in Kansas City, gaining recognition for directing the first Missouri band to participate in the Tournament of Roses Parade in 1960. Recognition came to the Central band in 1964 under the Sewards when they performed during half-time of a nationally televised St. Louis Cardinals football game in the pouring rain, which obliterated the yard lines. Fans were amazed with the band's performance under such adverse conditions, and the Cardinals doubled the money promised for their transportation. The Seward duo initiated a marching band festival in 1964, which provided competition in street and field performance for high school bands. The Sewards left in 1966 to become directors at Richmond High School, Kenneth's hometown.

Joseph A. Labuta, Director
1966–1967

Joseph A. Labuta assumed the position of director in the fall of 1966. He, too, had been a student of K. K. Anderson, graduating in 1953. He earned his doctorate degree at the University of Illinois. After one year at Central, he accepted a position as professor of music at Wayne State University in Detroit, Michigan.

Paul A. Montemurro, Director
1967–1972

The next director (1967) was Paul A. Montemurro, also a product of Central. A student of

Thomas Birch, Montemurro graduated in 1958 and completed the Master of Arts degree at Missouri University in 1961. Montemurro personally recruited talented high school musicians for Central. Because of his vigorous efforts and the band's favorable publicity at several professional football games, the number of music majors increased to one hundred in 1970, the largest enrollment in the history of the Conservatory.

An excellent jazz musician, Montemurro initiated the First Annual Stage Band Festival in March 1969. Success was immediate because a large number of high school bands participated, and especially because Clark Terry, a well-known jazz soloist and other jazz personalities were secured by Montemurro for the festival.

The Concert Band also grew in size and quality under the leadership of Montemurro. In January 1971 an invitation was accepted for the band to perform at the Southwest Division of the Music Educators National Conference in Albuquerque, New Mexico. Reaction to the performance was one of wonder at how a church-related college, plagued by limited funds and enrollment, could produce such a high degree of quality. A year earlier, a former member of the Boston Symphony, Rosario Mazzeo, had appeared on campus and acclaimed the band as among the finest in the country.

In 1972, Montemurro left Central to join the faculty at Oklahoma State University (121).

Keith House, Director
1972–1995

Keith House, a graduate of Central in 1949, under the guidance of Keith K. Anderson, became the sixteenth director since 1910 to lead the Central College bands. House earned a Master of Music Education degree from the University of Kansas in 1958 and was teaching as a high school band director in Lee's Summit, Missouri when he returned to his alma mater.

Under his leadership, the Central Methodist College bands continued their high quality of musicianship, and the 1977 annual tour marked the fifty-second consecutive tour since K. K. Anderson revived the practice begun in 1912 by N. W. Brickey. In 1974, the Concert Band was selected to perform for the combined Central and Southwest Divisions Convention of the Music Educators National Conference in Omaha, Nebraska.

Under his direction, the band recorded four albums that are included in the *Heritage of the March*, a series of recordings that have been distributed throughout the world.

House was appointed Dean of the Swinney Conservatory of Music in 1985.

In 1986, Keith House was honored by the Missouri Bandmasters Association by his election into the MBA Hall of Fame. In 1998, the Missouri Music Educators Association presented him with the Hall of Fame award. Unofficially he was the "Dean of Missouri Band

Directors." Professor House retired from Central Methodist University in 1995 and died on August 26, 2006. At his funeral on the campus of the University, a band of alumni honored him one last time with *Barnum and Bailey's Favorite March* played as the recessional.

Following the retirement of Keith House in the spring of 1995, Dr. Ron Shroyer served as Director of Bands for the 1995–96 school year. Marie Breed was hired in the summer of 1996 and was Director of Bands for the 1996–97 season. In the fall of 1997, Dr. Mary I. Woodbury was named as Director of Bands. She served through the 1999–2000 school year. Native Missourian Dr. Tom Ruess was named Director of Bands in the fall of 2000 and served until the end of the 2006–2007 school year. Larry Bennett, a Central graduate of 1969, was the interim director during the 2007–2008 school year. Skip Vandelicht assisted Bennett with the band and was appointed to the full-time position of Director of Bands in the fall of 2008–2009. Vandelicht was a Central graduate in 1977 and Director of Bands in the Fayette R-III School District (122).

Director of Bands

Norvill Brickey & Robert Carroll, Student Directors	1910–1913
Leonard Davis, Student Director	1913–1914
G. B. Lombardo	1915–1916
A. DeLos McCampbell	1916–1919
Charles Orrin Ransford	1919–1921
Lendon A. Enloe	1921–1922
Warren Chandler Middleton	1922–1923
Edwin F. Peters	1923–1925
Keith King Anderson	1925–1952
Thomas E. Birch	1952–1964
Kenneth and Nancy Seward	1964–1966
Joseph A. Labuta	1966–1967
Paul A. Montemurro	1967–1972
Keith House	1972–1995
Ron Shroyer	1995–1996
Marie E. Breed	1996–1997
Mary Woodbury	1997–2000
Tom J. Ruess	2000–2007
Larry Bennett / Skip Vandelicht	2007–2008
Skip Vandelicht	2008

Central College Band – 1911
Robert William Carroll, Student Director

Central College Marching Band – 1928
Keith K. Anderson, Director

Central College Band – 1935
Three different bands:
The Cadet Military Band, The Girls Band, The College Band

Central College Concert Band – 1949
Keith K. Anderson, Director
Band included future Central band directors:
Joe Labuta, Keith House, Ken & Nancy Seward

Jefferson College
Hillsboro
The College

Jefferson College, informally known as JeffCo, is a public, two-year community college founded in 1963. In addition to the main campus in Hillsboro, Jefferson College operated two additional sites: Jefferson College Arnold and Jefferson College Northwest in High Ridge, Missouri.

The Band

The band program at Jefferson College was established in 1966 by Robert Priez. It started as a class, meeting for one hour twice a week. Enrollment varied each semester, placing demands on the conductor to often find musicians outside the college to fulfill instrumentation needs.

Since 1999, the band membership is open to community members, with the band size averaging sixty to seventy players per semester. The band presents four concerts per year featuring literature both challenging and enjoyable for the audience and band members (123).

Directors

1966	Robert Priez
1967–1875	John Arnn
1975–1985	Huby Moore
1985–1990	Matt McCready
1990–1991	David Butler
1991–1993	Al Sherman
1993–1995	Kim Shelly
1995–1996	Melissa Marks
1996–1999	No band
1999–2008	Joe Pappas
2008	Randy Hodge

Missouri Southern State University
Joplin

Formerly
Joplin Junior College
Missouri Southern State College

The College / University

Missouri Southern State University was founded in 1937 as Joplin Junior College with 114 students and nine faculty members. In 1964, residents of Jasper County approved a 2.5 million dollar bond issue to begin construction on a new campus on the site of the current university. Classes were first held on the new campus in the fall of 1967 with 2,399 students and 95 faculty members. In 1977, the school was renamed Missouri Southern State College and officially became a state assisted four-year college and part of the State of Missouri's higher learning education system. In 2003, the Missouri General Assembly authorized the renaming of the college to Missouri Southern State University – Joplin, and in 2005 the university dropped Joplin from its name. In 1967, the campus was home to only six buildings. Since that time the campus grew to more than forty structures and a student population of over 5,500 students.

The Band

The Joplin Junior College band was established in 1940 under the direction of T. Frank Coulter. Coulter was the director of the Joplin High School band and a respected music educator in the state. The first drum major was Russ Holden and the first twirling drum major was Jack Holden. "The band, embryonic in years, but titanic in ability," described the early band in the college yearbook, *Crossroads* (124). Fifteen members are shown in a 1943 photograph.

The band was presented in uniforms for the first time in 1941. Many activities including the band were suspended in 1944 due to the war. A much smaller orchestra and choir still performed under the direction of Mrs. Alta Cowen Dale. In 1945 the band once appeared briefly on the college's campus, only to dwindle to small chamber instrumental ensembles until the early '60s. In 1962 the college fielded not only a concert band but a stage band as well. The program continued to thrive until 1968 when the new "Lion Pride Marching Band" was reestablished after a long absence. Complete with new uniforms, the band performed for sporting events and community activities.

G.K. Renner, writing about the history of the school—"Southern had been without a marching band since the early years of the Joplin Junior College and its absence was seen as hurting the college's image, but the cost of the program had held up its implementation" (125).

In 1982, Director Pete Havely added a flag/rifle/dance squad to the band and changed to the corps-style marching. The band program at Missouri Southern continued to flourish and added the MSSU Wind Ensemble to its offerings for band students in 2006.

Directors

T. Frank Coulter	1940–1944, founder
William Dale	1945–1946
Jerrold Perkins	1947–1949
Virginia Myers	1950–1962
Russell E. Benzamin	1963–1966
William Taylor	1967–1968
Delbert Johnson	1969–1977
Jim Johnson	1978–1979
Pete Havely	1979–2003
Rusty Raymond	2003

Joplin Junior College – 1943
T. Frank Coulter, Director

Missouri State University
Springfield

Formerly
Missouri State Normal School # 4
Southwest Missouri State Teachers College
Southwest Missouri State College
Southwest Missouri State University

The College / University

Missouri State University was founded in Springfield in 1905 as the Missouri State Normal School # 4. During its early years, the institution's primary purpose was the preparation of teachers for the public schools in southwest Missouri. The first name change came in 1919 when the school became Southwest Missouri State Teachers College.

By the mid-1940s the university had expanded its instructional program beyond teacher education to include the liberal arts and sciences; and as a result, the Missouri legislature, in 1947, authorized an official change in the institution's name to Southwest Missouri State College.

By 1972, as additional programs were implemented at the undergraduate level, and with the development of graduate education, the name became Southwest Missouri State University. In 2005, by an act of the Missouri Legislature, the name was changed to Missouri State University.

The Band

In the fall term of 1908, the State Normal School #4 band consisted of fifteen members under the instruction of Professor Martin C. Schricker. Schricker was a member of the music department and a German immigrant. He gained his musical training at Leipzig Conservatory in Berlin.

Ozarko, the yearbook of 1908, describes the band:

> The band is an important addition to the school. It has furnished splendid entertainment for the school at several chapel periods during the winter. The excellent music of the boys at the annual autumn picnic was a source of pleasure the entire day. The band has been present at all the athletic contests, and has contributed much to the enthusiasm and the school spirit. The band has cheered the Normal students in victory and consoled them in defeat. In the societies and entertainments of the school high grade solo work is furnished by the individual members of the band.

On one Saturday evening in April of this school year the band boys gave a concert in the Normal Chapel. This concert was recognized as one of the best student efforts of the year. There were several splendid solo numbers on the program.

The boys were proud this spring when the Knight Templers, order No. 40, of Springfield, chose them to lead in the parade at the State Association at Carthage, considered the 'Band Mecca' of the time. The boys in their new uniforms and with their inspiring music compared well with the boys of other reputable bands of the state. The band is ever an important factor in the school curriculum (126).

Clayton C. Kinsey became the band director in 1909, and Sidney Myers is listed as the director in 1914–1926. Myers was also the director of the school's orchestra.

In 1932, Winston Lynes was listed as Director of Bands. Wayne Glenn profiles Lynes in *The Ozarks' Greatest Hits*:

Lynes was born in Warsaw, Missouri in 1906. When he was 12 years old, he began playing the cornet and trumpet. By this time the family was living in Springfield where Lines became a member of the famous Boy Scout Band which was reputed to be the largest Scout Band in the country. A big thrill for him came when he was chosen to do a cornet solo in 1924 on WGN radio in Chicago. In 1924, Lynes, at age 17, was selected as the first trumpeter in the 75-piece Springfield Orchestra (127).

Ozarko, the yearbook of 1943, describes Lynes' marching band creativity:

The college has seen the band performing intricate march routines and moving quickly into unusual formation. On the day the football team beat Maryville, an "M" was formed by band musicians. Two weeks later the "M" was turned upside down in honor of Warrensburg.

At one game during the football season, the band was striding in splendid order, playing a throbbing march, when a member collapsed on the field. The audience gasped. Band members hurried to him, and as he was carried away, they gave a cheer in memoriam. A new band member was substituted and the band continued, undaunted. The collapse may have been another of Mr. Lynes' striking and original ideas (128).In 1935 the college yearbook indicates a band of 33 members under Lynes' direction. In addition, the college included al all female drum and bugle corps, each performing at football games, basketball games, and track meets.

Wayne Christenson became band director from 1937–1938 during a leave of absence by Winston Lynes. Lynes returned to the band in 1939, and in 1941 there were 71 members, with Lloyd Blakely, future Music Department chairman, playing first chair clarinet.

In 1957 the band numbered 55 members under Lynes' direction. Elton Burgstahler was the director of the marching band. Lynes also directed the ROTC band of 35 members.

Howard Liva was Director of Bands in 1966, and Dan Palen became director for one year in 1971. Robert Scott was appointed Director of Bands in 1972, coming from Northeast Missouri State College. In his first year at Southwest, Scott established the Ozarko Show Band Contest, naming the contest after the school's yearbook. In 1973 he established the SMS Jazz Festival.

Tony DiBartelomeo became director of the marching band in 1983, and he and Scott shared the Concert Band duties. Jerry Hoover was appointed Director of Bands in 1985. Hoover was the Director of Bands at New Mexico State University and a Missouri native, having taught at Cabool, Lebanon, and Jefferson City high schools before moving to the band position at New Mexico State University. Dr. Belva Prather joined the band staff in 1993 as Associate Director of Bands and conductor of the Wind Ensemble (129).

Missouri State University Director of Bands

1908–1909	Martin C. Schricker
1909–1914	Clayton C. Kinsey
1914–1932	Sydney Myers
1932–1937	Winston Lynes
1937–1939	Wayne Christeson
1939–1964	Winston Lynes
1964–1966	Elton Burgstahler (ROTC)
1966–1969	Howard Liva
1969–1971	John Pressley (ROTC)
1971–1972	Dan Palen
1972–1983	Robert Scott
1983–1985	Tony DiBartelomeo
1985–current	Jerry Hoover
1993–current	Belva Prather (Wind Ensemble)

Missouri State Normal School # 4 Band
(Undated)
Springfield-Greene County Historical Society photo

Missouri State Normal School #4 Band – 1909
Springfield
Clayton C. Kinsey, Director
Springfield-Greene County Historical Society photo

Missouri State Normal School #4 Band – 1913
Springfield
Clayton C. Kinsey, Director
Springfield-Greene County Historical Society photo

Southwest Missouri State University Pride Band – 1997
Jerry Hoover, Director

Missouri University of Science and Technology
Rolla

Formerly
Missouri School of Mines and Metallurgy
University of Missouri – Rolla

The University

The University of Missouri School of Mines and Metallurgy was founded in 1870—the first technological institution west of the Mississippi and one of the first in the nation. A product of the Morrill Act of 1862 and the land-grant movement of the late nineteenth century, the university was Missouri's response to the acute need for scientific and practical education in the developing nation.

Early curricula were focused on the state's mining industry. Missouri has the largest deposit of lead ore in the world located in the south central part of the state known as the "lead belt." By the end of the 1920s, studies included mining, civil, mechanical, electrical, chemical engineering, chemistry, metallurgy, mathematics, physics, and geology.

Graduate education and research began to assume greater emphasis on the campus during the 1950s. In 1964, recognizing its expanded nature and role, the name of the institution was changed to the University of Missouri – Rolla, joining Kansas City, St. Louis, and Columbia as part of the four-campus university system. In January 2008 the campus name was changed again and became the Missouri University of Science and Technology. The school remains part of the University of Missouri educational community.

The Band

"The first evidence of a regular instrumental music group at the Missouri School of Mines appears in the 1908 yearbook, *Rollamo*. The 'MSM Orchestra,' as it was called, was directed by C. W. Keniston, and consisted of eight pieces" (130). The development of a band did not come for another 23 years.

David Oakley, director of the Miners Band from 1960–1993, provides a historical tribute to the band in his unpublished account of *57 Years of Musical Miners*.

The first official band program was started in 1926, when John W. Scott, a Rolla musician and businessman, started the 'Miners Band.' Scott was a graduate of the school and a registered pharmacist in Rolla. Under his direction, regular rehearsals were conducted on the campus for the first time. In 1926 the band numbered 22, in 1927 the band numbered 24, and by 1928 the strength was up to 31 members.

Although a cooperative plan had been established by MSM and the ROTC to co-sponsor the band, the first appearance of the band in a military uniform came in 1930, and that was also the first year of mention of a formal concert for the group. The usual activities such as football trips and military parades were a part of the band on the campus. John W. Scott remained as director, a position he was to hold for 27 years.

In 1934 the band formed the 'M' for MSM on the football field for the first time, and in the same year presented its first good-will concert tour for the Rolla Chamber of Commerce. By 1935 the band had achieved some balance of instrumentation necessary for the concert music beginning to be available for the band. The 1937 *Rollamo* calls the band one of the outstanding campus groups.

After ten years in military uniforms, the band adopted its first school uniform consisting of a white shirt and trousers, with a cape in the school colors—silver and gold. In 1940 the uniform for the band returned to the military style due to World War II. Also, the band was at its largest size with thirty-six members. In 1945 the ROTC band is shown in the *Rollamo* with two girls marching with the band in military uniform. It is believed that this is the first time that the band became co-educational.

Scott continued as director until his death at age 80. In his 27 years directing the MSM band he was never paid for his service. After his death in 1950 the Scott family donated many of his unusual and antique instruments to the university. In addition, his extensive and well-catalogued library of band literature was given to the MUR band library.

In 1951 W. R. Phillips, a member of the faculty who taught English, became director of the band, succeeding John W. Scott. The MSM–ROTC band now numbered about 40 members and was closely tied to the military department. Phillips served as band director for two years. In 1954 William Parr, a graduate student, directed the band, which now had a membership of 30. In 1955 William Decker, director of the Rolla High

School Band, served as director of the MSM–ROTC on a part-time basis.

William Tetley, who became director of the Rolla High School Band in 1956, also came to MSM on a part-time basis to direct the band. For the first time in many years the band was sent on tour, and concerts were presented in Springfield and at the State Penitentiary. Tetley remained as director for a period of two years.

James W. Robbins, an instructor in the department of humanities, was appointed director in 1958. A new uniform was designed by Robbins, and with the approval of the military department, it replaced the military uniform. During 1959–1960, Captain Ralph M. Leighty, a member of the faculty of the military department, served as director of the band. During this time a separate concert and field band was established. Future growth of the band was indicated by the steady growth of the school.

In the fall of 1960 the school employed the first full-time music director, David L. Oakley. Previous directors had been members of other faculty departments. Oakley taught at high schools in Tennessee before coming to MSM. The first football show in 1960 was presented with 41 men on the field, and by the end of that semester a brass choir and dance band had been organized. By spring the concert band had 52 members and played three concerts on the campus. Under Oakley's direction four distinct band groups were established: military, concert, football, and dance bands. Some personnel were the same in each group. For many years the band had been an after-hours group, but for the first time the band was able to meet daily during the school day.

The fall of 1963 opened with the band performing at a professional football game for the St. Louis Cardinals. The band had 82 members and was featured at half-time on national television. There were now four girls in the band. In the first semester of 1964 the band passed a hundred in membership. The concert band was auditioned and its membership was set at 85 members. One of the highest honors for the band came in 1965 with the acceptance of an invitation to play at the New York World's Fair. The band presented six concerts over the three days at the Fair.

Few collegiate musical groups have been composed entirely of engineering students and applied science majors. However, UMR–ROTC bands have achieved recognition for excellence among such groups (131).

Missouri University of Science and Technology
Director of Bands

1926–1950	John Scott
1951–1953	W. R. Philllips
1954–1955	William Parr (Graduate student)
1955–1956	William Decker
1957–1958	William Tetley
1958–1959	James W. Robins
1959–1960	Cpt. Ralph M. Leighty
1960–1993	David Oakley
1993–1994	Doug Stotter
1994–1955	Tom Ruess
1995–1997	Patricia Childress
1997–2007	Donald K. Miller
2007–current	Robert Cesario

Missouri School of Mines and Metallurgy Band – 1926
John W. Scott, Director
Photo courtesy Susan Miller family collection

Missouri School of Mines R.O.T.C. Band – 1941
John W. Scott, Director
Photo courtesy Susan Miller family collection

Missouri Valley College
Marshall

The College

In 1874, the Cumberland Presbyterian Church established a church-related college in Missouri. A permanent education commission was established to plan and raise funds for the new college. Marshall, Missouri was selected as the site, and on June 30, 1888, a charter for the college was filed with the Missouri Secretary of State. The charter stated that the college was to be co-educational and under the control of the Synod of Missouri and Kansas of the Cumberland Presbyterian Church. The site for the new college in Marshall was chosen over Sedalia, Odessa, Independence, St. Joseph, and Fort Scott, Kansas. The city of Marshall provided 40 acres of land plus $162,000 in cash to attract the college. The city also boasted cheap fuel, good water, two railroads, no debts, and no saloons (132).

Band Directors

1933–1948	Artur T. Vawter
1948–1957	Louis Hanson
1962–1976	Rodney Polson
2007–current	Garry Anders

Missouri Valley College Band – 1949
Louis Hanson, Director
Mid-Continent Public Library archives photo

Northwest Missouri State University
Maryville

Formerly
Missouri State Normal School # 5
Northwest Missouri State Teachers College
Northwest Missouri State College

The College / University

Northwest Missouri State University was founded in 1905 when the Missouri Legislature created five districts in the state to establish teaching standards or norms in a state teacher college network.

Maryville was selected for the Northwest district. The town offered to donate 86 acres on the northwest corner of Maryville, the former site of a Methodist Seminary. The other towns in the normal school network were located in Kirksville, Cape Girardeau, Springfield, and Warrensburg.

The original mission of the school was to prepare students to become elementary school teachers. The first classes began on June 13, 1906, with a lab school teaching Maryville's children in the primary grades. The school eventually expanded to a full high school.

In 1919 the school was granted the name Northwest Missouri State Teacher's College, and offered a baccalaureate degree in teaching. In 1949 the name was changed to Northwest Missouri State College. On August 14, 1972, the school was granted university status. The name was changed to Northwest Missouri State University.

The Band

A college band has been in existence at Northwest Missouri State University virtually since the creation of the school. The first band started out as an "athletic band," with band members seated in the stands. The band did not march on the field. The main purpose of the group was still the same, however—to support the team and provide entertainment (133).

It was not until the year 1933 that the band became a completely uniformed group. The 1933 *Tower* yearbook states that the band "has played a big part in creating school spirit and pep in the student body" (134). During this time the director was H. O. Hickernell.

The band began to perform on the field in the 1940s, but only with members standing in a stationary position. In 1943, the marching band was referred to as musical soldiers, reflecting the war climate of the time. Beginning in 1949, John L. Smay is listed as the director of the band. Smay is credited with developing the first marching band at Northwest Missouri State College. The group he developed was the closest thing to a predecessor to the modern NWMSC marching band. In 1950, the band received new uniforms and Smay decided to offer open enrollment to any college student who played a band instrument. Previously the band had been reserved for music students and those who auditioned (135).

In 1955, Earle Moss succeeded John L. Smay as Director of Bands. Ward C. Rounds became director in 1960 with a band of thirty-five members. Rounds became part of the music department, and the marching band grew to one hundred and fifty members under his leadership (136).

Lance Boyd was director for one year in 1968 and is credited with giving the band the name "Bearcat Marching Band" or "BMB." Ward Rounds returned as the director in 1969 and held the position until Dr. Henry Howey replaced him in 1972 (137).

The late 1970s proved to be an unsettled period for the band, mostly due to the fact that the group had five different directors in six years. The first was Harold Jackson in 1976. Dr. Ernest Woodruff managed the band in 1977. Dr. Terry Milligan became the band director one year later. In 1979 until 1981, Dr. Guy D'Aurelio was appointed Director of Bands, making him the fifth director in five years.

In 1981 Alfred E. Sergel III became the next director and stayed for 23 years. During his time as director, the membership of the band steadily increased. Sergel started with 60 members and over the years built the band to over 160. In 1984 he established the Northwest Wind Symphony. The ensemble made its first of four appearances at the Missouri Music Educators annual conference in 1989. It was Sergel who is credited with the development and advancement of the band in his many years at NWMSU. He retired in July 2004 (138).

In 2004, Carl A. Kling succeeded Sergel and brought further recognition to the band program with a performance in the London, England, New Year's Day Parade. Kling resigned his position in 2010 to return to teaching in the public schools.

Northwest Missouri State University

Director of Bands

1933–1948	H. O. Hickernell
1949–1954	John L. Smay
1955–1959	Earl Moss
1960–1967	Ward C. Rounds

1968–1969	Lance Boyd
1969–1972	Ward C. Rounds
1973–1975	Henry Howey
1976–1977	Harold Jackson
1977–1978	Ernest Woodruff
1978–1979	Terry Milligan
1979–1981	Guy D'Aurelo
1981–2003	Alfred E. Sergel
2004–2010	Carl A. Kling

Northwest Missouri State College Band – 1953
John L. Smay, Director
Mid-Continent Public Library archives photo

Southeast Missouri State University
Cape Girardeau

Formerly
Missouri State Normal School # 3
Southeast Missouri State Teachers College
Southeast Missouri State College

The College

The Missouri State Normal School # 3 was founded in 1873 in Cape Girardeau as a teacher training institution, serving the southeast area of the state. Academic Hall, the copper-domed center of the campus, was completed in 1905 and sits on the site of a Civil War fort. It replaced the original Normal School building that was destroyed by fire in 1902. The original building housed classrooms, a gymnasium, and the library.

Missouri – The "Show Me" State

In 1899, Southeast's fifth president, Willard Vandiver, coined the phrase: "show me," which became the unofficial state motto. After serving as president of the State Normal School, Vandiver served in the US House of Representatives from 1897–1899. In a speech at a naval banquet in Philadelphia, he declared, "I come from a state that raises corn and cotton and cockleburs and Democrats, and frothy eloquence neither convinces nor satisfies me. I am from Missouri. You have got to show me" (139).

Through the years, the university has had several name changes to indicate a growth from a teacher training institution to a school with many diverse departments of instruction:

1873–1919	Missouri State Normal School # 3
1919–1946	Southeast Missouri State Teachers College
1946–1973	Southeast Missouri State College
1973–Present	Southeast Missouri State University

The Band

The Missouri State Normal Military Band was organized in the fall of 1907 under the direction of Earl G. Beck. Professor Beck was an instructor in violin and also directed the school orchestra. Before World War I the band was led by Professor Harry L. Albert. Under his direction musical groups made annual tours of Southeast Missouri towns. The college yearbook, *Sagamore*, lists William Eber Roller, Mus.B., as Director of Bands and Orchestras from 1921–1924. Yearbooks of the college from 1924–1930 do not show pictures of any bands on the campus.

The first picture of the college band, directed by Professor O. Lewis Wilcox, appears in the 1931 *Sagamore*. Wilcox was formerly director of the Central High School band in Cape Girardeau. He remained at Southwest Missouri State College for 26 years as director of bands until his retirement in 1957. The 1931 *Sagamore* describes the band program:

> The College Band completed a very successful year (1931). It is under the direction of a new leader, Prof. O. L. Wilcox, who was formerly in charge of the Central High School Band of Cape Girardeau. Its presentations included a very interesting chapel program, concerts at all football and basketball games and playing for many types of parades. Probably the most outstanding of these was the parade of the dedication of the stadium which included many out–of–town bands and local bands. The band also was taken to Carbondale on Halloween to play for the football game there between the two colleges. The band this year strutted out new uniforms which are probably the most attractive of any in this section. The members of the band received their tuition free this year (140).

The 1950 yearbook indicates that new red and black uniforms were worn for the first time that year.

Upon Wilcox's retirement in 1957, LeRoy Mason was named Director of Bands at SEMO. Mason was director from nearby Jackson High School from 1938–1957. Dr. Mark Scully, principal at Jackson High School, persuaded Mason to come to the university when Scully became president of the campus in 1956.

The *Sagamore* of 1976 wrote of Mason's accomplishments:

> Since 1957 SEMO football fans watched the Golden Eagles (Marching Band) perform under the direction of LeRoy Mason of the music department. This year, Mason will retire after serving the college for 19 years with an impressive record and a hard act to follow.
>
> Mason developed the college band into the marching team that has won national fame with 23 halftime appearances at professional football games, a Super Bowl performance in 1971, and the most national television time of any band over the last 16 years. The

Eagles honored their retiring director at homecoming with a special formation of 'LEROY MASON' and performed *A Jolly Good Fellow* on the field. Mason also acted as the grand marshal for the homecoming parade (141).

Following Mason's retirement in 1977, John Locke was appointed to the position of Director of Bands.

During Robert M. Gifford's tenure as Director of Bands from 1981–2004, the Golden Eagles grew from 70 members to 170 and continued the tradition of annual appearances for the St. Louis Football Cardinals, as well as the Atlanta Falcons and the Indianapolis Colts. The Golden Eagles also received invitations to perform for the Aloha Bowl and the Indianapolis 500 Race. The band was twice named the Best Dressed College Band in the nation by the National Association of Uniform Manufacturers. Assistant Directors of Bands during this period included James W. Erdman, Andrew Classen, Alzie Walker, and Barry W. Bernhardt.

During the same time period, the University's band program grew from three ensembles to eight performing groups, and the Symphonic Wind Ensemble performed at five MMEA Conferences as well as two CBDNA Divisional Conferences. The ensemble also performed ten world premiers and thirteen American premiers of works for contemporary wind band. The ensemble worked with composers and conductors such as Karl Husa, Norman Lockwood, Don Freund, Jim Croft, Ray Cramer, Richard Strange, Frigyes Hidas (Hungary), Laszlo Marosi (Hungary), Geir Knutson (Norway), Col. Jaroslav Horbal (Ukraine), Franco Cesarini (Switzerland), Alois Wimmer (Austria), and Evin Nigg (Switzerland).

Under Barry W. Bernhardt's leadership, the Golden Eagles Marching Band performed at the 1999 and 2006 Edinburgh Military Tattoo in Edinburgh, Scotland.

Southeast Missouri State University
Director of Bands

1907–1917	Earl G. Beck
1918–1920	Harry L. Albert
1921–1924	Eber Roller
1924–1930	Not available
1931–1957	O. Lewis Wilcox
1957–1977	LeRoy F. Mason
1977–1980	John R. Locke
1980–1981	A. Thad Hegerberg
1981–2004	Robert M. Gifford

| 2004–2010 | Barry W. Bernhardt |
| 2010–current | Martin C. Reynolds |

Missouri State Normal School # 3 Band – 1914
Earl G. Beck, Director
University Archives in Kent photo

Missouri State Normal School #3 Military Band – 1918
Harry L. Albert, Director
Cape Girardeau County Historical Society photo

Southeast Missouri State Teachers College
Combined military and college bands – 1930
Cape Girardeau County Historical Society photo

St. Louis Community College at Meramec
Kirkwood

The College

The St. Louis Community College district was established in 1964 to serve residents of St. Louis and St. Louis County. There are four campus sites: Forest Park (St. Louis City), Florissant Valley (Ferguson), Meramec (Kirkwood), and the newest campus in west St. Louis County (Wildwood). The Meramec campus encompasses 78 acres on a site formerly occupied by St. Joseph College. St. Joseph, a small private Catholic college founded in 1889, closed in early 1960 and the land was subsequently redeveloped for the Meramec Campus. With over 12,000 students, Meramec is the largest community college in Missouri.

In the earliest years of St. Louis Community College, even before the three campuses were built, classes were being held in various high schools around the district. The first music teacher was Frances Gillett, who traveled from school to school. When temporary buildings were erected on the corner of Big Bend and Geyer Road in suburban Kirkwood, Ms. Gillett became Meramec's only music faculty member. By 1966 she had formed a choir which she directed until her retirement in 1982.

The Band

As the college grew, Ms. Gillett wanted a full-time instrumental teacher who could develop a band program to serve the increasing number of instrumental music students. Gillett, a former faculty member at the University of Michigan, contacted the University of Michigan School of Music for a referral. Doctoral student Ron Stilwell was recommended and subsequently hired to begin the undertaking in 1968.

First Director

Ron Stilwell, a native of Columbus, Ohio, received a Bachelor of Science in Music Education degree from The Ohio State University, and then taught for five years in the Ohio public schools. Pursuing graduate studies at the University of Michigan, he earned the degree of Master of Music in Wind Instrument Performance and Doctor of Musical Arts in Clarinet Performance. During his first year of doctoral study, Stilwell was selected by the university band director, William D. Revelli, to serve as the Graduate Assistant Conductor of University Bands.

Dr. Stilwell started the first band program at Meramec Community College in 1968. The first meeting of what was then called the Concert Band was on September 17, 1968. There were 15 students at the first rehearsal, and the first piece attempted was *National Emblem March.*

Stilwell relates that the ensemble was so ragged that he had to use a police whistle to keep them playing in rhythm together. At that time, and until 1975, the group rehearsed in the afternoon and was comprised strictly of Meramec students.

During the first fall semester of 1968, the small ensemble served as a pep band at basketball games. The first performance as a concert group was for the District Board of Trustees in March, 1969, and the first public appearance was in April of that year. During the next four years the band grew to a maximum of 43 student performers and gave concerts not only on the campus but at various area high schools.

In the fall of 1975, upon Dr. Stilwell's returned from a sabbatical leave, the size of the band had declined to the point that the future was in doubt. At the same time, Stilwell received a call from the struggling Kirkwood Community Band asking if he would be willing to take over as conductor of their group. Instead, Stilwell proposed that the community group join the Meramec band on the campus. An evening rehearsal time was arranged to accommodate the new adult members. The name *Concert Band* was replaced with *Symphonic Band* as the two groups joined together.

Since its inception in 1968, the Meramec Symphonic Band has distinguished itself as something beyond the typical college/community band. The maturity of performance and the difficulty of the literature undertaken place it at an attainment level more typical of senior college ensembles.

The band was selected three times to appear at the annual convention of the Missouri Music Educators Association, twice under Stilwell's direction. He continued as the director until his retirement in 2003. In addition to building a concert band, Stilwell established a highly respected jazz program during his 35-year tenure.

Dale Skornia became director of the band in 2003 for three years followed by Jason Rinehart, one year, and Gary Gackstatter in 2007 (142)

St. Louis Community College at Meramec
Director of Bands

Dr. Ronald Stilwell	1968–2003
Dale Skornia	2003–2005
Jason Rinehart	2005–2006
Gary Gackstatter	2007

St. Louis Community College at Meramec Band – 1970
Ron Stilwell, Director
St. Louis Community College archive photo

Truman State University
Kirksville

Formerly
Missouri State Normal School # 1
Northeast Missouri State Teachers College
Northeast Missouri State College
Northeast Missouri State University

The University

Joseph Baldwin opened the North Missouri Normal School and Commercial College in 1867. In 1870 Missouri's General Assembly gave Baldwin's private college the distinction as the First District Normal School. It was the first institution of higher education authorized by state law for the primary purpose of preparing teachers for public schools. Later, additional Normal Schools would be authorized in Maryville, Warrensburg, Springfield, and Cape Girardeau, Missouri.

Although the state legislature granted Joseph Baldwin's school in Kirksville the title of Missouri State Normal School # 1, thirteen years earlier, in 1857, St. Louis established Harris Teachers College, a normal "type" school to train teachers for placement in the city's elementary schools. The same type of teacher training institution, Stowe Teachers College, was established in St. Louis for colored students in 1890.

In 1919 the First District Normal School became known as the Northeast Missouri State Teachers College. Another name change came in 1967 when the school was known as Northeast Missouri State College. In 1972 the college became Northeast Missouri State University. The new name, Truman State University, became official on July 1, 1996.

Often called "Kirksville State Teachers College" or "Kirksville State College," the city name of Kirksville was never part of the official name of the institution.

The Band

The Northeast Missouri State Teachers College band was started by Professors R. E. Valentine and Biggerstaff in 1928 to replace what reportedly was a "noisemaker at ball games" that had been organized informally by students in 1923. The band of 1928 was more than a concert organization as it was known some decades later, but was used to enhance celebrations of various types throughout the campus and the community. The Teachers College Band could regularly be seen and heard at ball games, civic activities, and performed summer concerts sponsored by Kirksville merchants.

Valentine, the principal supporter of the band movement, said, "The popularity of bands in communities throughout the United States is increasing to such an extent that it seems only a few years until every town and hamlet will have its own band organization. I would say that there are some thirty-five or forty thousand high school orchestras and probably as many bands throughout the country. It is therefore quite fitting that we, as a teachers college, should be sponsoring a real band and preparing teachers to go out into the communities and carry on such activity" (143).

Paul Strub, Director
1947–1962

Paul Strub was a 1939 graduate of Northeast and became the band director in 1947. Strub taught in the St. Louis area and played trombone with the St. Louis Philharmonic Orchestra. He earned his doctorate degree from the University of Kansas. Strub was a dynamic individual and was successful in building a band program that included local concerts, tours to area high schools, and marching shows. He was elected president of the Missouri Music Educators in 1959 and was awarded the Missouri Bandmaster Association Hall of Fame Award in 1975.

A former Strub student, Mary Reed wrote her reminiscences in 2004. "I was a seventeen-year-old Williamsburg, Iowa girl who came to Kirksville State Teachers College on a band scholarship in 1948. Paul Strub was a wonderful band director. Our band hats and coats were furnished but we had to supply our own slacks, blouse, and tie. When wearing band uniforms we could wear slacks on campus, but other than that, slacks on campus were taboo. Cold legs were a given" (144).

In 1962, Strub's wife was in failing health and they moved to Portales, New Mexico, where he accepted a position as the department chairman of music education at Eastern New Mexico University. He died in 1964 in Portales after an unsuccessful gall bladder operation.

Tom Duden, Director
1962–1978

Another former student of Strub's was Tom Duden, who took over the direction of the band in 1962. During his leadership the band became known as the "Marching 100." In 1973 the Marching 100 was invited to present the halftime show at the Governor's Cup game between the Kansas City Chiefs and the St. Louis Football Cardinals. Duden was invited by Governor Christopher "Kit" Bond to showcase the Northeast band at that game held in St. Louis (145).

Dan Peterson, Director

1978

In 1978, Dan Peterson took directorship of the band. He had been a very successful band director in Iowa and initiated changes that would bring prominence to the band, which also added membership to the group.

The Northeast Missouri State University Showboat Gamblers made their debut at Stokes Stadium in the fall of 1978.

When Peterson joined the NMSU faculty he made his presence felt by instituting a style of marching shows that was on the cutting edge of the band world at the time. The style, called "corps style," involved formations on the football field that were designed with two elements in mind: to portray the emotions of the music with congruent formations, and to place musicians within these formations to maximize the sound potential of the ensemble. Whether the music was dark in nature or light in emotional content, the entire show—including carefully chosen flags whose colors reflected the mood of the music and a large battery of percussion instruments that provided support and energy for the horn section—was shaped according to the dictates of the emotions suggested by the music.

This new concept replaced the "Big Ten style" in which band members marched out onto the field in columns on the yard lines and subsequently moved from their straight lines to form various pictures throughout the show. The pictures were inspired by different songs—always chosen to correlate to a theme. Musicians would then stand in their picture formations and play one song for each picture. The corps style introduced almost constant motion on the field—a much more difficult show to produce, but one which projected a continuous intensity during the performance.

Dan Peterson recalled that the name Showboat Gamblers was actually chosen by three of the band members, all of whom had participated in drum corps. In searching for a new name for the marching band, the discussion led to choosing a name that would represent northeast Missouri. When the Mississippi River was mentioned, one of the students brought up the name Gamblers. Another person added Showboat to their name. Their theme song became "Shenandoah."

Peterson recalled, "When I came to Truman we were really the first of any college in the Midwest to march corps style. I came at a time when the students were ready for a change, and it was very popular with the students who were here. And what a recruiting tool we had for the first three years! At that time high schools were just beginning to look at the corps style, and to have a college doing that with college players who could really play…it was almost like movie-star status with what we were doing at that time" (146).

In the thirteen-year period from 1979–1992, the Showboat Gamblers became well-known throughout the Midwest as a result of marching clinics that Peterson and his graduate assistants produced. The Showboat Gamblers also enjoyed performing at both Kansas City Chiefs games and for the St. Louis Football Cardinals at Busch Stadium.

The change in the marching band's halftime shows that occurred with the advent of the corps style in the late 1970s was obvious to all football fans. Concerning the new style, Peterson said, "Everybody was ready for a change, band directors across the country were ready, and we just happened to be in the right spot to make that change. I don't think, because of the traditions that schools like the University of Iowa had—or the University of Missouri—that they could have even done what we did" (147).

Missouri Normal School #1 Band – 1917
Mid-Continent Public Library archive photo

Northeast Missouri State Teachers College Band – 1952
Paul Strub, Director
Mid-Continent Public Library archive photo

University of Central Missouri
Warrensburg

Formerly
State Normal School # 2
Warrensburg Teachers College
Central Missouri State College
Central Missouri State University

The University was founded in 1871 as State Normal School, District #2, and became known as Warrensburg Teachers College. The name was changed to Central Missouri State Teachers College in 1919, Central Missouri State College in 1946, and Central Missouri State University in 1971. In 1965, the institution established a graduate school. In 2005, Missouri Governor Matt Blunt signed into law a provision authorizing Central Missouri State University to change its name to the University of Central Missouri. The new name change was made on September 20, 2006.

The Band

The first band was formed during the 1899–1900 academic year by Robert Zoll, Instructor in Drawing. By 1904 there were two bands, and in 1909, under the direction of David W. Schlosser, the band was playing at chapel and for basketball games. The band acquired uniforms with navy-blue coats and caps in 1915, while R. J. Meyer was the director.

Don Essig, who established a strong reputation as a director of circus and vaudeville bands, served as conductor from 1920–1941. Essig acquired a very large collection of historic musical instruments and vaudeville-style sound-producing novelty devices such as alarm clocks, canes, etc. These are now a highly recognized permanent collection housed in the Kirkpatrick Library and Utt Music Building on the campus. During this period of time and continuing until the early 1960s, student groups toured the area presenting programs in high schools and communities using these instruments.

Clifton A. Burmeister became the Director of Bands in 1945 and established an excellent program when many World War II veterans with strong performance skills returned to school. Members of the band during that period included the following, who achieved state and/or national recognition:

247

Frank Fendorf, high school band director at Chillicothe and later Vice President of Wingert–Jones Music, Inc., in Kansas City, and Honorary Associate Member of the American Bandmasters Association;

Edgar Summerlin, composer of the first Jazz Mass, shown nationally on NBC Television;

William (Bill) Mack, high school band director at Park Hill, Director of Bands at Missouri Western University and President of the Missouri Music Educators Association;

Lowell H. Brunner, high school band director at Odessa and Lindbergh High School in St. Louis and Tom Price, high school band director at Cameron.

Fendorf, Mack, Brunner, and Price are all elected members of the Missouri BandmastersAssociation Hall of Fame. Mack, Brunner, and Price are elected members to the Missouri Music Educators Association Hall of Fame.

In 1947 the school was emerging from World War II and the Navy training program held on the campus was being deactivated. The college was in the process of developing a new 'school spirit,' and Dean I. L. Peters approached Clifton Burmeister, Director of Bands, and told him a school fight song was needed for the football game the next weekend.

The composition, *Go Mules!,* was written over the weekend by Burmeister and has been adopted as the official school fight song. The composer was a graduate of Northwestern University in Evanston, Illinois, and later said that he patterned the song after the Northwestern fight song. The original score is framed and is on display in the Utt Music Building Instrumental Rehearsal Room. The current arrangement was written by David Holsinger in 1967. Holsinger was a graduate assistant with the band and a composition major. The extended second ending was written by Dr. Russell Coleman the same year.

The University Alma Mater was the winning entry in a 1962 contest and was composed by William S. Stoney, a music department faculty member. The words are by Carole Grainer. The current arrangement was written by Dr. Russell Coleman.

The band program remained relatively stable until a new era began under the leadership of Dr. Eugene Rousseau (1962–1964). The university began to experience enormous growth, and larger numbers of instrumental music majors arrived on campus.

Dr. Russell Coleman became Director of Bands in 1964. The first time a band from Central played at a state, regional, or national event was in 1969 when the Concert Band was invited to present a concert at the Southwestern Division Conference of the Music Educators National Conference in St. Louis. Previously the only off-campus concerts by Central Bands were occasional tours to play at regional high schools. This concert established the Central Concert Band as a major ensemble at the state, regional, and later national level. Since that time, they have been invited to present concerts at ten MMEA programs, a second SWMENC concert, and Southwestern Division Conference program for CBDNA, and twice at the International Convention of the American Bandmasters Association. Nineteen members of the prestigious American Bandmasters Association have been guest conductors with the Concert Band. Clearly, the concert presented in St. Louis marked the beginning of a new era in the history of bands at Central.

Beginning in the mid 1970s the band developed a very close relationship with Frank Erickson and Claude T. Smith, nationally recognized composers of music for the concert band. The UCM Band recorded many of their new compositions for distribution by the Summit Publishing Company and the Wingert-Jones Publishing Company. The band also recorded over 150 new compositions for the Belwin Publishing Company for use in their promotions.

During his tenure as Director of Bands, Dr. Coleman was elected to membership in the prestigious American Bandmasters Association. After his retirement he was elected to the Missouri Bandmasters Association Hall of Fame and the Missouri Music Educators Association Hall of Fame.

In the Spring of 2010 the University Wind Ensemble presented a concert in Carnegie Hall in New York City under the direction of Dr. Scott Lubaroff.

The Marching Mules gained widespread recognition through their performances at professional sporting events. The first performance was for a Kansas City Chief's game in 1963, and since that time they have performed 40 times for the Chiefs at Municipal and Arrowhead Stadiums. Their performances have been covered by ABC, CBS, and NBC televisions. The Marching Mules performed four times for the St. Louis Football Cardinals. Performances for the Kansas City Royals and Kansas City Athletics Baseball teams include the opening game three times, the American League Championship Playoffs, and the World Series.

Graduates include numerous public school band directors, university applied music professors, and currently five university band directors. Two graduates of the program, Dr. David Holsinger and Dr. Gordon Ring, have been winners of prestigious national band composition contests (148).

University of Central Missouri
Director of Bands

1899–1909	Robert L. Zoll
1909–1911	David W. Schlosser
1911–1913	Orley H. See
1913–1918	R. J. Meyer
1918–1919	Josephine Dixon
1920–1941	Don Essig
1941–1945	Alfred Bleckschmidt
1945	Marion Davies
1945–1952	Clifton A. Burmeister
1952–1956	Frank W. Lidral
1956–1962	Donald O. Braatz
1962–1964	Eugene Rousseau
1964–1996	Russell Coleman
1996–2004	Patrick Casey
2004–2005	Robert Gifford, Acting Director
2005–current	Scott Lubaroff

Central Missouri State College – 1966
Russell Coleman, Director of Bands
40 high school bands with 2400 members
performing at Homecoming

Central Missouri State College – "Mules" – 1969
Russell Coleman, Director

University of Missouri
Columbia

Formerly
State University of Missouri Agriculture College and University

The University of Missouri has provided teaching, research, and service to the people of Missouri since it was founded in 1839. The first publicly supported institution of higher education established in the Louisiana Territory; the University of Missouri was shaped in accordance with the ideals of Thomas Jefferson, an early proponent of higher education. The first commencement was in 1843. There were only two graduates, but the ceremony lasted three hours. It wasn't until 1868 that women were admitted for the first time. In 1870 the University was accorded land-grant status under the Morrill Act of 1862, prompting the Legislature to authorize a school of agriculture and mechanical arts. The University played its first intercollegiate football game in 1890. The opponent was Washington University of St. Louis. The first African-American students were admitted to the University in 1950. In 1963 the University became a four-campus system in Rolla, St. Louis, and Kansas City.

The First Band

On July 1, 1885, Lieutenant Enoch H. Crowder arrived in Columbia to relieve Lieutenant John H. Haden as Professor of Military Science and Tactics. Crowder was a Missouri native, a West Point graduate, and a licensed attorney. It was through the efforts of this soldier, a non-musician, that fostered the beginning of bands at the University of Missouri.

Although he was a strict disciplinarian, Crowder was admired and respected by the students, and his military science program quickly gained momentum. His next plan was to form a cadet band. He knew little about music but realized the importance of having music for military drills and reviews. He approached the University Board of Curators for their support. On October 1, 1885, the Curators issued a warrant for $125 for the purpose of aiding and securing a brass band with the understanding that the instruments become the property of the University. It was with this financial commitment that the first University of Missouri Band was established (149).

Frederic Pannell, Director
1885–1903

With money and approval from the University Board of Curators, Crowder now had the task of securing a director for the band. He called upon the services of Englishman Frederick

Pannell, a respected musician and composer who taught music at nearby Christian College. He was, however, a choir director and organist with limited instrumental background. Lieutenant Crowder nonetheless persuaded him to be the director of the band and paid him twenty-five dollars a month of his own money to take the job. Pannell accepted with the stipulation that he retain his position on the Christian College faculty (150).

With funds from the University and donations, the band's first instruments were purchased. This included an E–flat bass, a B–flat bass, a baritone, two tenor and two alto horns, four B–flat cornets, three E–flat cornets, an E–flat clarinet, and two bass drums. With new instruments and the endorsement from the university, the twelve charter members were eager to begin with music that they individually bought.

In the spring of 1886 the band gave its first performance. Uniformed in Prince Albert style uniforms and "stove pipe" hats, the band's concert was enthusiastically received by the community as reported later in *The Columbia Evening Missourian* (151).

By the start of the new school year in the fall of 1886 the band grew in membership and was now officially and firmly established with the University. However, Lieutenant Crowder was still unable to secure a salary for the director, Professor Pannell. In a letter to the Board of Curators, Crowder asked for payment for the instructor of the Cadet Band, who had been compensated for his services personally by Crowder. Perhaps it was due to Crowder's legal background and enthusiasm for the band that his request was granted.

Although highly praised for his contribution to the band's progress, Director Pannell was plagued with administrative details combined with letters about broken windows in the band room and missing equipment. It is perhaps strangely coincidental that during Pannell's tenure the band's rehearsal was in the attic of Academic Hall until it burned to the ground in 1892.

Pannell's troubles were very possibly of his own making, for he often left the room during University ceremonies where the band was performing. This frequent habit irritated University officials so much that the Board of Curators included a stipulation in Professor Pannell's contract that read: "The director will remain until the close of the entertainment." Soon thereafter the band accompanied the university football team to St. Louis for its first game trip. The team lost by a 43–0 score, and the band dispersed and did not reassemble for a week (152).

Pannell, the University of Missouri's first Director of Bands, retired in 1903. The Board of Curators moved quickly to employ his replacement.

Burr H. Ozment, Director

1903–1910

Burr H. Ozment was hired on November 25, 1903, as Director of the Cadet Band at a salary of forty dollars a month. Ozment had been directing a university band in Baldwin, Kansas, prior to his appointment. The new director brought a new grace and enthusiasm to the band.

Ozment moved quickly to get the thirty-one member band on the road to musical credibility. In fact, the results were so noticeable that the 1904 yearbook *Savitar* reported:

> The University of Missouri has now, for the first time, a Military Band that is a credit to the institution. The success of the Band this year is due, first, to the efforts of the Commandant of Cadets to enroll only experienced men; secondly, to the training the members have received from a competent director—something a University band has never before had; and finally, to the interest taken by the individual members and the support given them by the student body (153).

Prior to the arrival of Ozment, the band's unmusical motto, "The more noise, the more spirit," was a mark of distinction for the band members but unacceptable by the university.

The year 1910 brought an end to Ozment's ride on the wave of success. Since 1907, Director Ozment had brought some of his cadets to St. Louis to play summer concerts at Suburban Park. He would direct, and the band members—all boys—would be paid enough to afford their expenses in the following school year. Ozment claimed that the park was an "open shop," but the local musicians' union disagreed. After confrontations with the union members and some unfavorable press coverage, Director Ozment was dismissed on June 30, 1910, by the University Board of Curators (154).

George Venable, Director
1910–1945

The University turned to George Venable in the fall of 1910 to take over the leadership of the band. Venable was already well-known in Columbia as the founder of the Stephens College Orchestra. He was a string player who immediately used his talents to organize the University Orchestra in his first year. In addition, he occasionally conducted the St. Louis Symphony Orchestra (155).

During the thirty-five years that followed, Venable brought a wealth of pride to the Military Corps. For over twenty of those years, since the beginning of the annual military inspection in the Seventh Corps Area, the University Cadet Band received an A+ rating. It remained the highest honors accorded by such organizations in the Big Six Conference. The Band's success at these inspections prompted Venable to create a second musical organization—

the University Drum and Bugle Corps. In 1922 this group, under the direction of Venable's drum major, boasted ten bugles and thirteen drums (156).

As the band grew in size and ability, Professor Venable sought to expose the band to more public performances outside of the military establishment. He decided that more trips outside Columbia were necessary and that the band needed to expand its repertoire to include the music of the great composers. In addition, the band traveled to several away football games each year. Venable made certain that each one of these trips included stops at area high schools for concert performances. These performances, along with those at horse shows, fairs, and meetings, resulted in a recruitment strategy that netted over two hundred applicants for the band's sixty-five positions (157).

The year 1934 brought innovation and surprise to the band's halftime performance. For the first time the band marched on the field not only to form the traditional "M," but also the letters of opposing schools, words, and various figures. No longer would it be merely precision military marching at halftime. The "new" show-type marching band had come to the Missouri gridiron. To support this new image, the 1936 band discarded its old capes in favor of white cross belts to compliment its white trousers, cadet blue blouses, and black and gold shakos. Totally new uniforms in the school colors of black and gold were purchased in 1938.

The events of the school year 1938–39 were especially important. The band was designated by the State of Missouri World's Fair Commission to represent Missouri at the World's Fairs in both New York City and San Francisco. This was perhaps the most outstanding highlight of the band's fifty-three year history (158).

By 1946, after three decades of unprecedented success, Venable stepped down as director. He accepted, on August 31, 1946, the position as Assistant Professor of Music on a limited service basis. He remained in that position until his death on February 28, 1963.

George C. Wilson, Director
1946–1957

Wilson was a graduate of the University of Illinois, where he served as the band librarian under Dr. A. A. Harding. His Master of Arts degree was from Teachers College, Columbia University, New York City, and his Doctor of Music was from Phillips University, Enid, Oklahoma.

Following graduation from the University of Illinois he accepted a post at Kansas State Teachers College until 1939. From 1939–1946, he was Associate Professor of Music and Director of Bands at the University of Arizona, Tucson. He was appointed Professor of Music and Director of Band and Orchestra at the University of Missouri in 1946 and remained at that post until 1957. He was violist in the University Faculty String Quartet.

Prior to his arrival, the band had been part of the cadet corps program of the Military Science Department. It was through Wilson's efforts that the band was moved to the Music Department of the university.

During the ten years that Wilson led the University band he started the High School Band Day, bringing many area high school bands together for a massed band performance prior to a MU football game. MU Band Day was founded by Wilson in 1946, his first year at the university. Band Day continued until 1970.

The marching band, under Wilson's direction, took full advantage of those who learned to march serving in the military during World War II. It was during his tenure as director of bands that the name "Marching Mizzou" was coined. In the concert area, with his orchestra background, Wilson brought a symphonic style to the band program.

The manuscripts of *Old Missouri, Every True Son, Fight, Tiger, and Old Missouri* all contain the initials of G.C.W. in the top right corner. The mysterious initials were not of the composer, but that of Dr. Wilson, who arranged the familiar university songs for use by the marching band.

After ten years at the University of Missouri, Wilson was selected to be the Vice President of the internationally known National Music Camp at Interlochen, Michigan. He later became Director of the camp. At the National Music Camp (later named the Interlochen Arts Academy) he was principal conductor of the High School Symphonic Band from 1957–1979 and principal conductor of the World Youth Symphony Orchestra from 1966–1979.

In 1985, the Missouri Music Educators Association presented him with the first Hall of Fame Award. Wilson was born in Champaign, Illinois, on September 28, 1908, and died at the age of 92 on February 24, 2001 in St. Louis, where he lived in retirement (159).

Charles Emmons, Director

1958–1966

Charles Emmons came to the university in 1958 from Amarillo, Texas, where he developed a very successful high school band and orchestra program.

During his tenure as Director of Bands at the University of Missouri the band program made monumental progress, appearing at state, regional, and combined regional conventions of Music Educators National Conference and the National Convention of the Music Teachers National Association. The Symphonic Band appeared at the regional convention of the College Band Directors National Association.

Marching Mizzou, under his direction, received national recognition with performances at bowl games on national television, and it was Emmons who designed the famous floating

"Flip Tigers," MIZZOU–TIGERS formation that was first introduced at the Orange Bowl in 1960. It has become the signature field formation of Marching Mizzou ever since.

"That sort of thing hadn't been done before," Emmons recalled. "One game I left out the floating MIZZOU–TIGERS formation and received so many letters of complaint that it has been a part of every half-time show" (160).

In 1966 Emmons became the chairman of the music department and retired in 1982. He died in Columbia, Missouri on November 21, 2000 at the age of 83.

Alexander Pickard, Director
1966–1982

When Emmons became chairman of the music department in 1966, Assistant Band Director, Dr. Alexander Pickard, succeeded his as director of the university bands. Pickard transformed the Golden Girls from a line of twirlers into a dance troupe and added a flag corps to accentuate the music.

Under his direction, the band traveled to Hawaii and to England to play at Wembley Stadium for the Football Cup Finals. During his tenure, Dr. Pickard recorded three albums—*Music at Mizzou* (1968), *The Bicentennial Album* (1976), and the *Music of Ol' Mizzou* (1981). During Pickard's leadership of the band program, Mini Mizzou was formed to perform at functions both within the university community and outside the greater Columbia area. In addition, he organized the MU Alumni Band that annually paraded at homecoming each year.

In 1982 Pickard was appointed assistant department chairman, and Dr. Dale Kennedy, former director of bands at Wichita (Kansas) State University, succeeded him as Director of Bands (161).

University of Missouri – Columbia
Director of Bands

1885–1903	Frederick Pannell
1903–1910	Burr H. Ozment
1910–1945	George Veneable
1946–1957	George C. Wilson
1958–1966	Charles Emmons
1966–1982	Alexander Pickard
1982–1987	Dale Kennedy
1988–2001	Dale Lonis
2002–2010	Thomas O'Neal

State University of Missouri
Agriculture College and University
Cadet Band – 1896
Frederick Pannell, Director
University of Missouri archive photo

University Military Band – 1920
George Venable, Leader
University of Missouri archive photo

University of Missouri Concert Band – 1958
Charles Emmons, Director
University of Missouri archive photo

MARCHING MIZZOU
Sugar Bowl - Half-time Show
January 1, 1966

P. A.	Action-Formation	Music
No PA	ENTRANCE Block Band	Drum Cadence
"Ladies and Gentlemen, The Pride of Missouri - MARCHING MIZZOU, Charles L. Emmons, Director Richard L. Hills, Ass't Director with Robert Hutcherson and Robert Williams Drum Majors."	↓ Waltz Step ↓	Missouri Waltz
Cue: Band halts. "And now a little drill."	Changing to	I Ain't Down Yet Everything's Coming up Roses
Cue: Band halts. "It's Tea For Two".	Kick Routine	Tea For Two
Cue: Band halts and bows. "Presenting our Champion Twirlers Miss Patti Gram and Mr. Denis Knock".	Facing West	Orange Bowl March
No PA	RAZZLE - DAZZLE DRILL ending in block	Bye Bye Birdie segue Say It With Music
Cue: Band halts in block. "Here is our Famous Floating MIZZOU - TIGERS".	**MIZZOU** to **TIGERS**	Fight Tiger

Washington University in St. Louis
The University

Washington University in St. Louis is a private research university located in suburban St. Louis. Founded in 1853, and named for George Washington, the university is made up of seven graduate and undergraduate schools. Because of numerous Washington Universities in the United States, the Board of Trustees added the phrase "in St. Louis" to the official name in 1976.

The University was conceived by 17 St. Louis business leaders concerned by the lack of institutions of higher learning in the Midwest. Financial problems plagued the new school for several decades after its founding. The institution had no backing of a religious organization or government support. The earliest name of the school was "Eliot Seminar," named for a Unitarian minister and grandfather of the Nobel Prize laureate poet T.S. Eliot. In 1854, the Board of Trustees changed the name to "Washington Institute." In 1856 the school adopted the name "Washington University."

The Band

The Department of Music was established in 1948 and the first band concert was presented in 1949 under the direction of George Doren. In 1951 Clark Mitze became the director of the band and held that position until 1965. From 1952–1965, two names became prominent in the effort to organize wind music concerts on the campus: Clark Mitze and Lewis Hilton. Both were professors in the music department. In his 14 years at Washington University Mitze was never given the title of Director of Bands. Hilton's interest was wind chamber music and Mitze's centered on the concert band. In later years Hilton became the first editor of *Research in Music Education* for the Missouri Music Educators Association. It was through the efforts of both Mitze and Hilton that each year saw either a wind chamber music concert or a band concert at Washington University. There is no record that the school had a marching band, although athletic teams had been part of the university since 1900.

In 1954 Mitze organized a band concert that featured well-known trumpeter Raphael Mendez. In 1956 a concert was presented to coincide with the Music Educators National Conference meeting held in St. Louis. A performance of Persichetti's *Symphony for Band*, commissioned by Washington University, premiered at the conference. According to the personnel roster of the concert programs, virtually all concerts were a collaborative effort between the university music students and selected instrumentalists from the community.

In 1965 Mitze left Washington University to take a position with the National Endowment for the Arts in Washington D. C. After his departure, Hilton continued to schedule wind chamber music concerts, but the bulk of wind music responsibilities—both band and additional chamber concerts—went to graduate students pursuing advanced degrees. Those included John Shoemaker (1966–1968), James Mabry (1967–1969), Robert Casey (1969–1971), and William Jacoby (1971–1792).

In 1972 the Music Department employed Dan Presgrave as the first "official" Director of Bands. Leigh Gerdine, the department chair, was interested in strengthening the band program that was in decline. Presgrave was a graduate of Ohio University (Bachelor of Fine Arts) and Washington University (Master of Music Education). The solution Presgrave offered was to audition students on campus and accept those qualified to play in a college band, and then open the auditions to the outside music community for proper instrumentation and strength. Non-students were expected to make the same commitment to rehearsals and musical goals as those enrolled at the university. Two band concerts and one chamber music concert were scheduled each semester.

The format was adopted in 1972, and by 1976 there were enough players auditioning for the wind ensemble that a second university band was formed, which also functioned as a "pep band" for athletic events. Later the pep band separated from the Department of Music and was sponsored by the athletic department.

The Washington University Wind Ensemble had a productive musical life span of 26 years from 1972–1998. This included five performance at the Missouri Music Educators Conference and three invitations and two performances at the College Band Directors National Association annual conference.

In 1998 a new department chair proclaimed that all music ensemble participants must be students enrolled in the university, and off-campus participants would not be allowed. As a result, the Washington University Wind Ensemble diminished into a small group of chamber winds (162).

Washington University in St. Louis
Band Directors

1949–1951	George Doren
1952–1965	Clark Mitze
1966–1968	John Shoemaker
1967–1969	James Mabry
1969–1971	Robert Casey
1971–1972	William Jacoby
1972–2010	Dan Presgrave

Washington University in St. Louis
Wind Ensemble – 1978
Dan Presgrave, Director

HIGH SCHOOL BANDS

Chapter 9

HIGH SCHOOL BANDS

———————⊸ ⊹⊱⊰⊹ ⊹⊱——————

In the early 1900s the emergence of bands as a club activity became part of the social fabric of the high school. The band began to take its place with other music interest groups, including orchestra and vocal ensembles, as part of the fine arts curriculum.

The first instrumental ensemble in Missouri public schools was an orchestra of eight members in 1896 at Central High School in St. Louis (163). The earliest recorded high school band in Missouri (1900) was the Missouri Training School (for boys) in Boonville with nine members, which included two bass horns, three tenor horns, two cornets, bass drum, and snare drum (164).

McKinley High School in St. Louis organized the first public high school band as recorded in the 1908 *Carnation* yearbook by editor J. Leemann:

The McKinley High School has always striven to be the predecessor—to lead while others follow—and this year, as always, fully attained its desire.

During the opening month of the school year, another organization was added to the list of McKinley societies. We feel free to assert that, of all the societies, this one is really a *school* organization; its aim being to benefit the entire school as well as the individual members. Henceforth McKinley athletics and the school in general will have the added feature of a Concert Military Band.

The original idea was presented by Leo Wolfsohn to Mr. Burr, who, being delighted with the plan, took up the work with the originator and, after the consent of Principal Morrison had been secured, the procuring of members and the equipping of the band was immediately commenced.

Of course, like all new things, the beginning is small, but it is gradually increasing and it is only a question of time before the band will be one of the most complete, and under the superior direction of Mr. Burr, one of the best.

Though the band is growing and steadily improving, we still feel the need of more material assistance. It is unnecessary for us to speak of the value of the band to the school; that readily appeals to every loyal student and we only beg the permission to solicit your membership (165).

Early pictures at McKinley and other high schools as well, indicate that the school was co-educational, but many clubs and subjects were segregated by gender. Math and science classes were male-dominated, as was the Glee Club, Latin Club, and Debate Team. Women had their own activities to pursue, such as the Ukulele Club, Dulcimer Club, Sewing Club, and dance organizations. The orchestra was one exception to this cultural division. Both men and women participated. The band was a male activity. This could be attributed with the association that bands had with the military and later with athletic events.

St. Louis McKinley High School Band – 1908
First high school band in Missouri
Mr. Burr, Director
The Carnation yearbook photo

Rolla High School Band – 1913
John Scott Director
Susan Miller family collection photo

Liberty Odd Fellows Home Band – 1920
Photo courtesy David W. Short

Lincoln High School Band – Kansas City– 1920
State Historical Society of Missouri Photo

Central High School Band – St. Louis – 1922
C. H. Kelbaugh, Director
St. Louis Public Library archive photo

Northeast High School Band – Kansas City – 1923
Mid Continent Public Library photo

Springfield High School Band – 1923
Richie Robertson, Director
Springfield-Greene County Historical Society photo

Webster Groves High School Band – 1924
William B. Heyne, Director
Echo yearbook photo

Jackson High School Band – 1925
A. W. Roloff, Director
Silver Arrow yearbook photo

Cape Central High School Band – 1925
Miss Frieda Rieck, Director
Girardot yearbook photo

Normandy High School Band – 1926
Mr. Hollman, Director
Saga yearbook photo

Webster Groves High School Band – 1926
Hans J. Lemcke, Director
Former member of Sousa's Band
Echo yearbook photo

DeSoto High School Band – 1928
Yearbook photo

Billings High School Band – 1928
Yearbook photo

St. Charles High School Band – 1929
Mr. Snyder, Director
Yearbook photo

Maplewood High School Band – 1930
Mr. Van Meter, Director
Maple Leaves yearbook photo

Ferguson Junior High School
Drum and Bugle Corps – 1931
Ferguson Historical Society photo

Harrisonville High School Band – 1932
Picture taken on the steps of the
Cass County court house

Missouri Day massed bands at American Royal
Kansas City – 1933
Wentworth Military Academy, Lexington High School, Maryville, Joplin,
Raytown, Marceline, Hamilton, Humansville, Mount Vernon
State Historical Society of Missouri photo

Ferguson High School Band – 1935
John Crockett, Director
Ferguson was first high school in St. Louis County (1877)
Ferguson Historical Society photo

Kansas City Central High School Band – 1936
W. C. Schlager, Director
Kansas City Public Library photo

Kansas City Westport High School Band – 1939
Mid Continent Public Library archive photo

Camdenton High School Band – 1939
Mr. Jeffers, Director
The Tiger yearbook photo

Cape Central High School Band 1940
William Shivelbine, Director
Girardot yearbook photo

Washington High School Band – 1945
Roena Beckman, Director
Photo courtesy Gene Hunt

De Soto High School Band – 1945
Photo Courtesy Blaine Olson

Wardell High School Band – 1945
Joe English, Director

William Chrisman High School Band – 1947
Independence
Mid Continent Public Library archive photo

Caledonia High School Band – 1948
Yearbook photo

Sikeston High School Band – 1948
Keith Collins, Director
Photo courtesy Robert Collins

Nixa High School Band – 1949
Yearbook photo

Liberty High School Band – 1949
Yearbook photo
Mid Continent Public Library archive photo

Lilbourn High School Band – 1950
W. L. Giddens, Director
Photo courtesy Dennis Nail

Lincoln High School Band – 1951
Joplin

Lamar High School Band – 1952
Hubert Owens, Director
Yearbook photo

Illmo-Fornfelt High School Band – 1952
Yearbook photo

El Dorado Springs High School Band – 1952
Vernon Wade, Director
Yearbook photo

Perryville High School Band – 1953
Robert Adams, Director

Holcomb High School Band – 1954
Bryan Parnell, Director
Photo courtesy Dennis Nail

Kirkwood High School Band – 1955
Burton Isaac, Diector

Emerson-Philadelphia High School Band – 1957
Don Mozingo, Director
Photo courtesy Jeff Mozingo

Douglass High School Band -1959
Last Douglass High School band before closing of school in 1959
Hannibal Public Library photo

Sikeston High School Freshman Band – 1960
Ed Carson, Director
Photo courtesy Robert Collins

Ruskin High School Band – 1960
Tournament of Roses Parade
Kenneth and Nancy Seward, Directors
Photo courtesy Michael Tope

Palmyra High School Band – 1961
Don Mozingo, Director
Photo courtesy Jeff Mozingo

University City High School Band – 1964
Roger Warner, Director
First Missouri band to perform at Midwest Band Clinic
Yearbook photo

Lee's Summit High School Band – 1972
Keith House, Director
Mid Continent Public Library archive photo

Kennett High School Band – 1980
Dennis Nail, Director
Yearbook photo

Parkway West High School Band – 1984
John Baker, Director
Photo courtesy Bob Waggoner

NATIONAL
BAND
CONTEST

Chapter 10

THE NATIONAL BAND CONTEST

School bands in the early 1900s were organized as clubs, often to provide encouragement at athletic events. Latin clubs, debate societies, glee clubs, and orchestras found their way into the educational curriculum before the band.

In 1923, Edgar B. Gordon brought attention to the band's prominence when he addressed the Music Supervisors National Conference held in Cleveland. "The high school band is no longer an incidental school enterprise prompted largely by the volunteer services of a high school teacher who happens to have had some band experience…" (166). He advocated that: "[band] be assigned to a definite place in the school schedule with a daily class period under a trained instructor and with credit allowed for satisfactory work done" (167).

C. G. Conn

Charles G. Conn was a businessman and bandleader who "had been making rubber stamps in Elkhart, Indiana in 1875 when he experimented with adding rubber to his trumpet mouthpiece" (168). Seeing an opportunity with the interest in band instruments, Conn moved from mouthpiece manufacturing to producing brass instruments. He located his new business along the St. Joseph River in Elkhart. As a civic leader, Conn owned the *Elkhart Truth* newspaper and later became mayor of Elkhart, a state legislator in Indiana, and then United States Senator. In 1915, the C.G. Conn Band Instrument Company was sold to C. D. Greenleaf (169).

After World War I, band programs became integrated into the school curriculum and the popularity of the town band began to decline. The emergence of radio and the recording industry as an entertainment medium became a concern of the music industry that produced sheet music, pianos, and musical instruments.

The National Band Tournament

1923

The Music Industries Chamber of Commerce represented publishers, manufacturers, and retail dealers. In 1923 their annual convention was to be held in Chicago. Entertainment for the convention was the responsibility of the Chicago Piano Club that year. Industrial music groups were in vogue at the time and Victor J. Grabel, director of the Western Electric Company band, suggested the idea of a band contest for the convention.

With quality instruments now being made in America and band programs incorporated into the school music curriculum, the industry viewed the band contest as an opportunity for increased sales.

The contest idea was endorsed and Carl D. Greenleaf, president of C.G. Conn, Ltd., agreed to organize and raise funds for the event. Greenleaf was president of the Band Instrument Manufacturers' Association, and through his efforts $10,000 for the contest was raised (170).

The Association engaged the services of an advertising agent, Patrick Henry, to publicize the contest. The newspapers called the event a tournament, and winners would be offered $6,000 in cash prizes plus new instruments, medals, and ribbons. Additional stories announced that 6,000 high school students from 200 schools across the nation would participate. To stimulate interest, Henry wrote that bands would be playing jazz, and some even had girls among their ranks. The entrance of a Negro band from Hannibal, Missouri drew attention to the diversity of the contest.

Douglass High School

Douglass High School in Hannibal was the only high school in Marion and Ralls County to serve the education of African-American students. Hannibal is located in both counties. Douglass opened in 1878 and closed with the court ordered desegregation act in 1955. The 1923 the Douglass High School band was under the direction of the high school principal, Martin A. Lewis. Douglass was the only band from Missouri to participate in the National Band Contest. At the contest of 1923, twenty-six high school bands and four grammar school bands participated. Douglass came in last in the high school competition.

In 1923 the appearance of the Douglass High School band was a bold educational and cultural accomplishment for the students and their director. The Wabash Railroad provided passenger service from Des Moines to Chicago through Hannibal. The band used the railroad to travel to Chicago, since charter buses were a future form of transportation. Housing in Chicago for the boys was provided at the Navy Pier while girls stayed at the YWCA. There were no girls in the Douglass band.

The National Band Tournament of 1923
"35 Carefully Selected Bands"

When only 35 school bands applied to play in the band tournament, public relations maverick Patrick Henry pronounced: "… 200 bands had been eliminated, by preliminary competitions, and that 35 carefully selected bands would appear…" (171). Half of the bands in the contest were from Chicago and the surrounding area. Five bands did not show up.

The first National Band Contest was neither well-organized nor well run. A panel of judges was announced to adjudicate the event. Only one judge showed up. Lieutenant William H. Santelmann, director of the United States Marine Corps Band in Washington, D.C., provided the only evaluation for the contest. Directors were unhappy that only one person judged their band when a panel of experts had been advertised.

The first national contest did not require any prescribed music, and each band played from its individual repertory. In addition, bands of any size could participate. The smallest band had 25 members from Paw Paw, Michigan, and the largest with 80 members was from Fostoria, Ohio. Fostoria High School, under the direction of John W. Wainwright, won the $1,000 first prize. Joliet grammar school, directed by Guido Mattel, won first place and $1,000 in their division, which included only four bands.

Future Contests

Music merchants, sponsors of the contest, considered their first efforts a success and planned to continue their sponsorship in the future. Their goal of increased sales of instruments and music could be realized through school band competitions. The Committee on Instrumental Affairs of the Music Supervisors National Conference (later MENC) endorsed future national competitions but wanted their organization to be more involved in future events.

After considerable deliberation it was agreed that the 1924 contest would be served by three music groups. The National Bureau for the Advancement of Music would provide executive services. The Music Supervisors National Conference would enforce rules regarding adjudication, selection of judges, repertoire, and entrance qualification. The Band Instrument Manufacturers Association agreed to underwrite the cost of the contest.

"The 1924 contest specified that a series of elimination contests, first in the several states and then in each of five regions, precede a national competition. The committee was also reluctant to conduct a series of contests unless they could be made educational. Therefore, a repertoire list was developed from which a required number would be chosen each year and from which participating bands might select a second number" (172).

The 1924 contest did not materialize, nor did the one scheduled for 1925. "In 1926, 15 states conducted official contests. Three regional contests ensued and the national contest was held in Fostoria, Ohio, with 13 bands representing 10 states" (173). Fostoria was selected as the host city based on their first place ranking in the 1924 band tournament. Fostoria placed second in 1926 with first place honors going to Joliet Township High School directed by A. R. McAllister. Other participants included:

> Ogden, Utah
> Louisville, Kentucky
> Ashtabula Harbor, Ohio
> Council Bluffs, Michigan
> Houston, Texas
> Lockport, New York
> Lowell, Massachusetts
> Marion, Indiana
> Paw Paw, Michigan

An important outcome from the Fostoria contest in 1926 saw the founding of the National School Band Association.

Subsequent Contests

The success of the 1926 National Band Contest was duplicated and enlarged through the next decade. The 1928 contest saw the standardization of instrumentation, and the following year bands were divided into Class A or Class B according to size. Due to economic conditions, the 1932 and 1933 contests were not held. It was in 1933 in Evanston, Illinois that divisional ratings were introduced, changing the competitive climate of the event significantly (174).

The 1934 contest was held in Des Moines, and Cleveland hosted the 1936 event. The National Band Contest had grown so large by 1938 it was decided that regional contests would replace a national event. The number of bands was not the only factor that changed the format. Music administrators were concerned about the competitive nature of the event, and school districts were as concerned about the cost and loss of classroom time. Kansas City became a regional host city and the Hotel Muehlebach became the contest headquarters.

Retrospective… "The results were amazing"

Emil A. Holz, in his dissertation "The School Band Contest of America of 1923," provides the importance of this one national event for the future development of bands:

> The Schools Band Contest of America, conceived as an entertainment and promotional project, impelled leaders in music education and in the music industry to work together

toward long-range goals by spectacular means. The results were amazing. Instrumental music was firmly established in the public schools of America. Enrollments increased phenomenally and performance standards reached heights unattainable by the casually organized band and orchestras of the 1920s. For all its faults, the 1923 band tournament changed the course of music education history (175).

MARCHING
BAND
FESTIVALS

Chapter 11

MARCHING BAND FESTIVALS

The early town bands were concert groups performing for community and civic events. These concerts were played on the town square or in a shady grove during the summer months. Some groups did not continue marching in the traditional military style except to lead an occasional parade or funeral procession. Several exceptions may be found in the records of town bands, especially the Carthage Light Guard Band which was featured performing a "fancy drill" at a band tournament held in Clinton. High School marching band festivals or contests became popular after World War II.

Jackson Band Festival
Established–1945

LeRoy Mason, band director at Jackson High School, organized the first high school marching band festival in 1944. The festival brought bands together to perform individually and then together in a massed band finale. On September 9, 1945, the Jackson Board of Education discussed the possibility of making the band festival an annual event. Mason had come to Jackson in 1939 after teaching in Riverview Gardens for three years. The Jackson marching festival led to the establishment of the Southeast Missouri High School Band Association. With the success of the Jackson Band Festival, other schools in the area later established their own contests. However, the Jackson Band Festival continues each fall as organized in 1944.

Northeast Missouri Marching Band Festival
Established–1949

The Northeast Missouri Marching Band Festival was established in 1949 by J. M. Dillinger, Director of Bands at Hannibal High School. The event led to the establishment of the

Mark Twain Bandmaster's Association. The festival was a non-competitive event and was designed by Dillinger to provide smaller schools an opportunity to perform. The format was to have each school march on the field and play one selection, and then all bands assembled on the field with a guest director.

A program from the 3rd Annual Festival in 1951 listed the following participating schools:

Bowling Green	Charles Wells, Director
Canton	Raymond Martin
Hannibal	J. M. Dillinger
LaGrange	Richard Pettibone
Louisiana	Douglas Emerson
Salisbury	John Culler
Shelbina	Joe Mustion

Four States Marching Band Festival – Carthage
Established–1966

Robert Stanfield, the Carthage High School band director, organized the Four State Marching Band Festival in 1966. It drew school from Missouri, Oklahoma, Arkansas, and Kansas. As the festival grew it was incorporated into the Carthage Maple Leaf Festival, a week-long civic event.

Southeast Missouri Band Association Marching Band Contest
Established–1969

The Southeast Missouri Band Association Marching Band Contest was started in 1969 and was held in addition to the Jackson festival. Ron Nall of Cape Girardeau and Bil Salyer of Poplar Bluff organized the 1969 contest, which was held at Caruthersville High School. The contest rotated among various schools for several years until a permanent site was established at Charleston High School. In 1997 the Southeast Missouri High School Band Association celebrated the 53rd festival at four different sites—Poplar Bluff, Jackson, Kennett, and Perryville.

Washington High School Marching Festival
Established–1969

In the fall of 1969 the Four Rivers Conference sponsored a marching band festival which was limited to conference schools. The event was held at the Washington City Park football field. Gene Hunt, band director at Washington High School, was the festival manager.

The first Four Rivers Conference Invitational Marching Band Festival was held on October 11, 1969. The festival judges were John Patterson, Columbia Hickman High School, Darrell Hendon, Fulton High School, and Carl Walker, East Central College. Field competition winners were:

Class L:

    1 – Washington

    2 – Parkway West

    3 – Herculaneum

Class M:

    1 – Pacific

    2 – St. Clair

    3 – Hermann

Since the 1969 festival drew very few conference bands, it was decided in the fall of that year to change the format to an invitational event drawing from outside the original Four Rivers Conference.

In 1970 the name was changed to the Washington High School Marching Band Festival. Hunt remained the festival manager until 1993 when he retired from teaching. Troy Bunkley became the festival manager in 1994.

The 25th Anniversary Festival program listed 111 different schools that had participated in the Washington High School Marching Band Festival through the years.

Carrollton Band Day

Established–1970

Carrollton High School band director, Robert Ward, was the founder of the band festival which started in the fall of 1970. Ward was the Band Day director for six years (1970–1976) followed by Murphy Tetley for four years (1977–1981). Ron Schuler directed the event for 25 years (1982–2007) followed by Dave Phillips (2008), all being the Director of Bands at Carrollton High School.

Greater St. Louis Marching Band Festival

Established–1971

In the fall of 1969, Howard Stamper, President and CEO of Banquet Foods, was chairman of the music committee for the annual VP Parade in St. Louis. The parade started in the late 1800s as a fall festival with floats and marching bands to celebrate a successful harvest. Stamper suggested a field contest for those bands participating in the 1969 parade, but before the plan could be implemented Mr. Stamper passed away.

In his memory, the first contest was held in the fall of 1971 with eight bands at Francis Field on the campus of Washington University. Paris, Illinois was the first place winner. Year number two was rained out.

The festival continued under the joint sponsorship of the VP Music Committee and the Music Department of the University of Missouri St. Louis as part of the Extension Division. Dr. Warren Bellis, Director of Bands at UMSL, was named Festival Chairman. C. Herbert Duncan, Coordinator of Fine Arts Education for the Normandy School District, served as the Festival Coordinator.

Various high school football fields were used for the festival in the early years until Lindenwood College in St. Charles offered their new Astroturf field which had been donated by the St. Louis Football Cardinals. The festival began to expand into a morning session for bands not involved in the VP Parade. This enthusiastic growth reached the point where the Lindenwood stadium was too small. Fortunately, this point coincided with the decision to move the parade from September to July 4th.

In 1984 the Greater St. Louis Marching Band Festival moved to Busch Stadium in downtown St. Louis. 50 bands participated from three states with 5,000 participants. Over 10,000 watched the all day event.

In June of 1994, Dr. Warren Bellis, co-founder of the festival, died after serving as Festival Director for 22 years. C. Herbert Duncan became Festival Director one year prior.

The St. Louis Baseball Cardinals announced in 1995 that Busch Stadium would no longer be available for non-baseball events. The stadium was revamped for baseball only. Only a few blocks away a new indoor facility was being built and in 1996 the Greater St. Louis Marching Band moved to the Dome at America's Center. For five years the facility was named the Trans World Dome and in 2002 it was renamed the Edward Jones Dome. The use of an indoor facility with practice and warm-up rooms gave bands a premium venue for performances. Thirteen to fourteen thousand people annually watch the festival.

Music Bowl – Missouri
Established–1978

The national Music Bowl program was founded in 1977 by Beatrice Foods Company to recognize and support high school marching band programs as well as local charitable organizations.

Music Bowl–Missouri was introduced in 1978 and held on the campus of Central Missouri State University in Warrensburg. Dr. Russell Coleman, Director of Bands and Chair of the Department of Music, was the regional Music Bowl director. Through the early 1980s, the national Music Bowl contest grew to 13 regional events covering most of the 50 states. The Music Bowl concept also expanded to include a national competition. Regional winners were invited to march in the annual Orange Bowl Parade in Miami, and then perform in the Great Bands of the Orange Bowl to determine a national winner.

The Beatrice Foods Company was sold and dissolved in 1988. All regional Music Bowl festivals were discontinued with the exception of Missouri. Central Missouri State University continued to host the Music Bowl event until the retirement of Dr. Coleman. The university elected to change the name in 1999 to the *Festival of Champions* and used the event as a fundraiser for band scholarships.

Music Bowl Champions:

1978	Normandy	Robert Boedges, Director
1979	Winnetonka	Charles Menghini
1980	Jefferson City	Tabor Stamper
1981	Poplar Bluff	Bill Salyer
1982	Winnetonka	Charles Menghini
1983	Jefferson City	Gene Kirkham
1984	Kickapoo	Bill Palen
1985	Willard	Rhonda King
1986	Willard	Rhonda King
1987	Parkway West	John Baker
1988	Kickapoo	Bill Palen
1989	Kickapoo	John Robichaud
1990	Parkway West	John Baker
1991	Willard	Chris Church
1992	Willard	Chris Church
1994	Blue Valley	Martin Dunlap
1995	Willard	Chris Church
1996	Blue Valley	Martin Dunlap
1997	Jenks, Tulsa, Oklahoma	Bob Early

Ozarko Marching Band Competition

Founded–1972

The Ozarko Marching Band Competition was founded by Director of Bands, Robert Scott, at Southwest Missouri State University in 1972. The name *OZARKO* was taken from the university yearbook of the same name. After serving nine years as Director of Bands, Scott was named as Head of the Music Department in 1982. In 1985 the name of the event was changed to Ozarko Invitational Marching Festival under Director of Bands, Jerry Hoover.

Missouri Marching Band Festivals

Bi-State Marching Invitational	Potosi
Blue Springs Marching Invitational	Blue Springs
Carrollton Band Day	Carrollton
Carthage Maple Leaf Marching Festival	Carthage
Central Methodist University Band Day	Fayette
Central Rebel Invitational	Park Hills
ELDO Marching Festival	El Dorado Springs
Farmington Marching Invitational	Farmington
Francis Howell Central Coliseum Classic	St. Charles
Francis Howell Invitational	St. Charles
Greater St. Louis Marching Band Festival	St. Louis
Kahoka Parade of Champions	Kahoka
Lafayette Contest of Champions	Wildwood
Lee's Summit North Marching Festival	Lee's Summit
Marching Mizzou Champion of Champions	Columbia
Marching Warriors Marching Festival	St. Charles
Maple Leaf Marching Festival	Carthage
Missouri Day Marching Festival	Trenton
Missouri Western Tournament of Champions	St. Joseph
Odessa Marching Invitational	Odessa
Ozark Mountain Marching Festival	Reeds Spring
Ozarko Invitational Marching Festival	Springfield
Raytown Round-Up Marching Festival	Raytown
Route 66 Marching Festival	Rolla

Southeast Missouri Bandmasters Band Festival	Charleston
Ste. Genevieve Marching Festival	Ste. Genevieve
Sullivan Marching Festival	Sullivan
University of Central Missouri Festival of Champions	Warrensburg
Valhalla Marching Band Festival	Springfield
Washington High School Marching Festival	Washington
Webstock Marching Festival	Webb City
Wright City Wildcat Pride Field Competition	Wright City

Jackson Marching Festival – 1955
Massed bands in outline of State of Missouri
honoring Valle High School
Photo courtesy of Dennis Nail

MUSIC
PUBLISHING

Chapter 12

MUSIC PUBLISHING AND THE CLASSIC CONCERT BAND

Andrew Glover

Chief Operating Officer

C. L. Barnhouse Company

The label "Classic Concert Band" was developed by conductor/composer/instrumentalist Leonard B. Smith to describe the concept, style, and scope of a musical tradition most popular in the half-century, dating roughly 1880–1930. It was best exemplified on a popular scale during this era by John Philip Sousa, and also then and subsequently by Edwin Franko Goldman, Arthur Pryor, and Dr. Smith himself. An exploration into the concept of "Classical Concert Band" would be an immense project, but its core identity focused on the content of musical programming. In the most basic sense, Sousa viewed himself as an entertainer. His desire was to reach and entertain thousands of common citizens through the performances of his band, which was admittedly comprised of many of the finest wind and percussion artists of his day. He was there to entertain, primarily; if concertgoers were educated or artistically enriched in the process, it was an added benefit.

In his book, *On Conducting the Professional Concert Band*, Leonard Smith wrote:

> People attend band concerts because they enjoy music and wish to be entertained. They seek a comfortable setting or surrounding because they enjoy good music, well performed. The variety in band programming can make for an entertainment which is highly pleasurable and can be most appealing (176).

Programming

Sousa, Pryor, Goldman, and Smith all understood that proper programming—the selection of music and the pacing of it in concert—was the most essential element in pleasing the audience. While each of these conductors had his own tastes and judgments, programming of this style and era commonly centered on these kinds of music:

- Marches
- Light classical works, transcribed for band
- Featured soloists or ensembles with band accompaniment
- Popular music of the day
- Novelty selections

Much of the music used by bands of this era was transcribed from other mediums, primarily orchestral literature. Sousa was also keen to utilize popular music of the day. Famously, he performed Scott Joplin rags at the St. Louis World's Fair of 1904, to an auspicious response.

Town Band

Sousa, Pryor, Goldman, and others were headliners in this "business band" circuit, a moniker suggested by Harry Schwartz in "Bands of America." However, the Classic Concert Band was very much a part of thousands of communities all across the country. In the era before radio and television, and even when sound recording was in its infancy, live music was a prominent part of local culture.

Town bands, which were composed largely of amateur and adult musicians, and which predated the school band programs, provided musical entertainment to local citizens. These bands, in all sizes and levels of musical skill, performed for civic events, parades, and gave concerts for the entertainment of all. These town bands emerged as a distinctive part of the American sociological and cultural landscape. In 1910, if you wanted to hear music, you had two basic options: make it yourself, or go hear it performed by someone else. Millions of Americans received their introductions to "classical" music by hearing the local town band battle its way through "The Emperor Waltz" or the "Minuet in G."

From a purely musical standpoint, while Sousa's main objective was to attain commercial success through entertaining mass audiences, his band enjoyed a reputation of the finest in musical quality. Sousa's Band featured many of the best players of his day, and Sousa could afford to acquire the finest players. The bands of the average American small town enjoyed no such luxury. These were usually volunteer groups, with the leader perhaps receiving a stipend generated from local donors. As such, the musicians ranged in skill, to a considerable degree. Sousa's band could play Wagner's "Tannhauser Overture" or Strauss' "The Blue Danube Waltz" on a musical par with the major orchestras of the day, but such works were beyond the musical scope of the typical American town band. Carl Fischer, John Church, Theodore Presser, and other firms published many Sousa marches, as well as literal and difficult arrangements of many classical works transcribed for band by arrangers, including Mayhew Lake, L. P. Laurendeau, V. F. Safranek, M. C. Meyrelles, and others. It is reasonable to assume, from the success of these publishers during this era, than there were indeed some bands capable of playing such difficult works. It's also logical to assume that many bands attempted works well beyond their reach. Others had to explore alternative solutions.

The problems caused by this phenomenon were not lost on a group of composers and publishers who set about to address it. Recognizing that the typical town band was several steps below the Sousa Band in musical ability, many easier works were created and published. Composers such as George D. Barnard, George Rosenkrans, Charles J. Rockwell, and Joseph Gorton wrote music which was much closer to the skill level of the average town band. Many of these composers were leaders of bands which likely were not very experienced, and hence they composed music appropriate to the ensemble out of necessity.

Early Band Publications

The earliest published works of Karl L. King, one of the most prolific composers of band music, came into print in 1909. They present an interesting combination of difficulty level. King wrote tremendous difficult marches, including some for various circus bands with which he was associated:

Robinson's Grand Entrée	1911
Barnum and Bailey's Favorite	1913
Sells Floto Triumphal	1914

At precisely the same time, King was composing and publishing a wealth of marches, waltzes, serenades, and lighter original works at what we would today consider the "Grade 2 or 2 ½ level."

The Avenger	1910
Fidelity	1911
Pride of Arizona	1912

Marches such as these sold as briskly as the "heavier" works. When King was growing up in Ohio, he played in many bands—some quite exceptional, others not so. Undoubtedly he recognized the need of music for both kinds of bands.

The Music Publishing Industry

It is interesting to note that today's world of band music publishing is largely driven by the market, which is composed in strong majority by school bands at all levels from elementary through college and university. The industry focuses much of its effort on designing products appropriate to the skill level of these various ensemble types. The school band movement is a relatively new phenomenon, first gaining major momentum in the 1930's. But the notion of composing and publishing music for bands of lower levels of ability and experience is one which actually predates the school band movement by a generation.

The Classic Concert Band declined in popularity as times changed. Audio recording and the innovations of radio and television could be considered part of this reason. The world of bands evolved from existing almost exclusively in the professional and adult town and factory band area, then into the school band movement. Today's community bands, however, continue the general concept of Classic Concert Band by entertaining citizens in communities all across America. The most successful of these, at least from the audience perspective, are those ensembles who remember that their role is to entertain through the performance of music. Programming, of course, is the key (177).

Editor's note:
Andrew Glover is Chief Operating Officer for C. L. Barnhouse Company, music publishers since 1886. He graduated from Webster Groves High School (Ed Carson, band director) and Central Methodist University (Keith House, band director). His primary instrument is the euphonium.

While still in college, Glover performed each summer with the famous Detroit Concert Band, conducted by Leonard B. Smith. He was with this band for three seasons and recorded extensively with that ensemble. Glover is producer and director of the CD recording, *On the Bandstand,* by the Town Square Cornet Band. While in high school Glover organized a circus band which reunites annually to perform in the 4th of July parade in St. Louis. The band rides on a specially designed replica of a circus band wagon pulled by a team of horses.

"Music Publishing" was written for this publication.

KANSAS CITY
SHEET MUSIC
COLLECTION

Chapter 13

THE KANSAS CITY SHEET MUSIC COLLECTION

1874–1996

The Kansas City Sheet Music Collection contains over 660 song titles published in Kansas City, Missouri, from 1874–1996. This collection is part of the University of Missouri Library System's Digital Library.

The most significant Kansas City publisher of sheet music was J. W. Jenkins' Sons Music Company, which published from the 1880s to the 1940s. Jenkins' Sons published on a national level and is perhaps best known as the publisher of Euday L Bowman's *Twelfth Street Rag*. The collection includes several notable compositions, one of which is Scott Joplin's *Original Rag*, published by the Hoffman Music Company in 1899.

The collection includes several compositions that celebrate Kansas City itself. Of particular historical relevance are pieces about the Kansas City A's baseball team, Fairyland Park, the Plaza lights, Electric Park, and the city in general.

Included in the collection with reference to Kansas City:

> *Kansas City Blues*
> *Kansas City High School Cadet March*
> *Kansas City My Home Town*
> *Kansas City Pep*
> *Kansas City's Triumphal March*

Several Kansas City composers are included in the collection, such as Charles L. Johnson and Lucien Denni, who formed their own publishing companies in order to publish sheet music.

Some of the more unusual publishing companies from the Kansas City area represented in the collection include the Kansas City Talking Machine Company and the Jones Dry Goods

Store, the latter publishing music during the first decade of the 1900's. Publications by the Woodland Music Company represent the most recent works in the collection, containing the collegiate sports composition of Milo Finley and items by Martha Fay (178).

All photos: Used by permission of the University of Missouri – Kansas City Libraries, Dr. Kenneth J. LaBudde, Department of Special Collections.

Used by permission of the University of Missouri-Kansas City Libraries,
Dr. Kenneth J. LaBudde Department of Special Collections

Used by permission of the University of Missouri-Kansas City Libraries,
Dr. Kenneth J. LaBudde Department of Special Collections

Used by permission of the University of Missouri-Kansas City Libraries,
Dr. Kenneth J. LaBudde Department of Special Collections

Used by permission of the University of Missouri-Kansas City Libraries,
Dr. Kenneth J. LaBudde Department of Special Collections

Used by permission of the University of Missouri-Kansas City Libraries,
Dr. Kenneth J. LaBudde Department of Special Collections

RESOURCES

RESOURCES

Chapter 1
Introduction

1. M. L. Mark and C. G. Gary, *A history of American music education,* 2nd edition, Reston, VA: Music Educators National Conference, 1999.

2. R. Hellyer, Harmoniemusik, In *Harmoniemusik,* Retrieved February 27, 2005 from Groves Music Online website.

3. R. Camus, Mixed wind bands, In *Band*, section 4, Retrieved March 5, 2005 from Groves Music Online: http://www.grovemusic.com.offcampus.lib.washington.edu.

4. Ibid.

5. R. K. Hansen, *The American wind band: A cultural history,* Chicago: GIA Publications, 2005.

6. F. L. Battisti, *The winds of change,* Lerch Creek, CT, Meredith Music Publications, 2002.

7. Camus.

8. Ibid.

9. Hansen.

10. Ibid.

11. United States Army Bands, General Pershing and army bands, *US army bands in history,* chapter 7, Retrieved March 10, 2005 from United States Army Bands, website: http://bands.army.mil.

12. Ibid.

13. Claude A. Phillips, *A History of Education in Missouri*, Jefferson City, Hugh Stephens Printing Company, 1911, 2–3.

14. Ibid. 6–7.

15.   Ibid. 6–7.

16.   Ibid. 6–7.

17.   Selwyn K. Troen, *The Public and the Schools—1838 to 1920*, University of Missouri Press, Columbia, 1975, 10.

18.   Harris–Stowe State University, online, http://www.hssu.edu, 2008.

Chapter 3

Town Bands

19.   Anne Marvin, "Facing the Music: The Turn-of-the Century Hometown Band," Kansas Historical Society, Topeka, (1998), http://www.kshs.org/features/feat 198.htm.

20.   David E. Fulmer, *The Lafayette Raconteur*, "Cornet Bands and Brass Bands in Lafayette County, Lafayette County Historical Society, Vol. 1, No. 2, unpublished, undated.

21.   "Band concert draws three thousand," *Shelbina Torchlight*, Shelbina, 1907.

22.   "Novinger Band at Crystal Lake Park," *Macon Republican*, Macon, 1907.

23.   "Novinger Through the Years," Adair County Library, unpublished, undated.

24.   E. M. Violette, "History of Adair County," 1911, Kirksville.

25.   "Marble Hill band records, 1875–1902," The Western Historical Manuscript Collection, Missouri University of Science and Technology, Rolla, folder 67.

26.   "21st Annual Plattsburg Chautauqua, August 21–29, 1926," Clinton County Historical Society, Plattsburg, 20.

27.   "Plattsburg Chautauqua—1926," Buchanan County Historical Society, St. Joseph.

28.   Carol J. McDowell, *The History of the Band Program at Jackson High School,* Jackson, 1999.

29.   *History of the Band*, Cape Girardeau Municipal Band, concert program, unpublished.

30.   Karen L. Walker, *The Organization of the Cape Municipal Band, 1881–1927,* unpublished master's thesis, Southeast Missouri State University, Cape Girardeau, 2008.

31.   "Town Bands Entertain People," Cass County Democrat–Missourian, undated.

32.   Nancy Fagerness, "And the Band Played On," Missouri Wine Country Journal, Summer, 1995, 12.

33.   "The Band Plays On, 100 years of the El Dorado Springs Municipal Band," Preserve Our Past Society (POPS), El Dorado Springs, Missouri, 1985, unpublished.

34. Marvin Kottman, "Forest Green Band began 100 years ago," Salisbury County News, November 6, 1986.

35. Ibid.

36. Helen Russell, Plattsburg, personal letter to author, August 9, 2007.

37. *Annual Assembly of the Plattsburg Chautauqua Association,* 1906 printed program.

38. *Plattsburg Chautauqua Association,* 1909 printed program.

39. History Museum of Springfield—1901.

40. Bill Miller, "Band Music Enlivened Washington's Early Days," *The Washington Missourian,* April 23, 1964, 6C.

41. Nancy Fagerness, "And the Band Played On," *Missouri Wine Country Journal,* Summer, 1995, 11.

42. Ibid, 11.

43. "A Look Back," Gentry County Historical Society Bulletin, Albany, 1947.

44. Wayne Glenn, *Ozarks' Greatest Hits*, Nixa, 2005, 21.

45. Don Burns, "Springfield's Amazing Boy Scout Band," *Springfield*, March, 1981, 19.

46. *Musical Times,* Philadelphia, 1889.

47. *The Metronome,* New York, 1889.

48. "The Successful Director of the Carthage Light Guard Band," *Carthage Weekly Press,* 1891.

49. "The Band's Trip to Boston," *Carthage Weekly Press,* 1895.

50. George Stupp, "Here Comes the Band," A Short Historical Melange, unpublished, undated.

51. *Lafayette Raconteur, The,* Lafayette County Historical Society, Vol. 1., No. 2, unpublished, undated.

52. Harry R. Voigt, *Concordia, Missouri—A Centennial History,* 1960, unpublished.

53. Wayne Glenn, *Ozark's Greatest hits*, Nixa, 2005, 55.

54. Ibid, 55.

55. Claude Kendall, "How About Our Band," *Lawrence County Record*, April 4, 1907.

56. Author unknown, *The Band Story*, The Centennial History of Moniteau County Fair, 1866–1966, 22, unpublished.

57. Neil Newton, *The History of McGirk, Missouri, Band*, The Centennial History of Moniteau

County Fair, 1866–1966, 23, unpublished.

58.   Lawrence B. Hert, *A Band member Remembers,* The Centennial History of Moniteau County Fair, 1866–1966, 21, unpublished.

59.   *Granby News Herald*, June, 1950.

60.   *Pictorial history of Perry County*, Lutheran Historical Society, Altenburg, unpublished.

61.   Nancy Fagerness, "And the Bands Played On," *Missouri Wine Country Journal*, Summer, 1995, 10.

62.   Western Historical Manuscript, University of Science and Technology, Rolla, "Ozark Land and Lumber Company," folio R279.

63.   "Through the Years," Ste. Genevieve County Historical Society bulletin, Vol. 6, No. 3, 1957.

64.   Earl Kreder, *The St. Charles Bands, 1870–2004*, St. Charles Historical Society, 2006.

65.   "Webster Only St. Louis Community Continuing Band Concert Tradition," *St. Louis Globe Democrat,* July 24, 1957, St. Louis, 6A.

66.   Ralph Watters and Floyd Watters George, "Bandstand Reminder of Marshfield's Town Band Era," *Webster County Historical Society Journal*, June, 1983, No. 22, 1.

67.   Wayne Glenn, *Ozarks' Greatest Hits,* 2005, Nixa, 20.

68.   Kevin L. Lines, "A History of Missouri's Municipal Band Tax," unpublished, 1955.

Chapter 4

St. Louis World's Fair—1904

69.   Terry Austin, "Bands at the 1904 World's Fair,*.* " Virginia Commonwealth University, Gaylord Music Library, Washington University, St. Louis, Missouri, 23–25.

70.   Jane Anne Liebenguth, "Music at the Louisiana Purchase Exposition," *The Bulletin of the Missouri Historical* Society, Vol. 36, October 1979, St. Louis, 27–34.

71.   "The Musical Director," *World's Fair Bulletin*, Missouri Historical Society library, St. Louis, September, 1901.

72.   Richard I. Schwartz and Iris J. Schwartz, *Bands at the St. Louis World's Fair of 1904,* Washington University, St. Louis, 2003, dissertation.

73.   Western Historical Manuscript Collection, University of Science and Technology, Rolla, R.453, F.14.

74. Liebenguth, "Music at the Louisiana Purchase Exposition," 27–34.

75. Ibid, 27–34.

Chapter 5
Pioneers

76. Dan E. Adkison, *Establishment and Growth of the Wind Band at Central Methodist College,* Central Missouri State University, Warrensburg, 1977, 14–29, dissertation, used by permission.

77. James Robertson, "Minutes of the organizational meeting of Missouri school music directors," Columbia, 1934, unpublished.

78. Ibid.

79. Kimberly A. Whitehead, "The History of the Sikeston High School Band Program," Southeast Missouri State University, 2007, unpublished, dissertation.

80. Robert Holden, "T. Frank Coulter," researched from historical documents, yearbooks and interviews in Joplin, 2008, unpublished.

81. "The Successful Director of the Carthage Light Guard Band, *Carthage Weekly Press,* August 27, 1891.

82. Cory de Vera, "Emmons' Leadership Applauded," *Columbia Tribune,* November 22, 2000, 1A, obituary.

83. Renee Wilson, "The Effect of One Woman," Adair County Historical Society, Adair County Public Library Archives, 2, unpublished,

84. Ibid, 2.

85. Ibid, 3.

86. Ibid, 2.

87. "We Remember—J. R. Huckstep," Raytown Historical Society, April, 2005.

88. "A Big Band Coming from Germany," *Truth,* C. G. Conn publication, 1904.

89. "Lemcke, A Music Maker in Webster," *St. Louis Post Dispatch,* September, 1968, C2.

90. Ibid, C2.

91. "LeRoy F. Mason," *The Southeast Missourian,* Cape Girardeau, July 17, 1976, obituary.

92. Chris L. Rutt, *History of Buchanan County and the City of St. Joseph,* Biographical Publishing Company, Chicago, 1904, 128.

93.   Peter Lucia, "When Asbury Park Was a Musical Center," Asbury Park Press, April, 1996.

94.   Ibid.

95.   Rick Benjamin, "Arthur Pryor: Ragtime Pioneer," Paragon Ragtime Orchestra September, 2008, used by permission.

96.   Ibid.

97.   Don Burns, "Springfield's Amazing Boy Scout Band," Springfield Magazine, Vol. 2, No. 10, March, 1981, 19.

98.   Ibid, 20, 22.

99.   Ibid, Vol. 2, No. 11, April, 1981, 25.

100. Ibid, Vol. 3, No. 1, June, 1981, 36, 37.

101. Ibid, 37.

102. Clair Mann, *The History of Rolla, Missouri,* Phelps County Historical Society, Rolla, 1974.

103. Western Historical Manuscript Collection, University of Science and Technology, Rolla, 1905.

104. Tim Beveridge, "John Scott ex '89 still Directing Band," *MSM Alumnus,* Missouri School of Mines, Rolla, 1965.

105. Ibid.

106. David Oakley, *Fifty-seven Years of Musical Miners,* Missouri School of Mines, Rolla, 1974, unpublished.

107. Pam Smith Kelly, "A Daughter's Tribute," Claude T. Smith Publication, Inc. Olathe, Kansas, 2001, from CD recording liner note, used by permission.

Chapter 6

Band Associations

Jon S. Ferguson, Secretary, Phi Beta Mu—Lambda Chapter, "Minutes of the organizational meeting—January 8, 1959," retrieved from the archives of Lambda Chapter.

Archives of Lambda Chapter, Phi Beta Mu.

Robert Scott, personal recollection of the founding of the Missouri Bandmasters Association.

Carroll Lewis, *The Beginning of MBA,* transcribed from handwritten notes from the archives of Missouri Music Educators Association.

Missouri All–State Band, *"Missouri All-State Band: Yes, No or Maybe,"* undated and unsigned document from the archives of the Missouri Music Educators Association.

Archives of the Missouri Music Educators Association.

Chapter 7
Missouri Music Educators Association

108. Herman Byrd, "Missouri Music Educators Association—MMEA," Seminar Report, Southwest Missouri State University, Springfield, 1979, unpublished, used by permission.

Chapter 8
College and University Bands

109. "The Swinney Conservatory of Music," *Central Methodist College Bulletin,* XLVI, Fayette, March, 1977, 130.

110. Editorial, "A College Band," *The Collegian,* Central College, Fayette, October, 1908, 42.

111. Editorial, "Best Band in State," *The Collegian,* Central College, Fayette, November, 1911.

112. "Central College Band," *The Ragout,* Central College, Fayette, 1912, 93.

113. "A Letter," *The Collegian,* XLI, Central College, Fayette, March, 1913, 1.

114. "Howard–Payne Organizes a Band," *The Collegian,* XLVI, Central College, Fayette, November, 1917, 5.

115. Dan E. Adkison, "Establishment and Growth of the Wind Band at Central Methodist College," A thesis, Master of Arts in Music in the School of Fine Arts and Sciences, Central Missouri State University, August, 1977, unpublished, used by permission.

116. Skip Vandelicht, "Supplement to Establishment and Growth of the Wind Band at Central Methodist College / University," Fayette, June 2010.

117. Joe Pappas, Jefferson College, Hillsboro.

118. Missouri Southern State College, *Crossroads,* Joplin, 1940.

119. G. K. Renner, *In Pursuit of Excellence, Missouri Southern State College, 1937–1992,* Missouri Southern State College, 1992.

120. *Ozarko ,* Missouri State Normal School # 4, Springfield, 1908.

121. Wayne Glenn, *Ozarks' Greatest Hits,* Nixa, 2005.

122. Ibid, *Ozarko,* 1943.

123. Information from Robert Scott, former Director of Bands and Music Department Chairman.

124. *Rallamo,* Missouri School of Mines and Metallurgy, Rolla, 1908.

125. David L. Oakley, *57 Years of Musical Miners,* University of Missouri–Rolla, 1965, unpublished.

126. Gary Anders, Missouri Valley College band, Marshall, 2010.

127. Samantha J. Baier, interview with Carl A. Kling, Maryville, October 15, 2007

128. Tower, Northwest Missouri State College, Maryville, 1933, 110.

129. Ibid., 1950, 18.

130. Ibid., Baier, 2007.

131. Ibid., Baier, interview with Al Sergel, Maryville, October 2007.

132. Ibid., Baier, interview with Ernest R. Woodruff, Maryville, October 2007,139, Phyllis Rossiter, "I'm from Missouri—you'll have to show me," *Rural Missouri,* Volume 4 2 , Number 3, Jefferson City, March, 1989, 16.

133. Southeast Missouri State University, *History & Traditions,* retrieved from www.semo.edu/whyse/history.htm (2011).

134. Sagamore, Southeast Missouri State Teachers College, Cape Girardeau, 1931.

135. Ibid. (1976).

136. Ronald Stilwell, St. Louis Community College at Meramec, personal recollection, 2009.

137. David C. Nichols, *Founding the Future: A History of Truman State University,* Kirksville: Truman State University Press, 2006.

138. "Paul Strub, Band Director Deluxe," *Index,* Kirksville, Missouri, September 7, 1947.

139. Ibid., Nichols.

140. Dan Peterson, personal correspondence, July, 2007.

141. Ibid.

142. Russell Coleman, source material from university yearbook, *Rhetor* with additional information provided by Frank Fendorf and Scott Lubaroff.

143. University of Missouri, Minutes of Meeting of the Executive Board of Curators, October 1, 1885, handwritten.

144. David A. Lockmiller, *Enoch H. Crowder: Soldier, Lawyer, Statesman,* University of Missouri Studies, 1955, 41.

145. "University Band Formally Wore Prince Alberts and Stove Pipes," *The Columbia Evening Missourian,* November 23, 1920, Section 1, 2.

146. Ibid.

147. *Savitar*, University of Missouri, Columbia, 1904, 118.

148. Minutes of Meeting of Executive Board of Curators, University of Missouri, June 30, 1910.

149. Ibid., *Savitar* (1939) 321.

150. Ibid. (1924) 265.

151. Ibid. (1939) 321.

152. Ibid.

153. Suzanne Wilson Hayworth, personal reflections of her father, Brookfield, Wisconsin, 2008.

154. "Strike up the Band," *Missouri Alumnus,* Columbia, 2006.

155. Robert Spiegelman, "The University of Missouri Band: The Early Years—1885 to 1946," unpublished masters degree research project, Columbia, 1985, used with permission.

156. Dan Presgrave, Washington University in St. Louis, personal recollection, 2010.

Chapter 9

High School Bands

157. *The Red and Black* yearbook, Central High School, St. Louis, 1926.

158. Missouri State Historical archive, SHS #025908, Columbia.

159. J. Leeman, *The Carnation* yearbook, McKinley High School, Vol. 1, Number 1, St. Louis, 1908.

Chapter 10

The National Band Contest

160. Emil A. Holz, "The Schools Band Contest of America of 1923," *Journal of Research in Music Education,* Vol. 10, No. 1, Music Educators national Conference, Reston, Virginia, 1953, 3.

161. Ibid., 4.

162. Kristen Laine, *American Band,* New York: Penguin Group, 2007, 66.

163. Ibid., 67.

164. Holz, 7.

165. Ibid., 7.

166. Ibid., 10.

167. Ibid., 11.

168. Stephen L. Rhodes, "The American School Band Movement," *History of the Wind Band,* Lipscomb University, Nashville, 2007, www.lipscomb.edu/windbandhistory.

169. Ibid., Holz, 12.

Chapter 12
Music Publishing

170. Leonard Smith, *On Conducting the Professional Concert Band,* Detroit Concert Band Publication, Detroit, 1992, publication out of print.

171. Andrew Glover, Oskaloosa, Iowa, 2009, used by permission.

Chapter 13
Kansas City Sheet Music Collection

172. University of Missouri–Kansas City, Dr. Kenneth J. LaBudde Special Collections.

ACKNOWLEDGEMENTS

ACKNOWLEDGMENTS

———————

The author gratefully acknowledges the follow individuals and organizations for their contribution to the publication:

Editing	Lynda Harman, Nancy Remmert, Jean Weinstock
Cover and Graphic Design	Wade Howell, Howell Graphic Designs, St. Louis
Publishing Consultant	Hannah Lee, Twin Harbor Press, Minneapolis
Publication Financial Coordinators	Kurt Bauche, Missouri Bandmasters Association
	Tom Poshak, Lambda Foundation, Phi Beta Mu

College and university band directors
County historical societies of Missouri
High school band directors
Lambda Foundation / Phi Beta Mu
Missouri Bandmasters Association
Missouri Historical Society
Missouri Music Educators Association
Missouri State Archives – Jefferson City
Retired members of the band directors profession
State Historical Society of Missouri – Columbia
University of Missouri – Kansas City library
University of Missouri – St. Louis library
Western Historical Manuscript Collection – Rolla

Research Departments of:
    Cape Girardeau Public Library
    Kansas City Public Library
    Lutheran Historical Society

Mid Continent Public Library – Independence

Missouri History Museum – St. Louis

Missouri State University Library - Springfield

Southeast Missouri State University Library – Cape Girardeau

Springfield Greene County Museum

Springfield Public Library

St. Charles Public Library

St. Louis County Library

St. Louis Public Library

The State Historical Society of Missouri - Columbia

University of Central Missouri Library - Warrensburg

University of Missouri – St. Louis Library

Used by permission

Rev. Dan E. Adkison, "Establishment and Growth of the Wind Band at Central Methodist College," Central Missouri State University, 1977, unpublished dissertation.

Herman Byrd, "Missouri Music Educators Association – MMEA," Southwest Missouri State University, 1979, unpublished seminar report.

Russell Coleman, Music Bowl – Missouri, Central Missouri State University, 2010, correspondence to author.

Andrew Glover, *Music Publishing and the Classic Concert Band,* Oskaloosa, Iowa, 2008, unpublished contribution to the *History of Missouri Bands*.

Pam Smith Kelly, "A Daughter's Tribute," Claude T. Smith Publications, Inc., Olathe, 2001, CD liner notes.

Carol J. McDowell, *The History of The Band Program At Jackson High School,* Stewart Printing and Publishing Company, Marble Hill, 1999.

David L. Oakley, *57 Years of Musical Miners,* University of Missouri-Rolla, 1965.

Robert Spiegelman, "The University of Missouri Band: The Early Years, 1995-1946," University of Missouri – Columbia, 1985, unpublished senior research project.

Claude T. Smith, *Emperata,* Wingert Jones Music, Kansas City, Missouri, 1964.

Alexander R. Trevino, "A Revisionist View of Band Development in American Music Education," *NBA Journal*, Baton Rouge, National Band Association, 2007, Vol. 47, No. 3, 40-43.

Kimberly A. Whitehead, "The History of the Sikeston High School Band Program," Southeast Missouri State University, 2007, unpublished dissertation.

Research Contributors

James Albin, Chairman	Genealogy and Cemetery Committees, Moniteau County
Matthew Frederickson	Gasconade County bands
Bill Grace	Lafayette County bands
Byron W. Hanson	Interlochen Center for the Arts
Gene Hunt	Franklin County bands
Carla L. Jordan, Director	Lutheran Historical Society, Altenburg
Carroll Lewis	The origins of the Missouri Bandmasters Association
Kevin L. Lines	*A History of Missouri's Municipal Bands,* 1995
Susan Miller	Personal recollections and photos of John W. Scott
Larry Pohlman	Research from the Springfield-Greene County Library
Margaret Pryor	"World's Greatest Trombone Player" – Arthur Pryor
Robert Scott	Origin of the Missouri Bandmasters Association
Ronald Stillwell	St. Louis Community College at Meramec band history
Cindy Price Svehla	Cameron Municipal Band history

Proofreaders and Historical Contributors

Ron Allen, George Alter, Gary Anders, Kurt Bauche, Paul Baur, John Bell, Barry Bernhardt, Gary Brandes, Terry Boone, Leon Bradley, Ruth Brown, Robert Cesario, Russell Coleman, Robert Collins, Daniel Cotner, Linda M. Donohue, Wendell Doyle, Stephen H. Duncan, Pat Ellebracht, James T. Elswick, Frank Fendorf, Charles Ferguson, Matthew Frederickson, Lynn Seward Fryer, Robert Gifford, Wayne Glenn, Dave Goodwin, Bill Grace, Michele Hansford, Robert Hanson, Byron Hanson, Wynne Harrell, Suzanne Hayworth, Val Hayworth, Robert Holden, Jerry Hoover, Ilene House, Linda A. Huck, Nick Leist, Jacqueline Lewin, Dee Lewis, Linton Luetje, William Mack, Carla Maltas, Marvin Manring, Kate Massey, Bill Maupin, Gerald McCollum, Carol McDowell, Avalyn McGintey, Charlotte McIntosh, Christine Montgomery, Dennis Nail, Ronald Nall, David Nichols, Rob Nichols, Robert Nordman, Jim Norman, Jim Oliver, Tom O'Neal, Joe Pappas, John Patterson, Donna Pavelski, Dan Peterson, Alexander

Pickard, Larry Pohlman, William Popp, Mary Poshak, Tom Poshak, Belva Prather, Dan Presgrave, Margaret Sara Przybylski, Keith Reuther, Stephen Rhodes, Ed Roberts, Donna Russell, Helen Russell, Lee T. Schneider, Ron Schuler, Carla Schantz, Jill Schantz, Alfred E. Sergel, Steve Seward, Wendy Sims, Roger Slusher, Barbara Sparkman, Mary Strickrodt, Dale Sullens, Henry Sweets, Paul Swofford, Elaine Swofford, Dennis Swope, Murphy Tetley, Skip Vandelicht, Melody Vandelicht, Roger Warner.

Financial Contributors

Rodney and Diane Ackmann	Michael and Heather Hathaway
Bruce and Sara Barnett	Gene and Kay Hunt
Charles and Kathy Blackmore	Bill and Bev Maupin
Herman Byrd	Tom and Betty Meyer
Ryan Curtis	Cary and Dee Mogerman
Wade Dowdy	Tim Oliver
Wendell and Judy Doyle	John and Cheryl Patterson
Mallory Duncan	Donna Pavelski
Susan Duncan	Dan Peterson
Matthew Duncan	Jeff Roberts
Stephen, Juli and Mitchell Duncan	Jill and Craig Schantz
Frank Fendorf	Karin, Carla and Kyle Schantz
Gerald and Jackie Fuchs	Lee and Nina Schneider
Jean and Howard Funck	Robert and Alice Scott
Gene and Nancy Garza	Steve Shankman
David and Debbie Goodwin	David and Janet Taylor
Melissa Gustafson-Hinds	Keith and Sally Vinyard
Buddy and Karla Hannaford	Frank Viverito
Wynne and Betty Harrell	Paul and Deb Warnex

Corporate and Educational Financial Contributors

Band Instrument Service

Boonville Band Boosters

Central Methodist University Bands

Collinsville High School Band

Contemporary Productions

Farmington Band Boosters

Farmington Middle and High School Bands

Herculaneum High School Band

Missouri State University
  Kppa Kappa Psi / Epsilon Chi chapter

Missouri University of Science & Tech.
  Kappa Kappa Psi / Delta Xi chapter

Kirksville Band Boosters

Kirkwood Band Boosters

Lee's Summit West Band Boosters

Liberty Band Boosters

Lindbergh Bandstanders

Metro 8 District / MMEA

Meyer Music Company

Mid America Band and Orchestra

Missouri Bandmasters Association

Missouri State University Bands

Missouri University of Science Tech.
  Bands and Orchestras

MMEA District # 7 Junior High Bands

MMEA District # 7 High School Bands

Moniteau County School District

Nottelmann Music

O'Fallon Township High School Band

Parkway Central Music Parents

Parkway South Band Boosters

Pattonville Band Boosters

Sappington-Concord Historical Society

Shattinger Music Company

Shivelbine Music Store

St. Charles Municipal Band

St. Charles West Band Boosters

St. Louis Municipal Opera, Co. "The Muny"

Stanbury Uniform Company

Susan Miller Trust

Tipton Cardinal High School Band

Union High School Band Boosters

Washington Band Boosters

Webb City Band Boosters

Windsor Band Parents

Tributes

The author, Missouri Bandmaster Association and the Lambda Foundation of Phi Beta Mu would like to express their gratitude to the following for their financial contribution:

In Honor Of

Robert J. Boedges

Gary Brandes

Leon C. Bradley

Cathy Coonis

Gary Brandes

Roger and Donna Russell

Russell Coleman

University of Central Missouri Bands

Russell Coleman

Alice, Ronald and Allison Coleman

Russell Coleman

Roadkill Clarinet Quintet

Paul Copenhaver

Paul and Nancy Copenhaver

C. Herbert Duncan

Roger and Donna Russell

Frank Fendorf

J. W. Pepper & Sons, Inc.

Robert M. Gifford

Ann, Robert B. and Tim Gifford

Bob Hansen

Roger and Donna Russell

Gene Henderson

In appreciation for support of music education
in the Francis Howell School District
Roger and Donna Russell

Jerry Hoover

Doug, Lori, Amy and Andrew Hoover

Gene Kirkham

Robert, Julie, Emily, Kevin and Katie Hill
Andrew, Jill, Lucas and Tucker Flowers

Dee Lewis

Cathy Coonis, Lori Hutton, Rex McCargar

Meramec Community College Symphonic Band

Ron Stilwell

Don Mozingo

The Jeff Mozingo Family

Robert Nordman

Department of Music -University of Missouri – St. Louis

John Gray Patterson

Cheryl Patterson

John Patterson

Columbia Community Band

Alex Pickard

Marching Mizzou Alumni Band

Dr. Alexander Pickard

Friends and students of Dr. Pickard

Larry and Caroline Pohlman
Gretchen and Greg Pohlman

Ed Roberts
Gail, Jack, Jeff, Melissa and Scott

Ed Roberts
Harrisonville High School Band

Bob Scott
Jerry and Betty Hoover

Bob and Alice Scott
Larry, Caroline, Gretchen and Greg Pohlman

Bert E. Stanley
Toni Stanley Ratican, Kay Stanley Dixon
Sara Stanley Barnett, Mark Stanley

Paul Warnex, Deb Warnex, Cindy Price-Svehla
Liberty Band Boosters

Charles Wells and Raymond King
Bohart Music Company
Gerry and Jackie Fuchs

Nate Wisdom
Windsor Band Parents Association

125 Years of Missouri University Bands
University of Missouri Bands
Kappa Kappa Psi and Tau Beta Sigma

★ ★ ★

In Memory Of

★ ★ ★

Don Anderson
Bob, Will, Linda, Larry and Don Jr. Anderson

John Baker
Bob and Ann Waggoner
St. Ann Music, LLC

Warren Bellis
Lois Bellis

Warren Bellis
Gary Brandes

Warren Bellis
Donna and Roger Russell

Bill Brackman
Joyce Brackman

Bill Brackman
Tom and Mary Poshak

Jessica Brinker
Farmington High School Band

Ed Carson
Kaye, Carol, Ken and Keith Carson

Ed Carson
Andrew Glover

Russ Chambers
Larry and Caroline Pohlman

Jess Cole
Bob and Alice Scott

Keith Collins

David and Lucy Aufdenberg Dealy

Ron Curtis

Ryan, Steffanie and Derek Curtis

Ron Curtis

Robert J. Boedges

Ron Curtis

Roger and Donna Russell

Bettye Holland Daly

Roger and Donna Russell

Charles Emmons

Alex Pickard

Charles Emmons

Jim and Lana Widner

Bob Gray

Keith and Sally Vinyard

W. L. Giddens

Robert M. Gifford

Lewis Hilton

Roger Warner

Keith House

Andrew Glover

Keith House

Jane Hicklin

Carroll Lewis

Larry, Caroline, Gretchen and Greg Pohlman

Acknowledgments

Arch Martin

Bob and Alice Scott

Arch Martin

Missouri Association for Jazz Education

LeRoy F. Mason

Robert M. Gifford

LeRoy F. Mason

Donna Ackmann McCune Russell

Al McCune

Donna McCune Russell

Tom Price

Cameron Municipal Band

Betty J. Price Family

Bob Rippee

Camdenton High School Bands

Ward Rounds

Northwest Missouri State University

Summer Band Camp Staff

John W. Scott

David Miller, Caroline Miller, Susan Miller

Kenneth and Nancy Seward

Lynn and Harold Fryer

Robert Spiegelman

Lindbergh High School Bandstanders

Robert Spiegelman

Kurt, Sue, Kate and Kyle Bauche

Robert Spiegelman
Patrick Duff and Phillip Duff

Robert Spiegelman
Neil and Barb Finbloom

Robert Spiegelman
Bev and Bill Maupin

Robert Spiegelman
Alex Pickard

Claude T. Smith
Maureen Smith and Pamela Smith Kelly

Claude T. Smith
Bev and Bill Maupin

George Turmail
Tom and Mary Poshak

Charles Wells and Raymond King
Bohart Music Company
Gerry and Jackie Fuch

George C. Wilson
Val and Suzanne Wilson Hayworth

George Wingert and Merrill Jones
Joyce Martin

Phi Beta Mu Lambda Foundation
In Memory of

Robert Spiegelman
Lindbergh High School
2011

Michael and Bridget Baudrex, Charlie Blackmore, Mark and Lisa Blackmore, Steve and Karen Bynum, Roger and Karen Cash, Mike and Cathleen Danner, Denis, Ann and Joey Dennis, Ken and Joyce Drury, Francis Howell Central High School Band Boosters, Semon Frelich, Friends of the Lindbergh High School Flyerettes, Josephine Glaser, Irv and Sharon Gordon, William Greenblatt, Harvey and Esther Greenstein, Jack and Betty Grossman, Leo, Kim Hanewinkel and Ian Pelt, Marvin and Phyllis Harber, Gene Hunt, Sherry Kaplan, Kathy Karpu, Kennerly Elementary School Parent Teacher Organization, Donna Kohler, Leonard and Sandy Kornblum, Megan and Stephen Kovacs, Keith Krebek, Philip, Kathy and Donnie Lawson, Lindbergh School District Personnel Services, Ronald, Sharon and Joshua Loesch, Greg and Christine Luzecky, Hi and Cheryl Martin, Daniel and Beverlee Maschek, Bill and Bev Maupin, Charles and Jennifer McDonnell and Family, McKendree College Band, Daniel and Beverlee Meschek, Missouri Music Educators Association, Patricia Moore, Doug, Kathy, Amanda and Andrew Morrell, Joseph, Laura and Carolyn Mueller, John, Ruth, Eve and Jeff Panhorst, Joe Pappas, Judy Paskal, John, Jean, James and Daniel Reusch, Steve and Diane Rothman, Zel and Lorraine Rothman, Lyn and Joseph Sexton and Family, Irvine and Elaine Shore, Richard, Susan and Wil Spaeth, Adam Spirk, Edward, Mary and Ellen Strouth, Gerald and Margaret Syberg, Bob and Patricia Tobler, Bruce and Sherri Tons, Gerald and Ilien Towbin, Jim, Connie, Jeff and Lisa Walker, Alexia Bee Weitzel, Ben and Marilyn Whitehead, Jim, JoAnne and Curt Williams.

THE AUTHOR

C. HERBERT DUNCAN

Duncan started piano lessons at the age of eight while living in Fredericktown, Missouri. His father was the owner and publisher of the Madison County Press. In 1940 the family moved to Ferguson, Missouri, a suburb of St. Louis, where he attended the Ferguson schools and graduated from high school in 1948. During that time he was in the Ferguson High School band and orchestra under the direction of Wilford B. Crawford. For three years Duncan played in the St. Louis All-County Band and studied percussion with William Albers, a member of the St. Louis Symphony Orchestra.

He enrolled in Central College, Fayette, as a music education major in 1948 and played tympani in the college concert band and snare drum in the marching band for four years under the direction of Keith K. Anderson. Upon graduation from Central in 1952, with a Bachelor of Music Education degree, he obtained his first teaching position in Weston, Missouri. The following year he became the Director of Bands for the Normandy School District in suburban St. Louis, where he stayed for 30 years.

In the summer of 1953 he enrolled at the University of Kansas in Lawrence as a graduate school candidate. He taught percussion in the Midwestern Music and Art Camp while taking classes toward his advanced degree. He graduated with a Masters of Music Education degree in 1956. Duncan continued to be associated with the summer music camp at KU for the next 13 years as Camp Supervisor. In 1968 he founded the Lakewood Music Camp in Potosi which ran for twelve years.

In 1964, he was asked to start the band program at the newly established University of Missouri–St. Louis. He did this while maintaining his high school position. The program started with 12 people and grew to 65 students in three years.

The St. Louis Municipal Opera (The Muny) selected Duncan to organize a band for eleven different musicals, including six different productions of *The Music Man.* He originated

357

the VP Fair Honors Band which included outstanding performers from area high schools. The band played three concerts a day at the Gateway Arch during the week-long July 4th celebration.

The VP Fair Honors Band continued for 13 summers.

In 1971 he founded the Greater St. Louis Marching Band Festival along with the late Dr. Warren Bellis of the University of Missouri – St. Louis. The festival brought together 48 high school bands from three states to an indoor NFL stadium with adjudication by nationally recognized band directors. The festival celebrated its 40th anniversary in 2011.

Duncan has received the:

Phi Beta Mu Founders Award	1999
National Band Association Citation of Excellence	2006
Missouri Music Educators Association Hall of Fame Award	2006
Missouri Bandmasters Association Hall of Fame Award	2009

FINALE

FINALE

———◆◆◆◆———

Harold Hill:

"I always think there's a band, kid."

The Music Man
1957
Meredith Willson

(Flute & piccolo, The Sousa Band, 1921–1923)